Over 10 Million Copies in Print!

COMPREHENSIVE
CURRICULUM
of Basic Skills

GRADE
1

Math

Reading

Reading Comprehension

English

Writing

Thinking Kids®
Carson-Dellosa Publishing LLC
Greensboro, North Carolina

Thinking Kids®
Carson-Dellosa Publishing LLC
P.O. Box 35665
Greensboro, NC 27425 USA

Printed in the USA • All rights reserved.   ISBN 978-1-4838-2410-9
06-261171151

Reading

Reading Comprehension

English

Spelling

TABLE OF CONTENTS

READING

Name, Address, Phone Number

This book belongs to

Vivian

I live at

hes

The city I live in is

The state I live in is

My phone number is

Name _____

Review the Alphabet

Directions: Practice writing the letters.

Name _____

Review the Alphabet

Directions: Practice writing the letters.

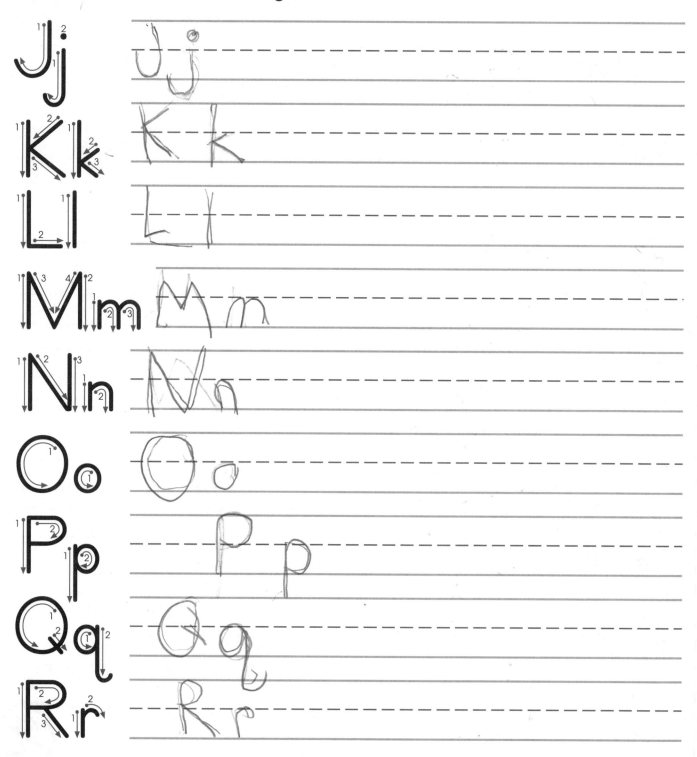

Name _____

Review the Alphabet

Directions: Practice writing the letters.

Ss   S s

Tt   T t

Uu   U u

Vv   V v

Ww   W w

Xx   X x

Yy   Y x

Zz   Z z

Comprehensive Curriculum - **Grade 1**

Name _____

Letter Recognition

Directions: In each set, match the lowercase letter to the uppercase letter.

a   C

f   H

c   J

h   E

e   A

j   F

g   D

b   B

i   M

d   G

k   I

l   L

m   K

Name _____

Letter Recognition

Directions: In each set, match the lowercase letter to the uppercase letter.

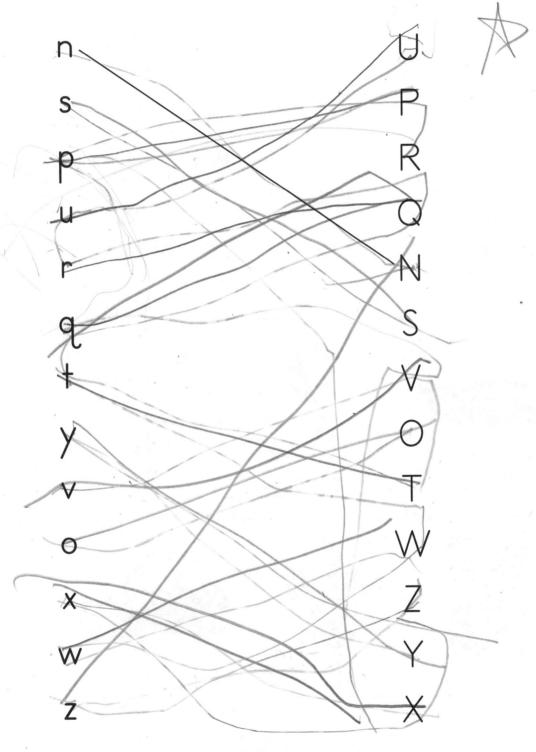

Name _____

Beginning Consonants: *Bb, Cc, Dd, Ff*

Beginning consonants are the sounds that come at the beginning of words. Consonants are the letters **b, c, d, f, g, h, j, k, l, m, n, p, q, r, s, t, v, w, x, y,** and **z**.

Directions: Say the name of each letter. Say the sound each letter makes. Circle the letters that make the beginning sound for each picture.

Bb   Cc   Dd   Ff

Bb Dd   Ff Cc   Cc Dd   Ff Bb

Bb Dd   Ff Cc   Cc Dd   Ff Bb

Beginning Consonants: *Bb, Cc, Dd, Ff*

Directions: Say the name of each letter. Say the sound each letter makes. Draw a line from each letter to the picture that begins with that sound.

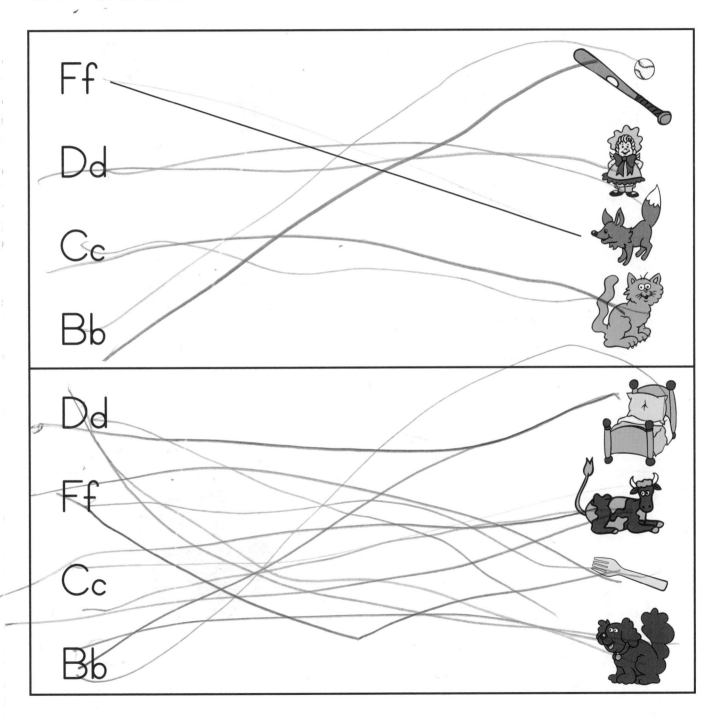

Name _____

Beginning Consonants: *Gg*, *Hh*, *Jj*, *Kk*

Directions: Say the name of each letter. Say the sound each letter makes. Trace the letter pair that makes the beginning sound in each picture.

Gg   Hh   Jj   Kk

Name _____

Beginning Consonants: *Gg, Hh, Jj, Kk*

Directions: Say the name of each letter. Say the sound each letter makes. Draw a line from each letter pair to the picture that begins with that sound.

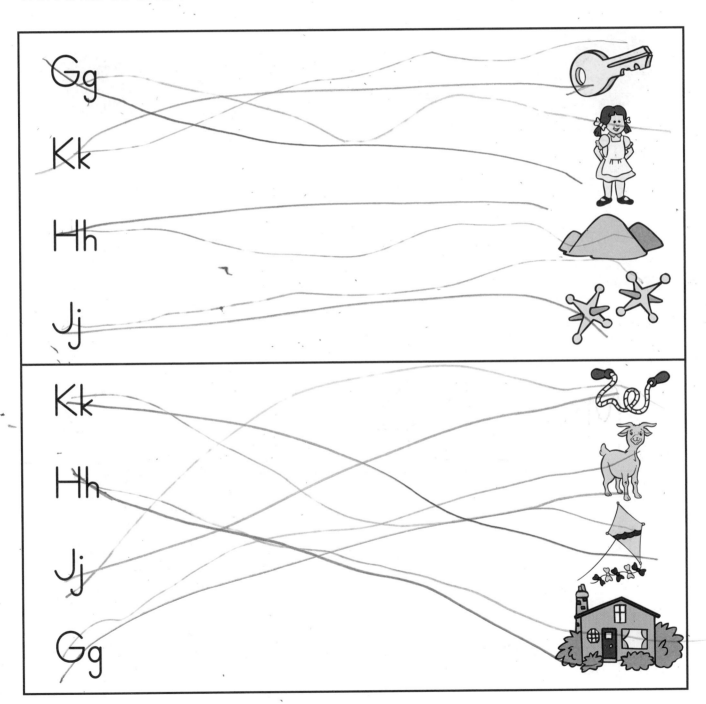

Comprehensive Curriculum - **Grade 1**

Name _____

Beginning Consonants: *Ll, Mm, Nn, Pp*

Directions: Say the name of each letter. Say the sound each letter makes. Trace the letters. Then, draw a line from each letter pair to the picture that begins with that sound.

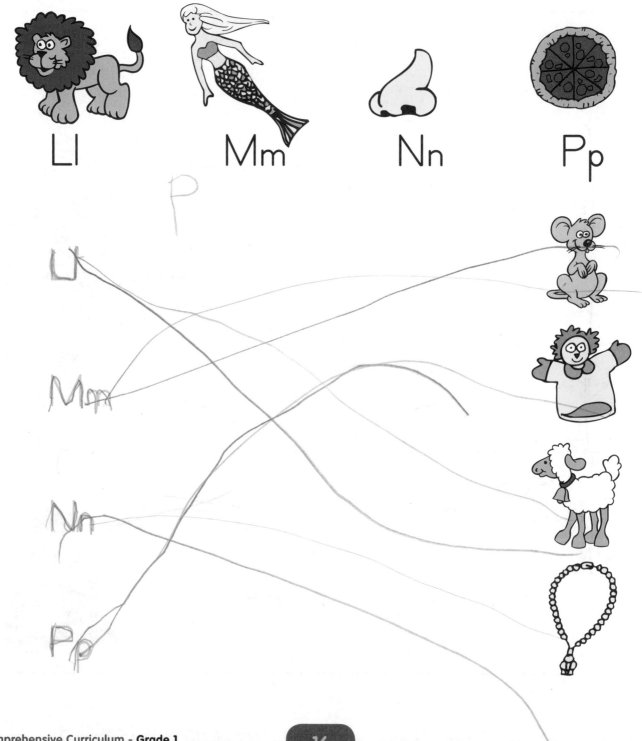

Beginning Consonants: *Ll, Mm, Nn, Pp*

Directions: Say the name of each letter. Say the sound each letter makes. Trace the letter pair that makes the beginning sound in each picture.

Ll   N   Mm   Nn   Pp

Mm   Ll

Mm   Pp

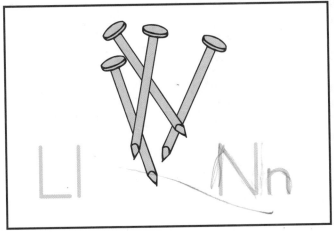

Ll   Nn

Pp   Mm

Beginning Consonants: *Qq*, *Rr*, *Ss*, *Tt*

Directions: Say the name of each letter. Say the sound each letter makes. Trace the letter pair in the boxes. Then, color the picture that begins with that sound.

Beginning Consonants: *Qq, Rr, Ss, Tt*

Directions: Say the name of each letter. Say the sound each letter makes. Draw a line from each letter pair to the picture that begins with that sound.

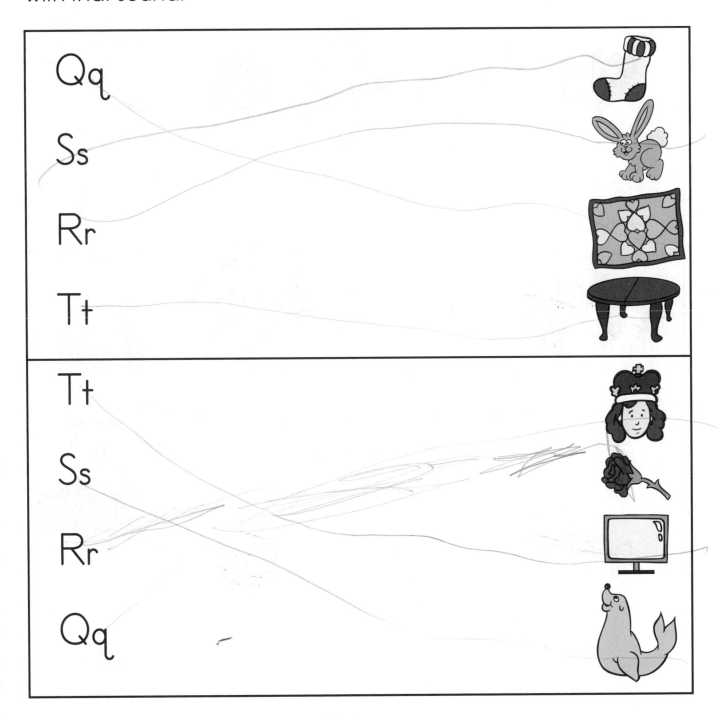

Beginning Consonants: *Vv, Ww, Xx, Yy, Zz*

Directions: Say the name of each letter. Say the sound each letter makes. Trace the letters. Then, draw a line from each letter pair to the picture that begins with that sound.

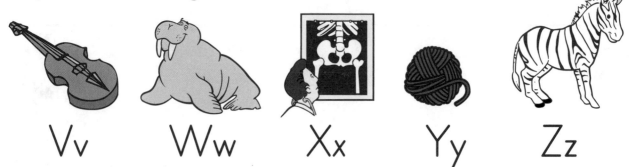

Vv　　Ww　　Xx　　Yy　　Zz

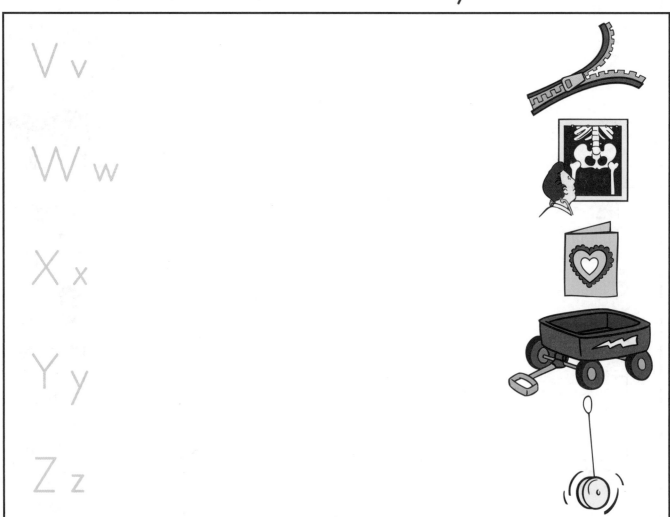

V v

W w

X x

Y y

Z z

Beginning Consonants: *Vv, Ww, Xx, Yy, Zz*

Directions: Say the name of each letter. Say the sound each letter makes. Then, draw a line from each letter pair to the picture that begins with that sound.

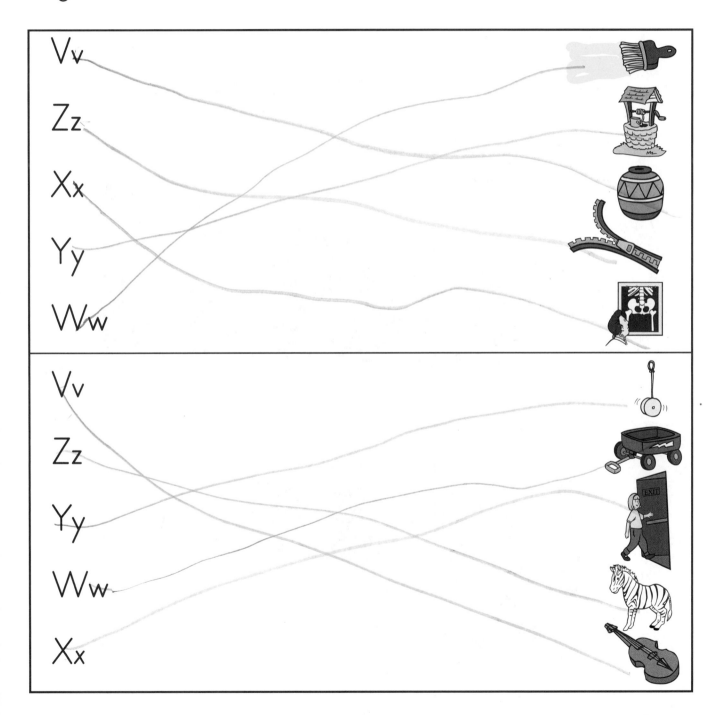

Review

Directions: Help Meg, Kent, and their dog, Sam, get to the magic castle. Trace each capital consonant letter and write the lower-case consonant next to it. Say the sound each consonant makes.

Review

Directions: Write the letter that makes the beginning sound for each picture.

C ar

Z ipper

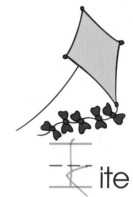

K ite

L etter

b oat

r ose

S un

h ouse

T urtle

g oat

J ar

d og

Name _____

Ending Consonants: *B*, *D*, and *F*

Ending consonants are the sounds that come at the ends of words.

Directions: Say the name of each picture. Then, write the letter that makes the **ending** sound for each picture.

Ending Consonants: *G*, *M*, and *N*

Directions: Say the name of each picture. Draw a line from each letter to the pictures that end with that sound.

Ending Consonants: *K*, *L*, and *P*

Directions: Trace the letter in each row. Say the name of each picture. Then, color the pictures in each row that end with that sound.

Ending Consonants: *R*, *S*, *T*, and *X*

Directions: Say the name of each picture. Then, circle the ending sound for each picture.

 r s t x

 r s t x

 r s t x

 r s t x

 r s t x

 r s t x

 r s t x

 r s t x

Beginning and Ending Consonants

Directions: Say the name of each picture. Draw a **blue** circle around the picture if it **begins** with the sound of the letter below it. Draw a **green** triangle around the picture if it **ends** with the sound of the letter below it.

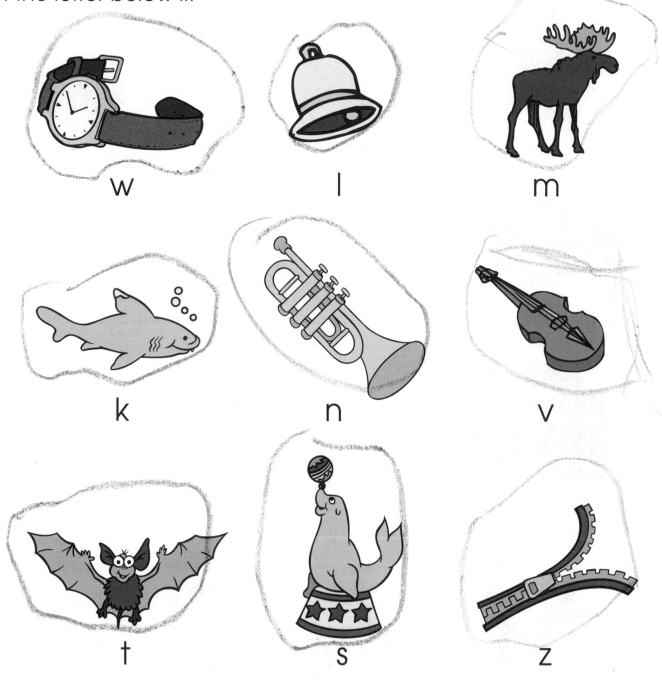

w

l

m

k

n

v

t

s

z

Beginning and Ending Consonants

Directions: Say the name of each picture. Draw a triangle around the letter that makes the **beginning** sound. Draw a square around the letter that makes the **ending** sound. Color the pictures.

o   r   t   f   d   w   v   t   b

x   c   r   t   g   d   d   a   k

l   m   h   x   g   r   p   t   v

Beginning and Ending Consonants

Directions: Say the name of each picture. Write the beginning and ending sounds for each picture.

b g

Pp 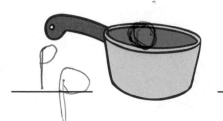 r

ra  ibbit

Cam  b

Chi  ck

Si  nk

gr  ass

s  x

Short Vowels

Vowels are the letters **a**, **e**, **i**, **o**, and **u**. Short **a** is the sound you hear in **ant**. Short **e** is the sound you hear in **elephant**. Short **i** is the sound you hear in **igloo**. Short **o** is the sound you hear in **octopus**. Short **u** is the sound you hear in **umbrella**.

Directions: Say the short vowel sound at the beginning of each row. Say the name of each picture. Then, color the pictures that have the same short vowel sound as that letter.

Name _____

Short Vowel Sounds

Directions: There are three pictures in each box. The words that name the pictures have missing letters. Write **a**, **e**, **i**, **o**, or **u** to finish the words.

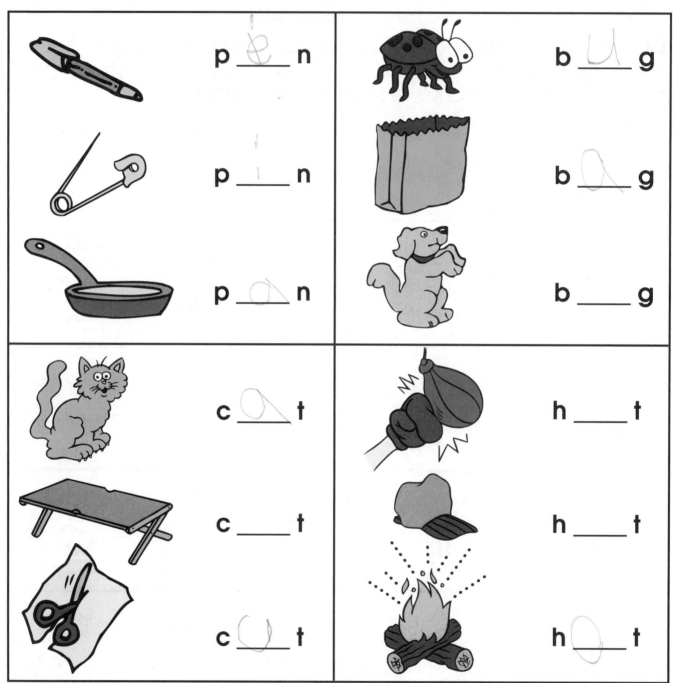

p _e_ n

p _i_ n

p _a_ n

b _u_ g

b _a_ g

b ___ g

c _a_ t

c ___ t

c _u_ t

h ___ t

h ___ t

h _o_ t

Long Vowels

Vowels are the letters **a, e, i, o**, and **u**. Long vowel sounds say their own names. Long **a** is the sound you hear in **hay**. Long **e** is the sound you hear in **me**. Long **i** is the sound you hear in **pie**. Long **o** is the sound you hear in **no**. Long **u** is the sound you hear in **cute**.

Directions: Say the long vowel sound at the beginning of each row. Say the name of each picture. Color the pictures in each row that have the same long vowel sound as that letter.

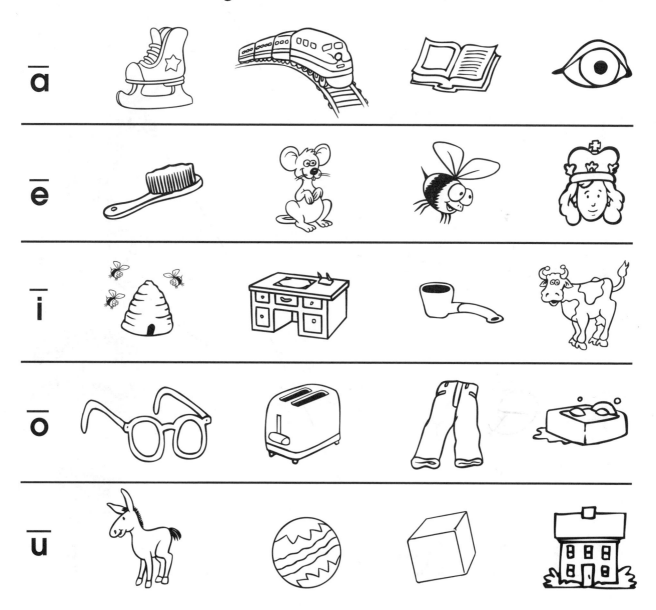

Long Vowel Sounds

Directions: Write **a**, **e**, **i**, **o**, or **u** in each blank to finish the word. Draw a line from the word to the picture.

c __a__ ke

r __o__ se

k __i__ te

k __e__ y

m __u__ le

Name _____

Words with *A*

Directions: Each train has a group of pictures. Write the word that names the pictures. Read your rhyming words.

These trains use the short **a** sound, as in the word **cat**:

These trains use the long **a** sound, as in the word **lake**:

Comprehensive Curriculum - **Grade 1**

Short and Long Aa

Directions: Say the name of each picture. If it has the short **a** sound, color it **red**. If it has the long **a** sound, color it **yellow**.

ă   ā

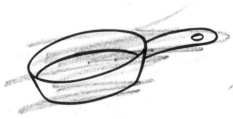

Words with *E*

Directions: Short **e** sounds like the **e** in **hen**. Long **e** sounds like the **e** in **bee**. Look at the pictures. If the word has a short **e** sound, draw a line to the **hen** with your **red** crayon. If the word has a long **e** sound, draw a line to the **bee** with your **green** crayon.

hen   bee

Short and Long *Ee*

Directions: Say the name of each picture. Circle the pictures that have the short **e** sound. Draw a triangle around the pictures that have the long **e** sound.

Words with *I*

Directions: Short **i** sounds like the **i** in **pig**. Long **i** sounds like the **i** in **kite**. Draw a circle around the words with the short **i** sound. Draw an **X** on the words with the long **i** sound.

pin

five

pig

slide

kite

lid

tie

bib

pie

Name _____

Short and Long *Ii*

Directions: Say the name of each picture. If it has the short **i** sound, color it **yellow**. If it has the long **i** sound, color it **red**.

ĭ

ī

Name _____

Words with O

Directions: The short **o** sounds like the **o** in **dog**. Long **o** sounds like the **o** in **rope**. Draw a line from the picture to the word that names it. Draw a circle around the word if it has a short **o** sound.

hot dog

fox

blocks

rose

boat

Comprehensive Curriculum - **Grade 1**

Short and Long Oo

Directions: Say the name of each picture. If the picture has the long **o** sound, write a **green L** on the blank. If the picture has the short **o** sound, write a **red S** on the blank.

_____

_____

_____

_____

_____

_____

_____

_____

Words with *U*

Directions: The short **u** sounds like the **u** in **bug**. The long **u** sounds like the **u** in **blue**. Draw a circle around the words with short **u**. Draw an **X** on the words with long **u**.

rug

cup

music

tub

suit

glue

bug

puppy

gum

Name _____

Short and Long *Uu*

Directions: Say the name of each picture. If it has the long **u** sound, write a **u** in the **unicorn** column. If it has the short **u** sound, write a **u** in the **umbrella** column.

ū

ŭ

_____   _____

_____   _____

_____   _____

_____   _____

_____   _____

Super Silent *E*

When you add an **e** to the end of some words, the vowel changes from a short vowel sound to a long vowel sound. The **e** is silent.

Example: rip + **e** = ripe

Directions: Say the word under the first picture in each pair. Then, add an **e** to the word under the next picture. Say the new word.

pet   _____   tub   _____

man   _____   kit   _____

pin   _____   cap   _____

Comprehensive Curriculum - **Grade 1**

Short and Long Vowels

Directions: Say the name of each picture. On each line, write the vowel that completes the word. Color the short vowel pictures. Circle the long vowel pictures.

a e i o u

 j _____ g

 t _____ pe

 l _____ af

 p _____ n

 l _____ ck

 c _____ t

 c _____ be

 b _____ ll

 k _____ te

 r _____ pe

Short and Long Vowel Sounds

Directions: Cut out the pictures below. If the vowel has a **long** sound, glue it on the **long** vowel side. If the vowel has a **short** sound, glue it on the **short** vowel side.

Short	Long

cut ✂ -

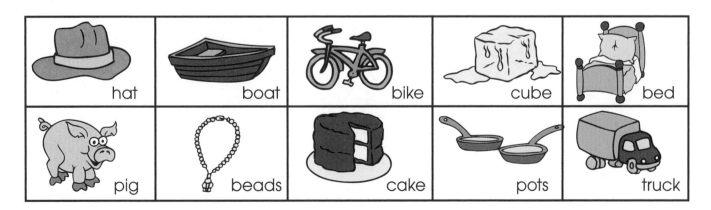

Page is blank for cutting exercise on previous page.

Review

Directions: Color all of the vowels black to discover something hidden in the puzzle.

```
j  e  j  g  w  d  q  n  j  c  g  c  u  b
k  g  u  m  b  j  h  c  h  w  l  o  d  s
r  c  z  i  l  p  q  s  b  k  i  n  z  f
g  k  w  x  e  d  a  e  f  e  l  x  q  k
v  r  f  j  p  i  o  u  a  g  n  f  s  b
d  n  v  m  a  e  e  i  u  u  h  b  s  f
u  a  e  i  e  u  a  i  u  e  a  e  i  u
l  z  k  i  u  u  a  a  e  e  i  m  w  z
q  h  r  a  e  u  e  i  a  e  e  c  c  b
i  u  u  e  o  a  o  u  o  i  i  o  o  u
t  x  b  h  a  i  e  o  u  a  d  v  r  l
c  h  f  s  j  e  i  e  i  f  f  k  j  v
n  m  d  t  e  g  a  o  t  i  j  m  x  h
t  p  g  i  c  v  h  n  g  d  o  p  r  l
l  h  o  k  q  f  r  p  s  j  t  u  g  v
```

What was hidden?

_____

Comprehensive Curriculum - **Grade 1**

Review

Directions: Circle the word if it has a long vowel sound.

Remember: A long vowel says its name.

feet

snake

cup

hose

tie

hat

dog

rake

bug

bone

bib

net

Review

Directions: On each line, write the vowel that completes the word.

a   e   i   o   u

 c__t

 sm__k_

 c__b

 m__m

 d__d

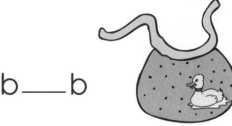 b__k_

 tr____

 p__n

 b__b

 d__ck

Review

Directions: Circle the **long vowel** words with a **red** crayon. Underline the **short vowel** words with a **blue** crayon.

Remember: The vowel is long if:
- There are two vowels in the word. The first vowel is the sound you hear.
- There is a "super silent e" at the end.

cub	red	coat
bite	cube	cage
cat	mean	rake
bit	cot	hen
leaf	feet	key
pen	web	bee
nest	boat	fox
rose	dog	pig

My Vowel List

Keep this list handy, and add more words to it.

short a
(ă as in **cat**)

_____

- - - - - - - -

_____

long a
(ā as in **train**)

_____

- - - - - - - -

_____

short e
(ĕ as in **get**)

_____

- - - - - - - -

_____

long e
(ē as in **tree**)

_____

- - - - - - - -

_____

short i
(ĭ as in **pin**)

_____

- - - - - - - -

_____

long i
(ī as in **ice**)

_____

- - - - - - - -

_____

short o
(ŏ as in **cot**)

_____

- - - - - - - -

_____

long o
(ō as in **boat**)

_____

- - - - - - - -

_____

short u
(ŭ as in **cut**)

_____

- - - - - - - -

_____

long u
(ū as in **cube**)

_____

- - - - - - - -

_____

Page is blank so student can remove and keep
list from previous page.

Consonant Blends

Consonant blends are two or more consonant sounds together in a word. The blend is made by combining the consonant sounds.

Example: floor

Directions: The name of each picture begins with a **blend**. Circle the beginning blend for each picture.

bl fl cl

cl fl gl

fl bl pl

fl cl gl

pl gl cl

gl fl sl

gl fl cl

sl fl cl

cl gl sl

Name _____

Consonant Blends

Directions: The beginning blend for each word is missing. Fill in the correct blend to finish the word. Draw a line from the word to the picture.

_____

_ _ _ _ _ _ _ _ _ _
_____ ain
_____

_ _ _ _ _ _ _ _ _ _
_____ og
_____

_ _ _ _ _ _ _ _ _ _
_____ ab
_____

_ _ _ _ _ _ _ _ _ _
_____ um
_____

_ _ _ _ _ _ _ _ _ _
_____ ush
_____

_ _ _ _ _ _ _ _ _ _
_____ esent

Consonant Blends

Directions: Draw a line from the picture to the blend that begins its name.

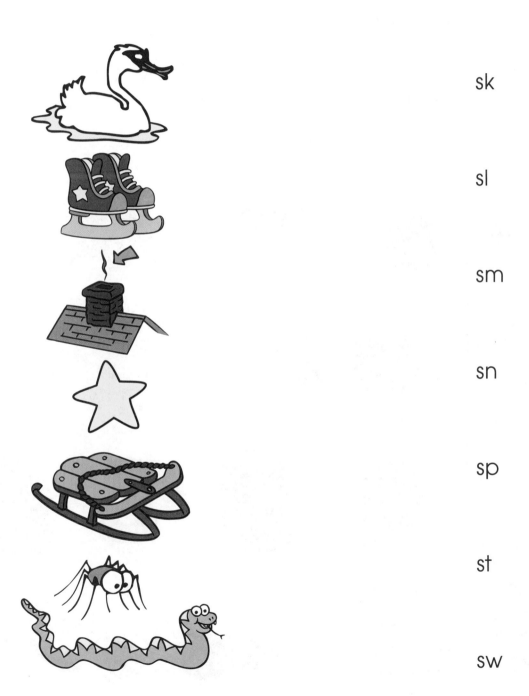

sk

sl

sm

sn

sp

st

sw

Consonant Teams

Consonant teams are two or more consonant letters that have a single sound.

Examples: sh and **ch**

Directions: Look at the first picture in each row. Circle the pictures in the row that begin with the same sound.

chair

shell

thumb

wheel

Beginning Blends and Teams

Directions: Say the blend for each word as you search for it.

```
b  l  o  s  l  e  d  a  b  f  t  k  a  i  n
l  b  r  e  a  d  x  s  t  o  p  i  x  a  p
o  l  g  u  f  e  n  p  s  p  i  d  e  r  i
c  l  o  w  n  a  w  l  p  z  j  c  r  a  b
k  t  c  e  n  t  h  s  t  e  g  l  q  c  r
d  h  b  r  e  a  e  j  w  k  x  o  w  h  y
h  u  s  n  a  k  e  m  d  j  l  c  m  a  j
v  m  i  u  k  l  l  s  k  u  n  k  c  i  f
i  b  g  l  o  b  e  m  h  n  o  q  t  r  r
b  f  l  j  x  s  y  a  z  s  l  e  d  o  o
s  h  e  l  l  w  k  l  f  s  s  v  u  p  g
h  a  r  l  c  a  d  l  l  v  w  k  z  s  n
o  z  y  q  s  n  l  t  a  h  n  r  u  m  q
e  f  l  o  w  e  r  a  g  l  o  v  e  e  r
w  g  m  b  c  e  n  m  o  p  d  o  f  l  g
p  r  e  s  e  n  t  r  a  i  n  b  p  l  i
```

Words to find:

block	frog	globe	crab
clock	glove	present	flower
train	flag	skunk	snake
swan	small	smell	spider
bread	sled	chair	shell
stop	wheel	shoe	clown
thumb			

Ending Consonant Blends

Directions: Write **lt** or **ft** to complete the words.

be _____

ra _____

sa _____

qui _____

le _____

Ending Consonant Blends

Directions: Draw a line from the picture to the blend that ends the word.

lf

lk

sk

st

Name _____

Ending Consonant Blends

Directions: Every jukebox has a word ending and a list of letters. Add each of the letters to the word ending to make rhyming words.

___and
b _____
h _____
l _____
s _____

___ent
b _____
d _____
t _____
w _____

___ump
b _____
d _____
j _____
p _____

___ink
p _____
s _____
l _____
th _____

___ing
r _____
s _____
st _____
k _____

___ank
b _____
r _____
s _____
t _____

Ending Consonant Blends and Teams

Directions: Say the blend for each word as you search for it.

```
b  e  l  t  l  e  m  m  i  l  k  r  p
b  r  l  z  m  a  a  i  u  v  r  i  n
r  r  d  u  m  p  s  h  n  x  i  t  a
i  b  p  i  n  g  k  p  i  b  n  g  w
n  m  k  i  q  i  w  e  n  t  g  d  s
g  t  h  i  n  k  n  c  e  s  i  r  h
e  e  i  k  i  f  h  r  c  d  x  e  e
t  c  s  j  b  c  l  a  s  p  n  m  l
e  r  i  e  l  o  m  n  i  y  e  p  f
n  b  n  b  a  n  d  k  g  o  s  f  k
t  a  g  l  n  a  l  a  n  d  t  e  d
x  d  c  o  k  u  z  j  e  l  u  m  p
r  a  f  t  b  r  h  s  h  r  i  n  k
```

Words to find:

belt	raft	milk	shelf
mask	clasp	nest	band
think	went	lump	crank
ring	blank	shrink	land
bring	tent	dump	sing

Name _____

Review

Directions: Finish each sentence with a word from the word box.

sting	shelf	drank	plant	stamp

1. Tom _____ his milk.

2. A bee can _____ you.

3. I put a _____ on my letter.

4. The _____ is green.

5. The book is on the _____ .

Rhyming Words

Rhyming words are words that sound alike at the end of the word. **Cat** and **hat** rhyme.

Directions: Draw a circle around each word pair that rhymes. Draw an **X** on each pair that does not rhyme.

Example:

soap
rope

red
dog

book
hook

cold
rock

cat
hat

yellow
black

one
two

rock
sock

rat
flat

good
nice

you
to

meet
toy

old
sold

sale
whale

word
letter

Name _____

Rhyming Words

Rhyming words are words that sound alike at the end of the word.

Directions: Draw a line to match the pictures that rhyme. Write two of your rhyming word pairs below.

_____   _____

- - - - - - - - - - - - - - -   - - - - - - - - - - - - - - -

_____   _____

_____   _____

- - - - - - - - - - - - - - -   - - - - - - - - - - - - - - -

_____   _____

ABC Order

Directions: ABC order is the order in which letters come in the alphabet. Draw a line to connect the dots. Follow the letters in ABC order. Then, color the picture.

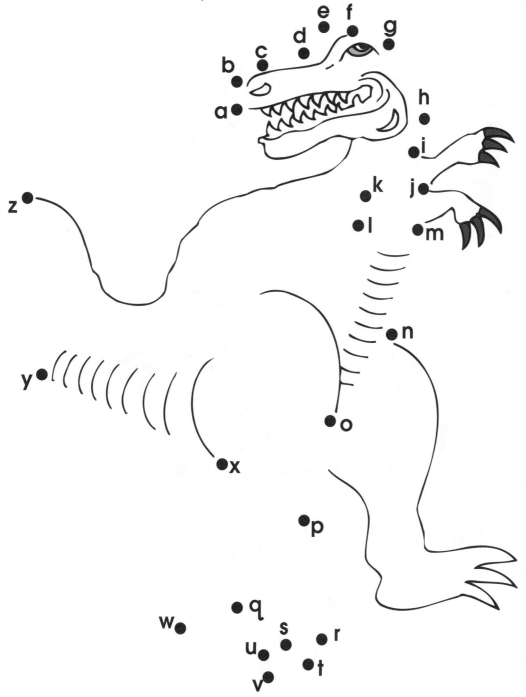

Name _____

ABC Order

Directions: Draw a line to connect the dots. Follow the letters in ABC order. Then, color the picture.

ABC Order

Directions: Circle the first letter of each word. Then, put each pair of words in ABC order.

ⓒar   ⓑird   moon   2   nest   fan

bird

car

card   dog   pig   bike   sun   pie

Name _____

ABC Order

Directions: Look at the words in each box. Circle the word that comes first in ABC order.

duck four rock	chair apple yellow	peach this walk
game boy pink	light come one	mouse ten orange
angel table hair	zebra watch five	foot boat mine
look blue rope	who dog black	book tan six

ABC Order

Directions: Cut out the foods Mom wants to buy when she goes shopping. Glue the words in ABC order on the shopping list.

Shopping List

✂ cut

steak

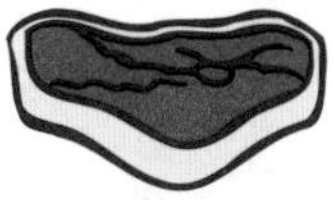

watermelon

bread

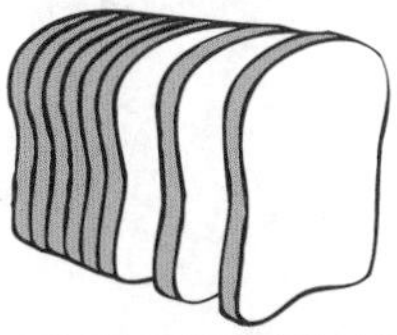

grapes

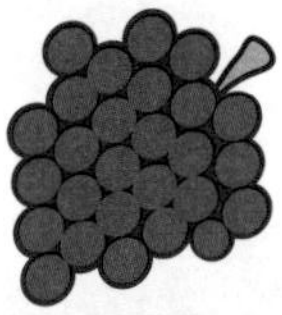

pickles

apples

milk

Page is blank for cutting exercise on previous page.

Sequencing: ABC Order

Directions: Put each group of words in ABC order by numbering them 1, 2, 3.

Example:

cold	**w**arm	**h**ot
1	3	2

small	**b**ig	**c**ute
___	___	___

doll

truck   **b**all

baby

sister   **f**amily

man

boy   **g**randma

Name _____

ABC Order

Directions: Put the words in ABC order. Circle the first letter of each word. Then, write 1, 2, 3, 4, 5, or 6 on the line next to each animal's name.

skunk _____

dog _____

butterfly _____

zebra _____

tiger _____

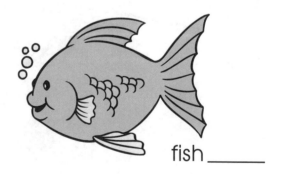

fish _____

Compound Words

Compound words are two words that are put together to make one new word.

Directions: Look at the pictures and the two words that are next to each other. Put the words together to make a new word. Write the new word.

Example:

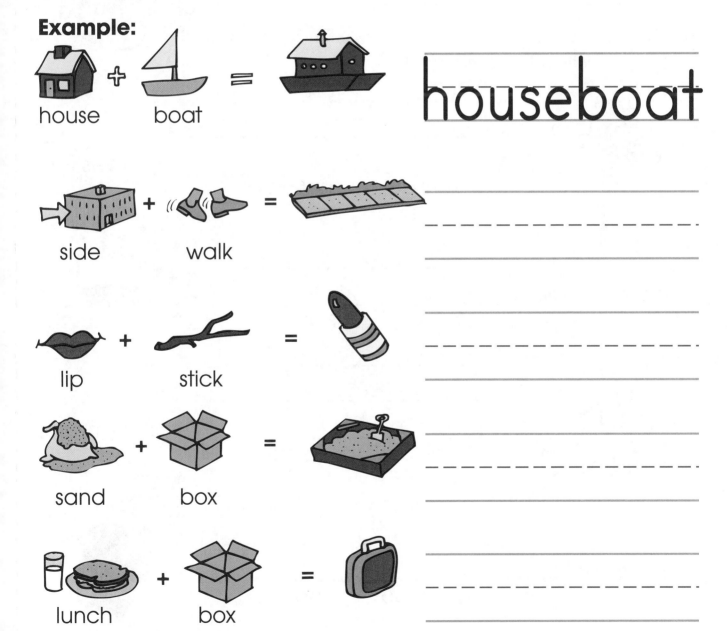

house   boat   =   houseboat

side   walk   =   _____

lip   stick   =   _____

sand   box   =   _____

lunch   box   =   _____

Compound Words

Directions: Circle the compound word that completes each sentence. Write each word on the line.

1. The _____ brings us letters.

           mailman   snowman

2. A _____ grows tall.

           sunlight   sunflower

3. The snow falls _____.

           outside   inside

4. A _____ fell on my head.

           raindrop   rainbow

5. I put the letter in a _____.

           mailbox   shoebox

Compound Words

Directions: Cut out the pictures and words at the bottom of the page. Put two words together to make a compound word. Write the new word.

☐ + ☐ = _____

☐ + ☐ = _____

☐ + ☐ = _____

☐ + ☐ = _____

cut ✂ -

| mail | snow | ball | bow |
| basket | man | rain | box |

Page is blank for cutting exercise on previous page.

Compound Words

Directions: Cut out the cards below. Turn them over. Take turns trying to make compound words. When a compound word is made, the player gets to keep the word.

Cut ✂ -

flash	snow	ball	sun
mail	house	plant	room
light	bow	light	card
base	shine	dog	box
rain	flake	thing	post
bath	house	in	house
any	side	day	birth

Page is blank for cutting exercise on previous page.

Names

Your name begins with a capital letter. People's names always begin with a capital letter.

Directions: Write your name. Did you remember to use a capital letter?

_____

- -

_____

Directions: Write each person's name. Use a capital letter at the beginning.

Zola

Katie

Marco

Jake

Write a friend's name.
Use a capital letter at
the beginning.

Names: Days of the Week

The days of the week begin with capital letters.

Directions: Write the days of the week in the spaces below. Put them in order. Be sure to start with capital letters.

Tuesday

Saturday

Monday

Friday

Thursday

Sunday

Wednesday

Names: Months of the Year

The months of the year begin with capital letters.

Directions: Write the months of the year in order on the calendar below. Be sure to use capital letters.

January	December	April	May	October	June
September	February	July	March	November	August

More Than One

Directions: An **s** at the end of a word often means there is more than one. Look at each picture. Circle the correct word. Write the word on the line.

two
dog   dogs

_____

_____

four
flower flowers

_____

_____

one
bikes   bike

_____

_____

three
toys   toy

_____

_____

a
lamb lambs

_____

_____

two
cat   cats

_____

_____

Name _____

More Than One

Directions: Read the nouns under the pictures. Then, write each noun under **One** or **More Than One**.

One

_____
_____
_____

barn

cows

ducks

horse

wagon

pigs

More Than One

_____
_____
_____

Comprehensive Curriculum - **Grade 1**

Name _____

More Than One

Directions: Circle the correct word to complete each sentence.

Remember: An **s** at the end of a word can mean more than one.

 I have two (apple, apples) .

 I can eat one (hot dogs, hot dog) .

 My dad has five (hats, hat) .

You can read four (book, books) .

 Six (letter, letters) are in the mailbox.

 One (plants, plant) needs water.

 Three (rabbit, rabbits) were pulled from the magician's hat.

More Than One

Directions: Choose the word that completes each sentence. Write each word on the line.

1. I have a _____ .

   dog   dogs

2. Four _____ are on the tree.

   apple   apples

3. I read two _____ today.

   book   books

4. My _____ is blue.

   bike   bikes

5. We saw lots of _____ at the zoo.

   monkey   monkeys

6. I have five _____ .

   balloon   balloons

Riddles

Directions: Read the word. Trace and write it on the line. Then, draw a line from the riddle to the animal it tells about.

long long

I am very big.
I lived a long, long time ago.
What am I?

giraffe

My neck is very long.
I eat leaves from trees.
What am I?

rabbit

I have long ears.
I hop very fast.
What am I?

dinosaur

Riddles

Directions: Read the word, and write it on the line. Then, read each riddle and draw a line to the picture and word that tells about it.

house

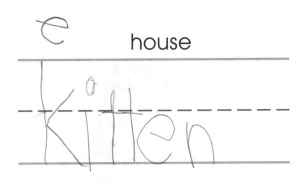

I like to play.
I am little. I am soft.
What am I?

house

kitten

I am big.
People live in me.
What am I?

kitten

flower

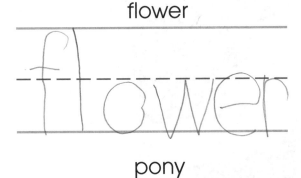

I am pretty.
I am green and yellow.
What am I?

flower

pony

I can jump. I can run.
I am brown.
What am I?

pony

Riddles

Directions: Write a word from the box to answer each riddle.

ice cream	book	chair	sun

There are many words in me.
I am fun to read.
What am I?

book

I am soft and yellow.
You can sit on me.
What am I?

chair

I am in the sky in the day.
I am hot. I am yellow.
What am I?

sun

I am cold. I am sweet.
You like to eat me.
What am I?

icecream

Picture Clues

Directions: Read the sentence. Circle the word that makes sense. Use the picture clues to help you. Then, write the word.

I ride on a
(bike)   hike   bike .

I ride on a
(train)   tree   train .

I ride in a
(car)   can   car .

I ride on a
(bus)   bug   bus .

I ride in a
jar   (jet)   Jet .

I ride in a
took   (truck)   truck .

Picture Clues

Directions: Read the sentence. Circle the word that makes sense. Use the picture clues to help you. Then, write the word.

I see the _bird_ .
(bird)   book

I see the _fish_ .
(fish)   fork

I see the _dogs_ .
(dogs)   dig

I see the _cats_ .
(cats)   coat

I see the _snake_ .
(snake)   snow

I see the _rat_ .
(rat)   rake

Picture Clues

Directions: Draw a line from the picture to its sentence.

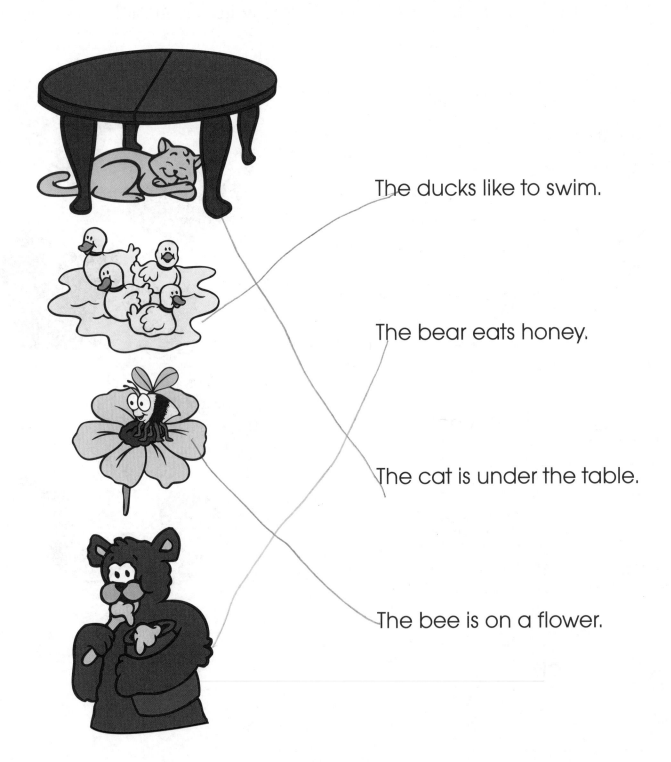

The ducks like to swim.

The bear eats honey.

The cat is under the table.

The bee is on a flower.

Picture Clues

Directions: Cut out the pictures below. Glue them next to the sentences.

The sun is yellow.

It is raining.

I can grin.

The bed is broken.

My pen and paper are here.

Cut ✂ --

Page is blank for cutting exercise on previous page.

Comprehension

Directions: Look at the picture. Write the words from the box to finish the sentences.

frog	log	bird	fish	ducks

The _frog_ can jump.

The turtle is on a _log_ .

A _bird_ is in the tree.

The boy wants a _fish_ .

I see three _ducks_ .

Comprehension

Directions: Read the poem. Write the correct words in the blanks.

A Flat Hat

The hat was on a mat.
A cat sat on the hat.
Now the hat is flat.

_____

The hat was on _____.

Who sat on the hat? _____

Now the hat is _____.

Following Directions: Color the Path

Directions: Color the path the girl should take to go home. Use the sentences to help you.

1. Go to the school and turn left.
2. At the end of the street, turn right.
3. Walk past the park and turn right.

Following Directions

Directions: Look at the pictures. Follow the directions in each box.

Draw a circle around the caterpillar.
Draw a line under the stick.

Draw an **X** on the mother bird.
Draw a triangle around the baby birds.

Draw a box around the rabbit.

Color the flowers. Count the bees.
There are _____ bees.

Classifying

Directions: Classifying is sorting things into groups. Draw a circle around the pictures that answer the question.

What Can Swim?

What Can Fly?

Classifying: These Keep Me Warm

Directions: Color the things that keep you warm.

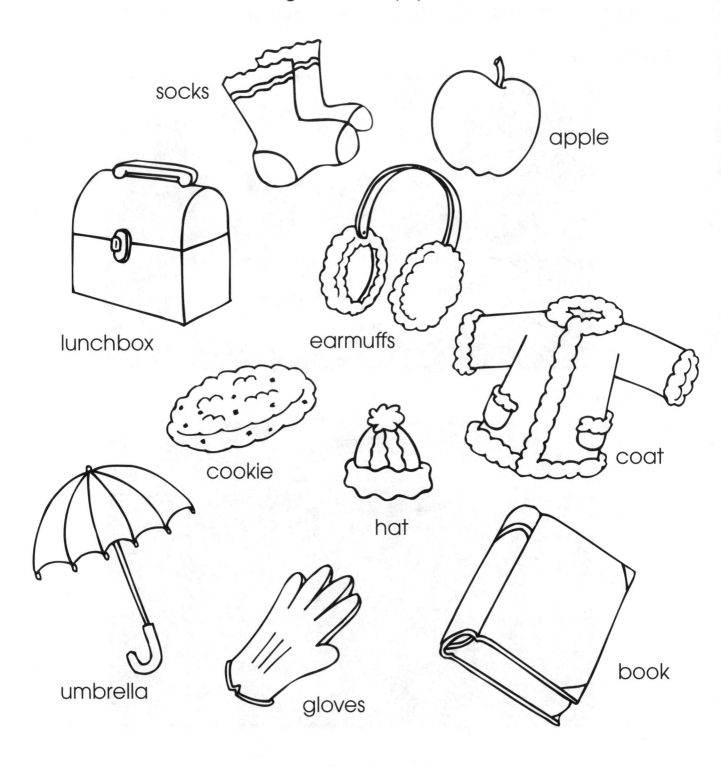

socks

apple

lunchbox

earmuffs

cookie

coat

hat

umbrella

gloves

book

Classifying: Objects

Help Dan clean up the park.

Directions: Circle the litter. Underline the coins. Draw a box around the balls.

Classifying: Things to Drink

Directions: Circle the pictures of things you can drink. Write the names of those things in the blanks.

milk

ice

soup and crackers

juice

water

banana

Classifying: Leaves

Directions: Cut out the leaves. Put them into two groups. Glue each group in a box on the top of the page. Write a name for each group.

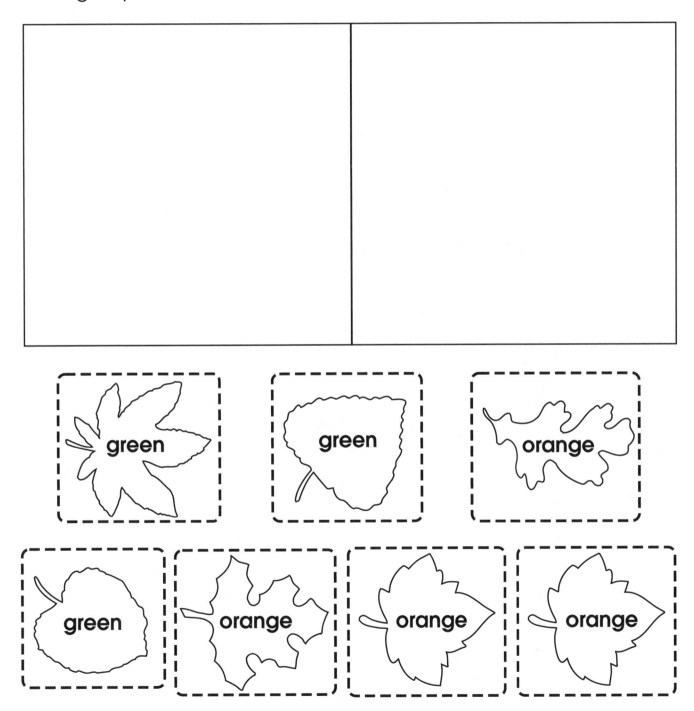

Comprehensive Curriculum - **Grade 1**

Page is blank for cutting exercise on previous page.

Classifying: Things to Chew

Directions: Draw a line from the pictures of things you chew to the plate.

soup

ice-cream bar

pizza

carrot

juice

GULP!

pasta

corn on the cob

milk

gum

Vocabulary

Directions: Read the words. Trace and write them on the lines. Look at each picture. Write **hot** or **cold** on the lines to show if it is hot or cold.

hot

hot _____

cold

cold _____

Vocabulary

Directions: Read the words. Trace and write them on the lines. Look at each picture and write **day** or **night** on the lines to show if they happen during the day or night.

day

day

night

night

Classifying: Night and Day

Directions: Write the words from the box under the pictures they describe.

stars	sun	moon	rays	dark	light	night	day

Classifying: Clowns and Balloons

Some words describe clowns. Some words describe balloons.

Directions: Read the words in the box. Write them in the correct columns.

float	laughs	hat	string
air	feet	pop	nose

clown

balloons

_____   _____

- - - - - - - - - - - - - - -   - - - - - - - - - - - - - - -

_____   _____

- - - - - - - - - - - - - - -   - - - - - - - - - - - - - - -

_____   _____

- - - - - - - - - - - - - - -   - - - - - - - - - - - - - - -

_____   _____

- - - - - - - - - - - - - - -   - - - - - - - - - - - - - - -

Comprehensive Curriculum - **Grade 1**

Similarities: Objects

Directions: Circle the picture in each row that is most like the first picture.

Example:

potato   **rose**   **tomato**   **tree**

shirt   **mittens**   **boots**   **jacket**

whale   **cat**   **dolphin**   **monkey**

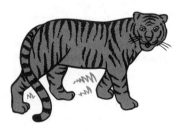   

tiger   **giraffe**   **lion**   **zebra**

Similarities: Objects

Directions: Circle the picture in each row that is most like the first picture.

Example:

| carrot | jacks | bread | pea |

| baseball | sneakers | basketball | bat |

| store | school | home | bakery |

| kitten | dog | fox | cat |

Comprehensive Curriculum - Grade 1

Classifying: Food Groups

Directions: Color the meats and eggs brown. Color the fruits and vegetables green. Color the breads tan. Color the dairy foods (like milk and cheese) yellow.

fish	bread	apple	cheese
crackers	carrot	orange	eggs
steaks	pear	milk	yogurt
ice cream	chicken	potato	pretzel

Same and Different: These Don't Belong

Directions: Circle the pictures in each row that go together.

Row 1   cookies   cake   beans   ice cream

Row 2   apple   banana   orange   cookies

Row 3   kite   dice   checkers   chess

Directions: Write the names of the things that do not belong.

Row 1 _____

Row 2 _____

Row 3 _____

Classifying: What Does Not Belong?

Directions: Draw an **X** on the picture that does not belong in each group.

fruit

| apple | peach | corn | watermelon |

wild animals

| bear | kitten | gorilla | lion |

pets

| cat | fish | elephant | dog |

flowers

| grass | rose | daisy | tulip |

Classifying: What Does Not Belong?

Directions: Draw an **X** on the word in each row that does not belong.

1.	flashlight	candle	radio	fire
2.	shirt	pants	coat	bat
3.	cow	car	bus	train
4.	beans	grapes	ball	bread
5.	gloves	hat	book	boots
6.	fork	butter	cup	plate
7.	book	ball	bat	milk
8.	dogs	bees	flies	ants

Classifying: Objects

Directions: Write each word in the correct row at the bottom of the page.

airplane   drum   radio   plate   car   pencil

spoon   crayon   chalk   fork   television   boat

Things we ride in:

_____

Things we eat with:

_____

Things we draw with:

_____

Things we listen to:

_____

Classifying: Names, Numbers, Animals, Colors

Directions: Write the words from the box next to the kinds of words they are.

Joe	cat	blue	Luis
two	dog	red	ten
Bella	green	pig	six

Name
Words

Number
Words

Animal
Words

Color
Words

Classifying: Things That Belong Together

Directions: Circle the pictures in each row that belong together.

Row 1   knife   key   fork   spoon

Row 2   orange   apple   candy   banana

Row 3   beach ball   soccer ball   baseball   apple

Directions: Write the names of the pictures that do not belong.

Row 1 _____

Row 2 _____

Row 3 _____

Classifying: Why They Are Different

Directions: Look at your answers on page 120. Write why each object does not belong.

_____

Row 1 _____

Row 2 _____

Row 3 _____

Directions: For each object, draw a group of pictures that belong with it.

shirt

_____

lettuce

Comprehensive Curriculum - **Grade 1**

Classifying: What Does Not Belong?

Directions: Circle the two things that do not belong in the picture. Write why they do not belong.

1. _____

_____

_____

_____

2. _____

_____

_____

Sequencing: Fill the Glasses

Directions: Follow the instructions to fill each glass. Use crayons to draw your favorite drink in the ones that are full and half-full.

full   **half-full**   **empty**

empty   **half-full**   **full**

Comprehensive Curriculum - Grade 1

Sequencing: Raking Leaves

Directions: Write a number in each box to show the order of the story.

Sequencing: Make a Snowman!

Directions: Write the number of the sentence that goes with each picture in the box.

1. Roll a large snowball for the snowman's bottom.

2. Make another snowball, and put it on top of the first.

3. Put the last snowball on top.

4. Dress the snowman.

Sequencing: A Recipe

Directions: Look at the recipe below. Put each step in order. Write 1, 2, 3, or 4 in the box.

HOW TO MAKE BREAD BUDDIES

Roll dough into balls and shapes. Connect pieces with a drop of water.

Mix 1 cup of water, 1 cup of salt, and 3 cups of flour.

Knead the dough.

Have an adult bake your bread buddy for 2-3 hours at 300°. Let it cool. Then, paint it!

What kind of bread buddy did you make?

_____

_ _

_____

Sequencing: How Flowers Grow

Directions: Read the story. Then, write the steps to grow a flower.

First, find a sunny spot. Then, plant the seed. Water it. The flower will start to grow. Pull the weeds around it. Remember to keep giving the flower water. Enjoy your flower.

1. _____ .

2. _____ .

3. _____ .

4. _____ .

5. _____ .

Sequencing: Make an Ice-Cream Cone

Directions: Number the boxes in order to show how to make an ice-cream cone.

Sequencing: Eating a Cone

What if a person never ate an ice-cream cone? Could you tell them how to eat it? Think about what you do when you eat an ice-cream cone.

Directions: Write directions to teach someone how to eat an ice-cream cone.

How to Eat an Ice-Cream Cone

_____

1. _____

_____

2. _____

_____

3. _____

_____

4. _____

Comprehension: Apples

Directions: Read about apples. Then, write the answers.

I like  . Do you?

Some  are red.

Some  are green.

Some  are yellow.

1. How many kinds of apples does the story tell about?

_____

- - - - - - - - - - - - - - - - - - - -

2. Name the kinds of apples.

_____   _____   _____

- - - - - - - - -   - - - - - - - - -   - - - - - - - -

3. What kind of apple do you like best?

_____

- - - - - - - - - - - - - - - - - - - -

Comprehension: Crayons

Directions: Read about crayons. Then, write your answers.

Crayons come in many colors.
Some crayons are dark colors.
Some crayons are light colors.
All crayons have wax in them.

1. How many colors of crayons are there?   many

few

2. Crayons come in _____ colors

and _____ colors.

3. What do all crayons have in them?

_____

Comprehension

Directions: Read the story. Write the words from the story that complete each sentence.

Jane and Will like to play in the rain. They take off their shoes and socks. They splash in the puddles. It feels cold! It is fun to splash!

Jane and Will like to _____ .

They take off their _____ .

They splash in _____ .

Do you like to splash in puddles?   Yes   No

Comprehension

Directions: Read the story. Write the words from the story that complete each sentence.

Ben and Eva have a bug. It is red with black spots. They call it Spot. Spot likes to eat green leaves and grass. The children keep Spot in a box.

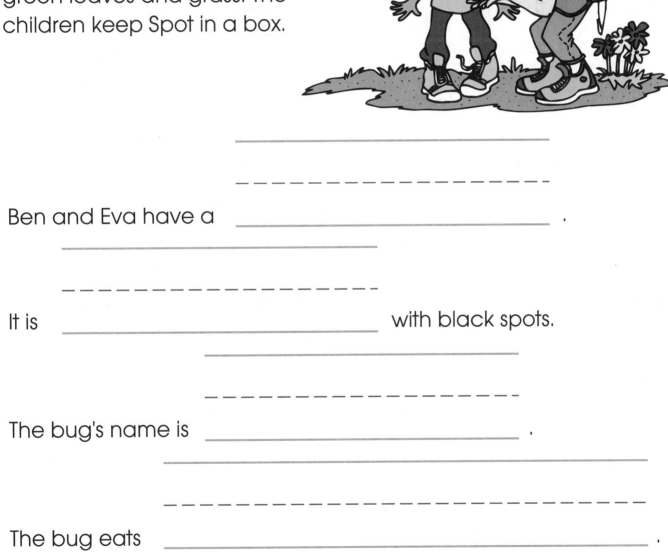

Ben and Eva have a _____ .

It is _____ with black spots.

The bug's name is _____ .

The bug eats _____ .

Comprehension: Snow Is Cold!

Directions: Read about snow. Circle the answers.

When you play in the snow, dress warmly. Wear a coat. Wear a hat. Wear gloves. Do you wear these when you play in the snow?

1. Snow is   warm.

                                              cold.

2. When you play in the snow, dress   warmly.

                                              quickly.

Directions: List three things to wear when you play in the snow.

_____

_ _

_____

_ _

_____

_ _

_____

Comprehension: Growing Flowers

Directions: Read about flowers. Then, write the answers.

Some flowers grow in pots. Many flowers grow in flower beds. Others grow beside the road. Flowers begin from seeds. They grow into small buds. Then, they open wide and bloom. Flowers are pretty!

1. Name two places flowers grow.

_____

_____

2. Flowers begin from _____ .

3. Then, flowers grow into small _____ .

4. Flowers then open wide and _____ .

Comprehension: Raking Leaves

Directions: Read about raking leaves. Then, answer the questions.

I like to rake leaves. Do you? Leaves die each year. They get brown and dry. They fall from the trees. Then, we rake them up.

1. What color are leaves when they die?

_____

_____

2. What happens when they die?

_____

_____

_____

_____

3. What do we do when leaves fall?

_____

_____

Comprehension: Clocks

Directions: Read about clocks. Then, answer the questions.

Ticking Clocks

Many clocks make two sounds. The sounds are tick and tock. Big clocks often make loud tick-tocks. Little clocks often make quiet tick-tocks. Sometimes, people put little clocks in a box with a new puppy. The puppy likes the sound. The tick-tock makes the puppy feel safe.

1. What two sounds do many clocks make?

_____   _____

_____ and _____

2. What kind of tick-tocks do big clocks make?

_____

_____

3. What kind of clock makes a new puppy feel safe?

_____

_____

Comprehension: Soup

Directions: Read about soup. Then, write the answers.

I Like Soup

Soup is good! It is good for you, too. We eat most kinds of soup hot. Some people eat cold soup in the summer. Carrots and beans are in some soups. Do you like crackers with soup?

1. Name two ways people eat soup.

_____   _____

- - - - - - - - - - - - - -   - - - - - - - - - - - - - -

_____   _____

2. Name two things that are in some soups.

_____   _____

- - - - - - - - - - - - - -   - - - - - - - - - - - - - -

_____   _____

3. Name the kind of soup you like best.

_____

- -

_____

Review

Directions: Read about cookies. Then, write your answers.

Cookies are made with many things. All cookies are made with flour. Some cookies have nuts in them. Some cookies do not. Some cookies have chocolate chips. Some do not. Cookbooks give directions on how to make cookies.

First, turn on the oven. Then, get out all the things that go in the cookies. Mix them together. Roll them out, and cut the cookies. Bake the cookies. Now, eat them!

1. Tell one way all cookies are the same.

_____

_____

2. Name one different thing in cookies.

_____

_____

3. Where do you find directions for making cookies?

_____

_____

Review

Directions: Read the story. Then, circle the pictures of things that are wet.

Some things used in baking are dry. Some things used in baking are wet. To bake muffins, first mix the salt, sugar, and flour. Then, add the egg. Now, add the milk. Stir. Put the muffins in the oven.

Directions: Tell the order to mix things when you bake muffins.

1. _____   4. _____

2. _____   5. _____

3. _____

Directions: Circle the answers.

6. The first things to mix are   dry.   wet.

7. Where are muffins baked?   oven   grill

Review

Directions: Read how to make energy balls. Then, answer the questions.

This snack is tasty and easy to make. You do not need to cook it. You will need a large bowl for mixing. You will need five things to make this snack.

Energy Balls

$\frac{1}{2}$ cup peanut butter

$\frac{1}{3}$ cup honey

$1\frac{1}{2}$ cups oatmeal

$\frac{1}{2}$ cup raisins

$\frac{1}{2}$ cup coconut flakes

Mix everything in the bowl. Roll the mix into small balls. If it is too sticky, get your hands damp.

1. What is third on the list of things needed?

_____

_____

2. How can you keep the mix from sticking to your hands?

_____

_____

Directions: Write what to do to make energy balls.

3. First, mix everything in a bowl. Then,

_____

_____

Comprehensive Curriculum - **Grade 1**

Comprehension: The Teddy Bear Song

Do you know the Teddy Bear Song? It is very old!

Directions: Read the Teddy Bear Song. Then, answer the questions.

Teddy bear, teddy bear, turn around.

Teddy bear, teddy bear, touch the ground.

Teddy bear, teddy bear, climb upstairs.

Teddy bear, teddy bear, say your prayers.

Teddy bear, teddy bear, turn out the light.

Teddy bear, teddy bear, say, "Good night!"

1. What is the first thing the teddy bear does?

_____

_____

2. What is the last thing the teddy bear does?

_____

_____

3. What would you name a teddy bear?

_____

_____

Sequencing: Put Teddy Bear to Bed

Directions: Read the song about the teddy bear again. Write a number in each box to show the order of the story.

Comprehension: A New Teddy Bear Song

Directions: Write words to make a new teddy bear song. Act out your new song with your teddy bear as you read it.

Teddy bear, teddy bear, turn _____ .

Teddy bear, teddy bear, touch the _____ .

Teddy bear, teddy bear, climb _____ .

Teddy bear, teddy bear, turn out _____ .

Teddy bear, teddy bear, say, _____ .

Comprehension: Balloons

Directions: Read the story. Then, answer the questions.

Some balloons float. They are filled with gas. Some do not float. They are filled with air. Some clowns carry balloons. Balloons come in many colors. What color do you like?

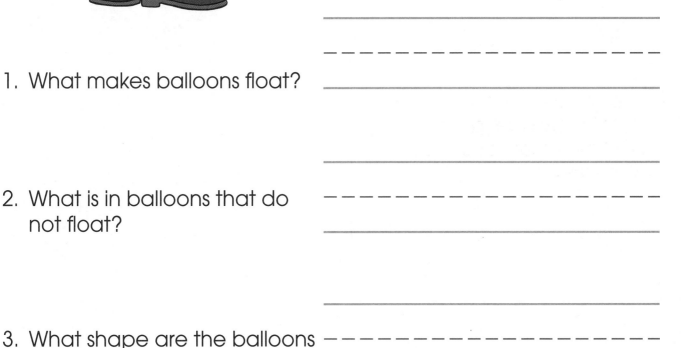

1. What makes balloons float? _____

2. What is in balloons that do not float? _____

3. What shape are the balloons the clown is holding? _____

Comprehension: Balloons

Directions: Read the story about balloons again. Draw a picture for the sentence in each box.

The clown is holding red, yellow, and blue balloons filled with air.

The clown is holding purple, orange, green, and blue balloons filled with gas.

Sequencing: Petting a Cat

Directions: Read the story. Then, write the answers.

Do you like cats? I do. To pet a cat, move slowly. Hold out your hand. The cat will come to you. Then, pet its head. Do not grab a cat! It will run away.

To pet a cat . . .

_____

1. Move _____ .

2. Hold out your _____ .

3. The cat will come to _____ .

4. Pet the cat's _____ .

5. Do not _____ a cat!

Comprehension: Cats

Directions: Read the story about cats again. Then, write the answers.

1. What is a good title for the story?

_____

_____

_____

2. The story tells you how to _____ .

3. What part of your body should you pet a cat with?

_____

_____

4. Why should you move slowly to pet a cat?

_____

_____

5. Why do you think a cat will run away if you grab it?

_____

_____

_____ .

Comprehension: Cats

Directions: Look at the pictures, and read about four cats. Then, write the correct name beside each cat.

Fluffy, Blackie, and Tiger are playing. Tom is sleeping. Blackie has spots. Tiger has stripes.

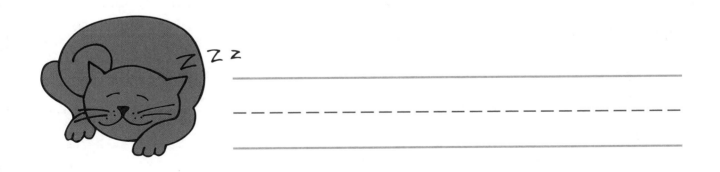

Comprehensive Curriculum - **Grade 1**

Same and Different: Cats

Directions: Compare the picture of the cats on page 149 to this picture. Write a word from the box to tell what is different about each cat.

| purple ball | green bow | blue brush | red collar |

_____

- -

1. Tom is wearing a _____ .

_____

- -

2. Blackie has a _____ .

_____

- -

3. Fluffy is wearing a _____ .

_____

- -

4. Tiger has a _____ .

Comprehension: Tigers

Directions: Read about tigers. Then, write the answers.

Tigers sleep during the day. They hunt at night. Tigers eat meat. They hunt deer. They like to eat wild pigs. If they cannot find meat, tigers will eat fish.

1. When do tigers sleep?

_____

_____

2. Name two things tigers eat.

_____

_____

_____

_____

3. When do tigers hunt? _____

Following Directions: Tiger Puzzle

Directions: Read the story about tigers again. Then, complete the puzzle.

Across:

1. When tigers cannot get meat, they eat _____ .

3. The food tigers like best is _____ .

4. Tigers like to eat this meat: wild _____ .

Down:

2. Tigers do this during the day.

Following Directions: Draw a Tiger

Directions: Follow directions to complete the picture of the tiger.

1. Draw black stripes on the tiger's body and tail.

2. Color the tiger's tongue red.

3. Draw claws on the feet.

4. Draw a black nose and two black eyes on the tiger's face.

5. Color the rest of the tiger orange.

6. Draw tall green grass for the tiger to sleep in.

Comprehension: How We Eat

Directions: Read the story. Use words from the box to answer the questions.

People eat with spoons and forks. They use a spoon to eat soup and ice cream. They use a fork to eat potatoes. They use a knife to cut their meat. They say, "Thank you. It was good!" when they finish.

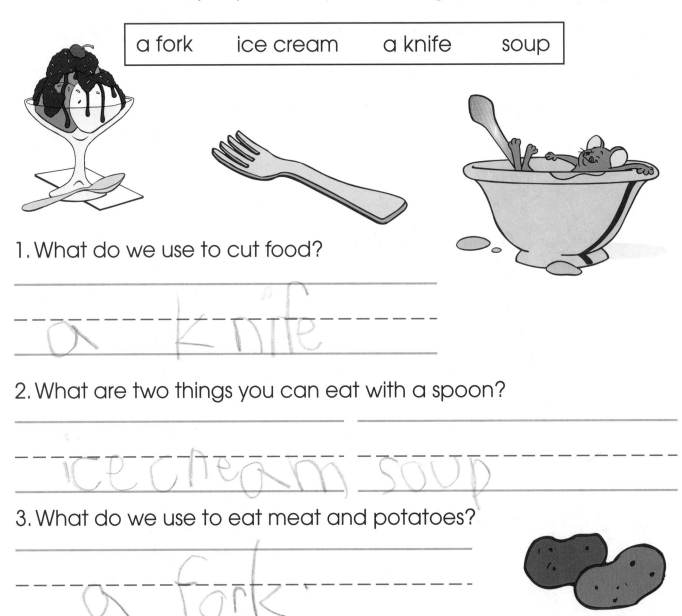

| a fork | ice cream | a knife | soup |

1. What do we use to cut food?

   a knife

2. What are two things you can eat with a spoon?

   ice cream soup

3. What do we use to eat meat and potatoes?

   a fork

Classifying: Foods

Directions: Read the questions under each plate. Draw three foods on each plate to answer the questions.

1. What foods can you cut with a knife?

2. What foods should you eat with a fork?

3. What foods can you eat with a spoon?

Comprehension: Write a Party Invitation

Directions: Read about the party. Then, complete the invitation.

The party will be at Dog's house. The party will start at 1:00 P.M. It will last 2 hours. Write your birthday for the date of the party.

Party Invitation

_____

Where: _____

Date: _____

Time It Begins: _____

Time It Ends: _____

_____

_____

Directions: On the last line, write something else about the party.

Sequencing: Pig Gets Ready

Directions: Number the pictures of Pig getting ready for the party to show the order of the story.

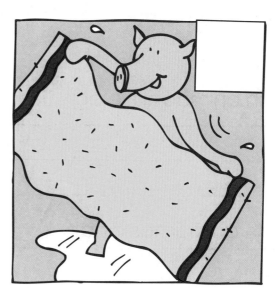

What kind of party do you think Pig is going to? _____

Comprehension: An Animal Party

Directions: Use the picture for clues. Write words from the box to answer the questions.

bear	cat
dog	elephant
giraffe	hippo
pig	tiger

1. Which animals have bow ties?

_____   _____

_ _ _ _ _ _ _ _ _ _ _ _ _   _ _ _ _ _ _ _ _ _ _ _ _ _

_____

2. Which animal has a hat?

_____

_ _ _ _ _ _ _ _ _ _ _ _ _ _ _ _ _ _

_ _ _ _ _ _ _ _ _ _ _ _ _ _ _ _ _ _

3. Which animal has a striped shirt?   _____

Classifying: Party Items

Directions: Draw a ☐ around objects that are food for the party. Draw a △ around the party guests. Draw a ○ around the objects used for fun at the party.

ice cream

fruit

games

tiger

noise makers

cake

garbage can

cat

hat

glasses

candle

bear

juice

balloons

giraffe

pig

pretzels

hippo

Comprehension: Play Simon Says

Directions: Read how to play Simon Says. Then, answer the questions.

SIMON SAYS, CLAP YOUR HANDS!

Simon Says

Here is how to play Simon Says: One kid is Simon. Simon is the leader. Everyone must do what Simon says and does but only if the leader says, "Simon says" first. Let's try it. "Simon says, 'Pat your head.'" "Simon says, 'Pat your nose. Pat your toes.'"

Oops! Did you pat your toes? I did not say, "Simon says," first. If you patted your toes, you are out!

1. Who is the leader in this game? _____

2. What must the leader say first each time? _____

3. What happens if you do something and the leader did not say, "Simon says"? _____

Comprehension: Play Simon Says

Directions: Read each sentence. Look at the picture next to it. Circle the picture if the person is playing Simon Says correctly.

1. Simon says, "Put your hands on your hips."

2. Simon says, "Stand on one leg."

3. Simon says, "Put your hands on your head."

4. Simon says, "Ride a bike."

5. Simon says, "Jump up and down."

6. Simon says, "Pet a dog."

7. Simon says, "Make a big smile."

Following Directions: Play Simon Says

Directions: Read the sentences. If Simon tells you to do something, follow the directions. If Simon does not tell you to do something, go to the next sentence.

1. Simon says: Cross out all the numbers 2 through 9.

2. Simon says: Cross out the vowel that is in the word **sun**.

3. Cross out the letter **B**.

4. Cross out the vowels **A** and **E**.

5. Simon says: Cross out the consonants in the word **cup**.

6. Cross out the letter **Z**.

7. Simon says: Cross out all the **K**s.

8. Simon says: Read your message.

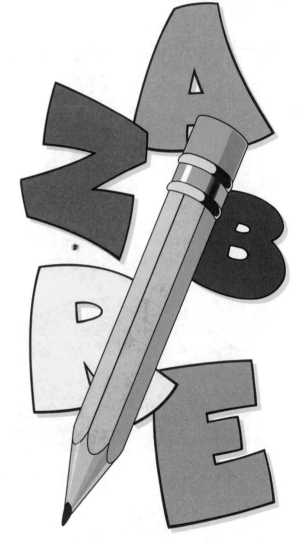

C 3 G U 7 P R U C P E K C P A 8 K K

6 T P U P J C 5 P O K 9 P B U P K K

Comprehension: Rhymes

Directions: Read about words that rhyme. Then, circle the answers.

Words that rhyme have the same end sounds. **Wing** and **sing** rhyme. **Boy** and **toy** rhyme. **Dime** and **time** rhyme. Can you think of other words that rhyme?

1. Words that rhyme have the same   end sounds.

                                        end letters.

> TREE, SEE
> SHOE, BLUE
> KITE, BITE
> MAKE, TAKE
> FLY, BUY

2. **Time** rhymes with   **tree**.

                              dime.

Directions: Write one rhyme for each word.

wing   boy

_____   _____

_____   _____

dime   pink

_____   _____

_____   _____

Rhyming Words

Many poems have rhyming words. The rhyming words are usually at the end of the line.

Directions: Complete the poem with words from the box.

My Glue

I spilled my _____.

I felt _____.

What could I _____?

Hey! I have a _____!

I'll make it _____.

The cleanest you've _____.

No one will _____.

Wouldn't that be _____?

blue	clue	scream	seen
glue	do	clean	mean

Classifying: Rhymes

Directions: Cut out the pieces. Read the words. Find two words that rhyme. Put the words together.

kite   my

tree   bell

buy   bee

well   white

Page is blank for cutting exercise on previous page.

Classifying: Rhymes

Directions: Circle the pictures that rhyme in each row.

Row 1

Row 2

Row 3

Directions: Write the names of the pictures that do not rhyme.

These words do not rhyme:

Row 1	Row 2	Row 3
_____	_____	_____

Comprehension: Babies

Directions: Read about babies. Then, write the answers.

Babies are small. Some babies cry a lot. They cry when they are wet. They cry when they are hungry. They smile when they are dry. They smile when they are fed.

1. Name two reasons babies cry.

_____   _____

_____   _____

_____   _____

2. Name two reasons babies smile.

_____   _____

_____   _____

_____   _____

3. Write a baby's name you like.

_____

_____

_____

Comprehension: Babies

Directions: Read each sentence. Draw a picture of a baby's face in the box to show if she would cry or smile.

1. The baby needs to have her diaper changed.

1

2. The baby has not eaten for a while.

2

3. Dad put a dry diaper on the baby.

3

4. The baby is going to finish her bottle.

4

5. The baby finished her food but is still hungry.

5

Comprehensive Curriculum - **Grade 1**

Sequencing: Feeding Baby

Directions: Read the sentences. Write a number in each box to show the order of the story.

The baby smiles.

Mom makes the baby's food.

The baby is put in his chair.

The baby is crying.

Mom feeds the baby.

Same and Different: Compare the Twins

Directions: Read the story. Then, use the words in the box and the picture to write your answers.

Ben and Ann are twin babies. They were born at the same time. They have the same mother. Ben is a boy baby. Ann is a girl baby.

mother	bow	boy	girl	hat	twins

1. Tell one way Ann and Ben are the same.

_____
_____
_____
_____

2. Ann and Ben are _____ .

3. Tell two ways Ann and Ben are different.

Ann is a _____ . Ben is a _____ .

Ann is wearing a _____ . Ben is wearing a _____ .

Comprehensive Curriculum - **Grade 1**

Comprehension: Hats

Directions: Read about hats. Then, write your answers.

There are many kinds of hats. Some baseball hats have brims. Some fancy hats have feathers. Some knit hats pull down over your ears. Some hats are made of straw. Do you like hats?

1. Name four kinds of hats.

_____   _____

_____   _____

_____   _____

_____   _____

Directions: Circle the correct answers.

2. What kind of hats pull down over your ears?

   straw hats

   knit hats

3. What are some hats made of?

   straw

   mud

Sequencing: Choosing a Hat

Directions: Write a number in each box to show the order of the story.

Comprehensive Curriculum - **Grade 1**

Name _____

Following Directions: Draw Hats

Directions: Draw a hat on each person. Read the sentences to know what kind of hat to draw.

1. The first girl is wearing a purple hat with feathers.

2. The boy next to the girl with the purple hat is wearing a red baseball hat.

3. The first boy is wearing a yellow knit hat.

4. The last boy is wearing a brown top hat.

5. The girl next to the boy with the red hat is wearing a blue straw hat.

Classifying: Mr. Lincoln's Hat

Abraham Lincoln wore a tall hat. He liked to keep things in his hat so he would not lose them.

Directions: Cut out the pictures of things Mr. Lincoln could have kept in his hat. Glue those pictures on the hat.

 letters

 candle

 penny

 one dollar

 bowl

 cat

 watch

paper

Page is blank for cutting exercise on previous page.

Comprehension: Boats

Directions: Read about boats. Then, answer the questions.

See the boats! They float on water. Some boats have sails. The wind moves the sails. It makes the boats go. Many people name their sailboats. They paint the name on the side of the boat.

1. What makes sailboats move?

_____

- -

_____

2. Where do sailboats float?

_____

- -

_____

3. What would you name a sailboat?

_____

- -

_____

Comprehensive Curriculum - **Grade 1**

Same and Different: Color the Boats

Directions: Find the three boats that are alike. Color them all the same. One boat is different. Color it differently.

Comprehension: A Boat Ride

Directions: Write a sentence under each picture to tell what is happening. Read the story you wrote.

Comprehension: Travel

Directions: Read the story. Then, answer the questions.

Let's Take a Trip!

Pack your bag. Shall we go by car, plane, or train? Let's go to the sea. When we get there, let's ride in a sailboat.

1. What are three ways to travel?

_____ _____ _____

_____ _____ _____

2. Where will we go?

_____

_____

3. What will we do when we get there?

_____

_____

Predicting: Words and Pictures

Directions: Complete each story by choosing the correct picture. Draw a line from the story to the picture.

1. Shawnda got her books. She went

   to the bus stop. Shawnda got

   on the bus.

2. Marco planted a seed. He watered it.

   He pulled the weeds around it.

3. Abraham's dog was barking.

   Abraham got out the dog food.

   He put it in the dog bowl.

Predicting: Story Ending

Directions: Read the story. Draw a picture in the last box to complete the story.

Predicting: Story Ending

Directions: Read the story. Draw a picture in the last box to complete the story.

Marco likes to paint.   He likes to help his dad.

He is tired when he's finished.

Predicting: Story Ending

Directions: Read each story. Circle the sentence that tells how the story will end.

Ann was riding her bike. She saw a dog in the park. She stopped to pet it. Ann left to go home.

The dog went swimming.

The dog followed Ann.

The dog went home with a cat.

Antonio went to a baseball game. A baseball player hit a ball toward him. He reached out his hands.

The player caught the ball.

The ball bounced on a car.

Antonio caught the ball.

Making Inferences: Baseball

Tess likes baseball. She likes to win. Tess's team does not win.

Directions: Circle the correct answers.

1. Tess likes

 football.   soccer.   baseball.

2. Tess likes to

 win.   lose.

3. Tess uses a bat.

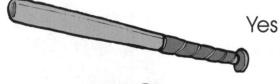   Yes   No

4. Tess is

 happy.    sad.

Making Inferences: The Stars

Layla looks at the stars. She sings a song about them. She makes a wish on them. The stars help Layla sleep.

Directions: Circle the correct answers.

1. Layla likes the

      moon.   sun.   stars.

2. What song do you think she sings?

    Row, Row, Row Your Boat

    Twinkle, Twinkle Little Star

    Happy Birthday to You

3. What does Layla "make" on the stars?

    a wish   a spaceship   lunch

Making Inferences: Feelings

Directions: Read each story. Choose a word from the box to show how each person feels.

happy	excited	sad	mad

1. Andy and Sam were best friends. Sam and his family moved far away. How does Sam feel?

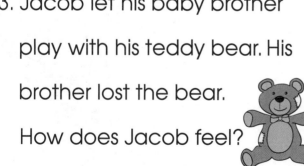

_____

_____

2. Deana could not sleep. It was the night before her birthday party. How does Deana feel?

_____

_____

3. Jacob let his baby brother play with his teddy bear. His brother lost the bear. How does Jacob feel?

_____

_____

4. Kia picked flowers for her mom. Her mom smiled when she got them. How does Kia feel?

_____

_____

Comprehension: Eating Ice Cream

Directions: Read the story. Write two things Sam could have done so he could have enjoyed eating his ice-cream cone.

It was a hot day. Sam went to the store and got an ice-cream cone. He sat at a table in the sun. Sam watched some friends play ball. Suddenly, his ice cream fell on the sidewalk.

1. _____

2. _____

Review

Directions: Write a sentence to complete this story.

1. Evan's dog runs away.

2. Evan chases it.

3. The dog runs into a store.

4. _____

_____

_____

_____

Directions: Read this story. Answer the questions.

Lea plays games with her little sister. Sometimes, Lea hides from her sister. Her sister calls her name over and over. Lea does not answer. Lea thinks it is funny.

1. Is Lea being nice or mean to her sister? _____

_____

2. Do you think her sister likes Lea to hide? _____

3. What would you do if you were Lea's sister?

_____

_____

Books

Directions: What do you know about books? Use the words in the box below to complete the sentences.

title	book	author
illustrator	pages	left to right
fun	library	glossary

The name of the book is the _____.

_____ is the direction we read.

The person who wrote the words is the _____.

Reading is _____!

There are many books in the _____.

The person who draws the pictures is the _____.

The _____ is a kind of dictionary in the book to help you find the meanings of words.

Nouns

A **noun** is a word that names a person, place, or thing. When you read a sentence, the noun is what the sentence is about.

Directions: Complete each sentence with a noun.

The _____ is fat.

My _____ is blue.

The _____ has apples.

The _____ is hot.

Nouns

Directions: Write these naming words in the correct box.

| store | zoo | child | baby | teacher | table |
| cat | park | gym | woman | sock | horse |

Person

_____ _____

_____ _____

Place

_____ _____

_____ _____

Thing

_____ _____

_____ _____

Name _____

Things That Go Together

Some nouns name things that go together.

Directions: Draw a line to match the nouns on the left with the matching nouns on the right.

toothpaste

washcloth

pencil

sock

salt

toothbrush

shoe

pepper

soap

paper

pillow

bed

Things That Go Together

Directions: Draw a line to connect the objects that go together.

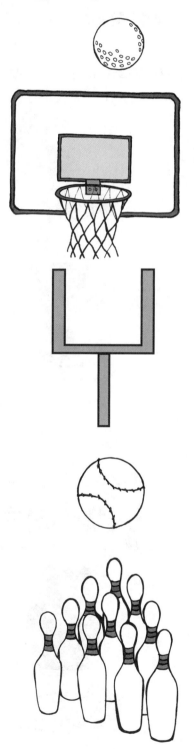

Verbs

Verbs are words that tell what a person or a thing can do.

Example: The girl pats the dog.
The word **pats** is the verb. It shows action.

Directions: Draw a line between the verbs and the pictures that show the action.

eat

run

sleep

swim

sing

hop

Verbs

Directions:
Look at the picture and read the words. Write an action word in each sentence below.

1. The two boys like to _____ together.

2. The children _____ the soccer ball.

3. Some children like to _____ on the swing.

4. The girl can _____ very fast.

5. The teacher _____ the bell.

Nouns and Verbs

A noun is a person or thing a sentence tells about. A verb tells what the person or thing does.

Directions: Circle the noun in each sentence. Underline the verb.

Example: The (cat) sleeps.

1. Jill plays a game on the computer.

2. Children swim in the pool.

3. The car raced around the track.

4. Mike throws the ball to his friend.

5. Monkeys swing in the trees.

6. Terry laughed at the clown.

Review

Directions: Cut out the words below. Glue naming words in the **Nouns** box. Glue action words in the **Verbs** box.

Nouns	Verbs

cut ✂ —

Page is blank for cutting exercise on previous page.

Review

Directions: Read the sentences below. Draw a **red** circle around the nouns. Draw a **blue** line under the verbs.

1. The boy runs fast.

2. The turtle eats leaves.

3. The fish swim in the tank.

4. The girl hits the ball.

Name _____

Words That Describe

Describing words tell us more about a person, place, or thing.

Directions: Read the words in the box. Choose the word that describes the picture. Write it next to the picture.

happy	round	sick	cold	long

Words That Describe

Directions: Read the words in the box. Choose the word that describes the picture. Write it next to the picture.

wet	round	funny	soft	sad	tall

Name _____

Words That Describe

Directions: Circle the describing word in each sentence. Draw a line from the sentence to the picture.

1. The hungry dog is eating.

2. The tiny bird is flying.

3. Horses have long legs.

4. She is a fast runner.

5. The little boy was lost.

Words That Describe: Colors and Numbers

Colors and numbers can describe nouns.

Directions: Underline the describing word in each sentence. Draw a picture to go with each sentence.

A yellow moon was in the sky.

Two worms are on the road.

The tree had red apples.

The girl wore a blue dress.

Name _____

Sequencing: Comparative Adjectives

Directions: Look at each group of pictures. Write 1, 2, or 3 under the picture to show where it should be.

Example:

tallest _3_   **tall** _1_   **taller** _2_

small _____   **smallest** _____   **smaller** _____

biggest _____   **big** _____   **bigger** _____

wider _____   **wide** _____   **widest** _____

Sequencing: Comparative Adjectives

Directions: Look at the pictures in each row. Write 1, 2, or 3 under the picture to show where it should be.

shortest _____   **shorter** _____   **short** _____

longest _____   **longer** _____   **long** _____

happy _____   **happier** _____   **happiest** _____

hotter _____   **hot** _____   **hottest** _____

Synonyms

Synonyms are words that mean almost the same thing. **Start** and **begin** are synonyms.

Directions: Find the synonyms that describe each picture. Write the words in the boxes below the picture.

small funny large sad silly little big unhappy	

Synonyms

Synonyms are words that mean almost the same thing.

Directions: Read the word in the center of each flower. Find a synonym for each word on a bee at the bottom of the page. Cut out and glue each bee on its matching flower.

cut -

Comprehensive Curriculum - **Grade 1**

Page is blank for cutting exercise on previous page.

Similarities: Synonyms

Directions: Circle the word in each row that is most like the first word in the row.

Example:

grin		(smile)	frown	mad
bag		jar	sack	box
cat		fruit	animal	flower
apple		rot	cookie	fruit
around		circle	square	dot
brown		tan	black	red
bird		dog	cat	duck
bee		fish	ant	snake

Synonyms

Synonyms are words that have the same meaning.

Directions: Read each sentence, and look at the underlined word. Circle the word that means the same thing. Write the new words.

1. The <u>little</u> dog ran.   tall   funny   small

2. The <u>happy</u> girl smiled.   glad   sad   good

3. The bird is in the <u>big</u> tree. green   pretty   tall

4. He was <u>nice</u> to me.   kind   mad   bad

5. The baby is <u>tired.</u>   sleepy   sad   little

_____   _____   _____

_____   _____   _____

_____   _____

_____   _____

Synonyms

Directions: Read each sentence, and look at the underlined word. Circle the word that means the same thing. Write the new words.

1. The boy was <u>mad</u>.	happy	angry	pup
2. The <u>dog</u> is brown.	pup	cat	rat
3. I like to <u>scream</u>.	soar	mad	shout
4. The bird can <u>fly</u>.	soar	jog	warm
5. The girl can <u>run</u>.	sleep	jog	shout
6. I am <u>hot</u>.	warm	cold	soar

_____   _____   _____

_____   _____   _____

_____   _____   _____

_____   _____   _____

Similarities: Synonyms

Directions: Read each sentence. Read the word after the sentence. Find the word that is most like it in the sentence, and circle it.

1. The flowers grew very tall.

 plants

2. Jan picked the apple from the tree.

 applesauce

3. Juan's van is dirty.

 truck

4. A dog makes a sound different from a cat.

 wolf

5. Dad put up a fence in the yard.

 gate

Similarities: Synonyms

Directions: Read the story. Write a word on the line that means almost the same as the word under the line.

Dan went to the _____ .
                         store

He wanted to buy _____ .
                         food

He walked very _____ .
                       quickly

The store had what he wanted.

He bought it using _____ .
                          dimes

Instead of walking home, Dan _____ .
                                       jogged

Antonyms

Antonyms are words that are opposites. **Hot** and **cold** are antonyms.

Directions: Draw a line between the antonyms.

closed

below

full

empty

above

old

new

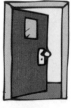

open

Opposites

Directions: Draw lines to connect the words that are opposites.

up	**wet**
over	**down**
dry	**dirty**
clean	**under**

Opposites

Opposites are things that are different in every way.

Directions: Draw a line between the opposites.

day

happy

big

open

front

little

closed

night

back

sad

Name _____

Antonyms

Directions: Find the two words that are opposites. Cut out the balloon basket, and glue it on the proper balloon.

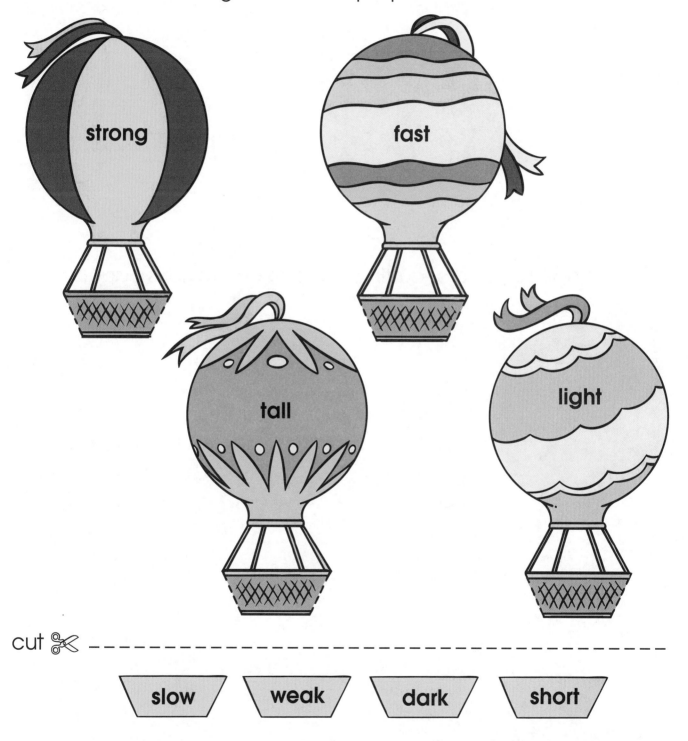

strong

fast

tall

light

cut ✂ -

slow   weak   dark   short

Page is blank for cutting exercise on previous page.

Opposites

Directions: Circle the picture in each row that is the opposite of the first picture.

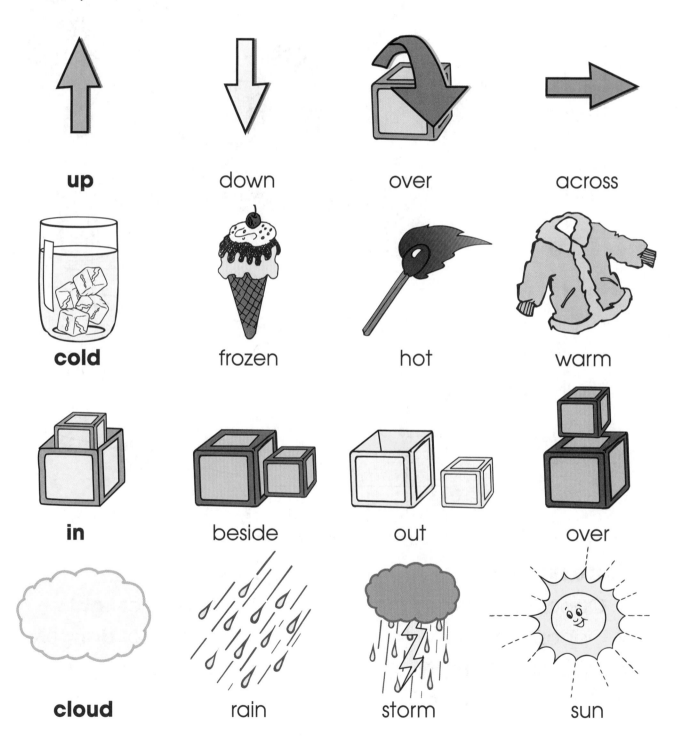

up	down	over	across
cold	frozen	hot	warm
in	beside	out	over
cloud	rain	storm	sun

Name _____

Opposites

Directions: Read each clue. Write the answers in the puzzle.

high   yes   left
heavy   tight
safe   full

Across:
1. Opposite of **low**
2. Opposite of **no**
4. Opposite of **empty**
6. Opposite of **loose**

Down:
1. Opposite of **light**
3. Opposite of **dangerous**
5. Opposite of **right**

Opposites

Directions: Cut out the pieces. Read the words. Find the pairs of words that are opposites, and put the pieces together. On the blank pieces, write your own pair of opposites.

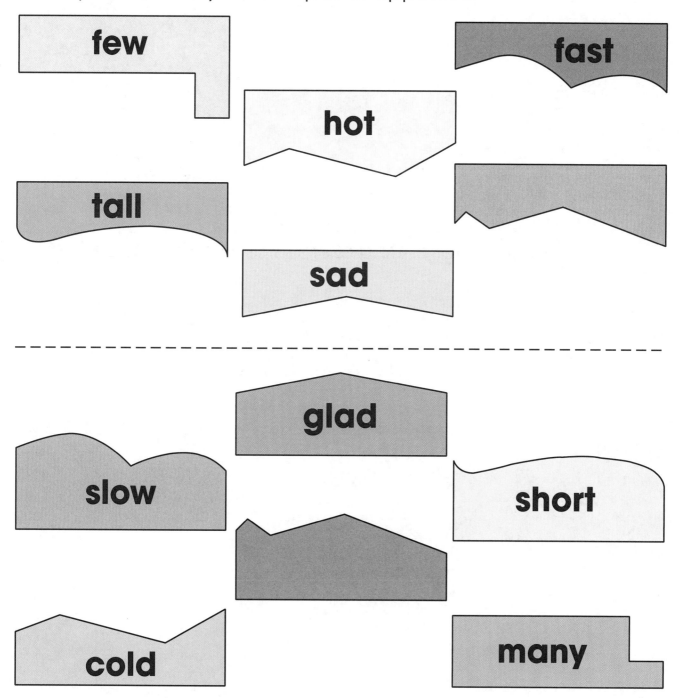

Page is blank for cutting exercise on previous page.

Opposites

Directions: Circle the two words in each sentence that are opposites.

1. Cold ice cream is good on a hot day.

2. Sam took off his wet socks and put on dry ones.

3. Do you like to run fast or slow?

4. The dog is black, and the cat is white.

5. The elephant looked really big next to the small mouse.

6. The tiny seed grew into a large plant.

Homophones

Homophones are words that **sound** the same but are spelled differently and mean something different. **Blew** and **blue** are homophones.

Directions: Look at the word pairs. Choose the word that describes the picture. Write the word on the line next to the picture.

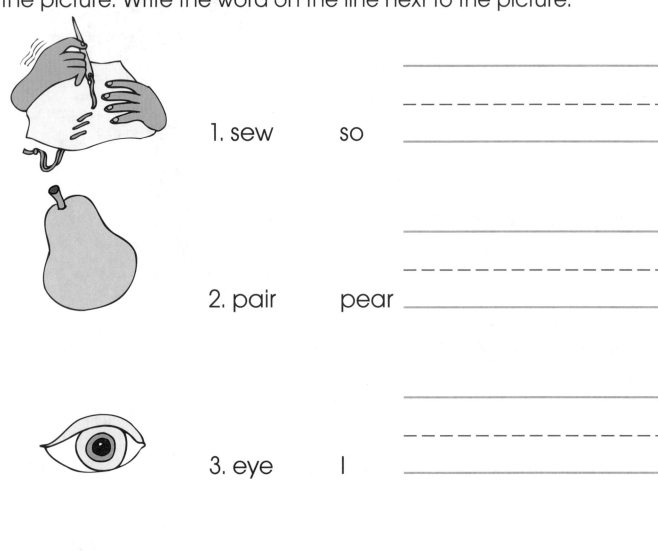

1. sew   so   _____

2. pair   pear   _____

3. eye   I   _____

4. see   sea   _____

Homophones

Directions: Read each sentence. Underline the two words that sound the same but are spelled differently and mean something different.

1. Ian ate eight grapes.

2. Kylie read *Little Red Riding Hood*.

3. I went to buy two dolls.

4. Five blue feathers blew in the wind.

5. Would you get wood for the fire?

Following Directions: Days of the Week

Calendars show the days of the week in order. Sunday comes first. Saturday comes last. There are five days in between. An **abbreviation** is a short way of writing words. The abbreviations for the days of the week are usually the first three or four letters of the word followed by a period.

Example: Sunday — Sun.

Directions: Write the days of the week in order on the calendar. Use the abbreviations.

Day 1	Day 2	Day 3
Sunday	Monday	Tuesday
Sun.		Tues.

Day 4	Day 5	Day 6
Wednesday	Thursday	Friday
	Thurs.	

Day 7
Saturday

Sentences

Sentences begin with capital letters.

Directions: Read the sentences, and write them below. Begin each sentence with a capital letter.

Example: the cat is fat.

T̵h̵e̵ ̵c̵a̵t̵ ̵i̵s̵ ̵f̵a̵t̵.

my dog is big.

_____
- -
_____

the boy is sad.

_____
- -
_____

bikes are fun!

_____
- -
_____

dad can bake.

_____
- -
_____

Word Order

If you change the order of the words in a sentence, you can change the meaning of the sentence.

Directions: Read the sentences. Draw a circle around the sentence that describes the picture.

Example:

The fox jumped over the dogs.
The dogs jumped over the fox.

1. The cat watched the bird.
   The bird watched the cat.

2. The girl looked at the boy.
   The boy looked at the girl.

3. The turtle ran past the rabbit.
   The rabbit ran past the turtle.

Word Order

Word order is the way words are arranged in a sentence so that they make sense.

Directions: Cut out the words, and put them in the correct order. Glue each sentence on another sheet of paper.

| I | like | bike. | to | ride | my |

| hot. | It | is | and | sunny |

| drink | I | can | water. |

| My | me. | with | plays | mom |

| tricks. | do | can | The | dog |

| you | go | store? | to | the | Can |

Page is blank for cutting exercise on previous page.

Word Order

Directions: Look at the picture. Put the words in order. Write the sentences on the lines below.

1. We made lemonade. some
2. good. It was
3. We the sold lemonade.
4. cost It five cents.
5. fun. We had

1. _____

2. _____

3. _____

4. _____

5. _____

Comprehensive Curriculum - **Grade 1**

Name _____

Word Order

Directions: Look at the picture. Put the words in the right order. Write the sentences on the lines below.

1. a Maya starfish. has
2. and Lily to Tyler swim. like
3. The shining. sun is
4. sand. the in Jack plays
5. cold. water The is

1. _____

2. _____

3. _____

4. _____

5. _____

Review

Directions: Put the words in the right order to make a sentence. Write the sentences on the lines below.

1. a gerbil. has Ann
2. is The Mike. named gerbil
3. likes eat. Mike to
4. play. to Mike likes
5. happy a is gerbil. Mike

1. _____

2. _____

3. _____

4. _____

5. _____

Telling Sentences

Directions: Read the sentences, and write them below. Begin each sentence with a capital letter. End each sentence with a period.

1. most children like pets
2. some children like dogs
3. some children like cats
4. some children like snakes
5. some children like all animals

1. _____

2. _____

3. _____

4. _____

5. _____

Telling Sentences

Directions: Read the sentences, and write them below.
Begin each sentence with a capital letter.
End each sentence with a period.

1. i like to go to the store with Mom
2. we go on Friday
3. i get to push the cart
4. i get to buy the cereal
5. i like to help Mom

1. _____

2. _____

3. _____

4. _____

5. _____

Asking Sentences

Directions: Write the first word of each asking sentence. Be sure to begin each question with a capital letter. End each question with a question mark.

1. _____ you like the zoo   **do**

2. _____ much does it cost   **how**

3. _____ you feed the ducks   **can**

4. _____ you see the monkeys   **will**

5. _____ time will you eat lunch   **what**

Asking Sentences

Directions: Read the asking sentences. Write the sentences below. Begin each sentence with a capital letter. End each sentence with a question mark.

1. what game will we play
2. do you like to read
3. how old are you
4. who is your best friend
5. can you tie your shoes

1. _____

2. _____

3. _____

4. _____

5. _____

Name _____

Periods and Question Marks

Directions: Put a period or a question mark at the end of each sentence below.

1. Do you like parades

2. The clowns lead the parade

3. Can you hear the band

4. The balloons are big

5. Can you see the horses

Review

Directions: Look at the picture. In the space below, write one telling sentence about the picture. Then, write one asking sentence about the picture.

Telling sentence:

_____

- -

_____

Asking sentence:

_____

- -

_____

Is and *Are*

Use **is** in sentences about one person or one thing. Use **are** in sentences about more than one person or thing.

Example: The dog **is** barking.
The dogs **are** barking.

Directions: Write **is** or **are** in the sentences below.

1. Jim _____ playing baseball.

2. Eli and Sam _____ good friends.

3. Cupcakes _____ my favorite treat.

4. Amina _____ a good soccer player.

Is and *Are*

Directions: Write **is** or **are** in the sentences below.
Example: Lexi __**is**__ sleeping.

1. Cats and dogs _____ good pets.

2. Luke _____ my best friend.

3. Apples _____ good to eat.

4. We _____ going to the zoo.

5. Pedro _____ coming to my house.

6. When _____ you all going to the zoo?

Vocabulary

Directions: Read the words. Trace and write them on the lines. Circle the word which completes each sentence. Write the word on the lines.

you and me _you and me_

I will play with _____ .   you   me

You can go with _____ .   you   me

Can you run with _____ ?   you   me

Vocabulary

Directions: Read the words. Trace and write them on the lines. Then, circle the word that completes each sentence. Write it on the line.

over _over_ _____

under _under_ _____

The kite is _____ the tree.

over   under

The kite is _____ the tree.

over   under

Vocabulary

Directions: Read the words. Trace and write them on the lines. Then, circle the word that completes each sentence. Write it on the line.

above _above_

below _below_

The fish is _____ the water.
above   below

The fish is _____ the water.
above   below

Vocabulary

Directions: Read and trace the words. Then, circle the word that completes each sentence. Write it on the line.

inside   inside

outside   outside

The dog is _____ his house.

inside   outside

The dog is _____ his house.

inside   outside

Vocabulary

Directions: Read the words. Trace and write them on the lines. Then, circle the word that completes each sentence. Write it on the line.

up   up

down   down

The flag is _____ the pole.
     up   down

The flag is _____ the pole.
     up   down

SPELLING

B...U...G

Color Names

Directions: Trace the letters to write the name of each color. Then, write the name again by yourself.

Example:

orange   orange

blue   blue

green   green

yellow   yellow

red   red

brown   brown

Color Names: Sentences

Directions: Use the color words to complete these sentences. Then, put a period at the end.

Example: My new are  orange.

 green tree    blue bike    yellow chick   red ball

1. The baby is 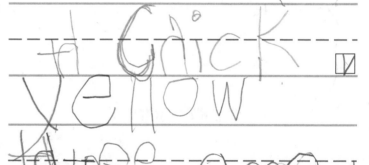 yellow chick ✓

2. This  is tree green ✓

3. My  is big and red ✓

4. My sister's  is bike ✓

Comprehensive Curriculum - Grade 1

Color Names: Sentences

Directions: Some of these sentences tell a whole idea. Others have something missing. If something is missing, draw a line to the word that completes the sentence. Put a period at the end of each sentence.

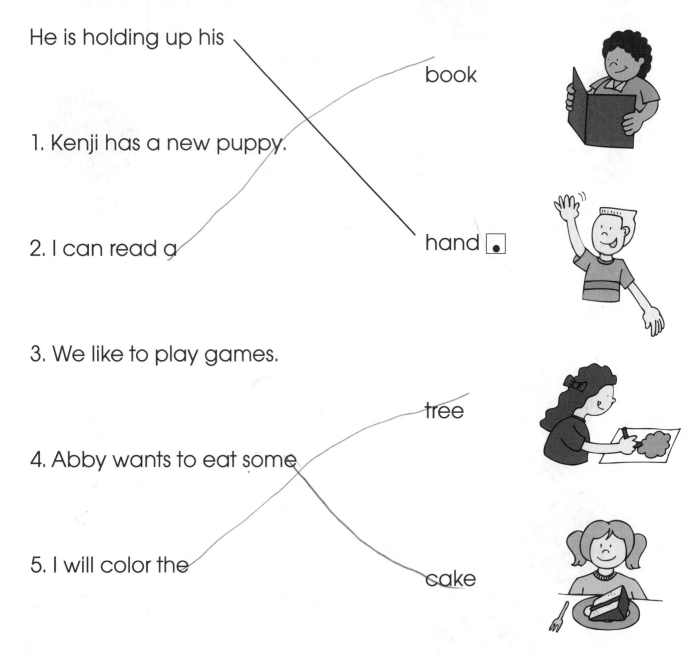

He is holding up his

book

1. Kenji has a new puppy.

2. I can read a

hand .

3. We like to play games.

tree

4. Abby wants to eat some

5. I will color the

cake

6. This is my birthday.

Name _____

Color Names: Capital Letters

A sentence begins with a capital letter.

Directions: The words by each picture are mixed up. Write them to make a sentence that tells about the picture. Begin each sentence with a capital letter, and end it with a period.

Example: coat she has a red

She has a red coat.

1. box sees he a blue

He sees a blue box

2. her is yellow flower

Her flower is yellow

3. red draws he a door

He draws a red door

Name _____

Color Names: Crossword Puzzle

Directions: Complete each color name. Some words go down, and some go across. Try to spell each word by yourself.

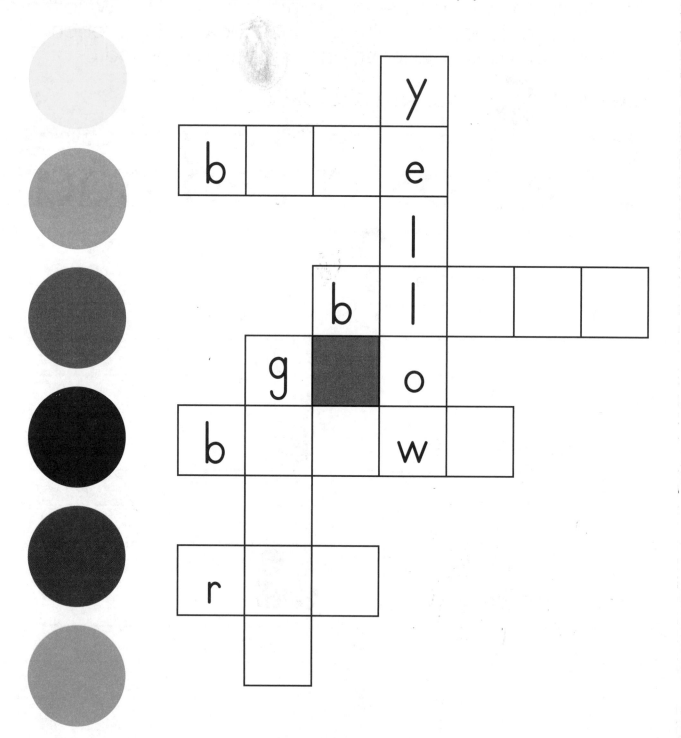

Color the Eggs

Directions: Read the words. Color the pictures with the correct colors.

Name _____

Finish the Pictures

Directions: Read the words. Finish the pictures.

a red ball

a black hat

a yellow sun

a pink kite

an orange balloon

a blue umbrella

Animal Names

Directions: Fill in the missing letters for each word.

Example:

frog   frog

fish   fish

dog   dog

bird   bird

cat   cat

Animal Names

Directions: The letters in the name of each animal are mixed up. Write each word correctly.

Example:

g f o r _____ frog

t a c _____

o d g _____

i f s h _____

d i b r _____

Animal Names: Beginning Sounds

Directions: Say the name of each animal. Write the beginning sound under its name. Find two pictures in each row that begin with the same sound as the animal. Write the same first letter under them.

Example:

frog
f

_____ f _____ _____ f _____ _____ _____ f _____ _____

cat

_____ _____ _____ _____ _____

fish

_____ _____ _____ _____ _____

dog

_____ _____ _____ _____ _____

bird

_____ _____ _____ _____ _____

Animal Names: Sentences

A **sentence** tells about something.

Directions: These sentences tell about animals. Write the word that completes each sentence.

Example:

My _frog_ jumps high.

1. I take my _____ for a walk.

2. My _____ lives in water.

3. My _____ can sing.

4. My _____ has a long tail.

Animal Names: Sentences

Directions: Finish writing the name of each animal on the line. Draw a line from the first part of the sentence to the part that completes it. Put a period at the end of each sentence.

Example:

A green frog _____ jumps in the water ▪

1. Ken's c _____ barks a lot □

2. My friend's d _____ climbs trees □

3. Owen's f _____ sits on his finger □

4. My little b _____ swims in the water □

Review

Directions: Use the words in the pictures to write a sentence about each animal. Put a period at the end of each sentence.

Example: The eats bugs.

The frog eats bugs.

The  drinks milk

- -

The eats seeds

- -

The jumps out

- -

The  meet

- -

Things That Go

Directions: Trace the letters to write the name of each thing. Write each name again by yourself. Then, color the pictures.

Example:

car   car

truck

train

bike

plane

Name _____

Things That Go

Directions: Fill in the missing letters for each word.

Example:

car   car

pl_ne   __ _ane

b_k_   __ _i_e

tr_ _n   __ _ain

__ _uck   tr_ck

Things That Go

Directions: The letters in the name of each thing are mixed up. Unscramble the letters, and write each word correctly below.

Example:

r a c   car

a i t r n

e p l n a

k i b e

c k u t r

Name _____

Things That Go: Beginning Sounds

Directions: Say the name of each thing. Write the beginning sound under its name. Find two pictures in each row that begin with the same sound as the first picture. Write the same first letter under them.

Example:

car
C   C   C

 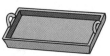 

truck

train

bike

   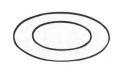

plane

Things That Go: Sentences

Directions: These sentences tell about things that go. Write the word that completes each sentence.

Example:

The ____**car**____ is in the garage.

1. The _____ was at the farm.

2. My _____ had a flat tire.

3. The _____ flew high.

4. The _____ went fast.

Name _____

Things That Go: Sentences

Directions: Finish writing the names of the things that go. Draw a line from the first part of the sentence to the part that completes it. Put a period at the end of each sentence.

Example:

The blue   bike

is in the bike rack [•]

1. The   c

climbed up the hill [ ]

2. Bob's   t

is in the garage [ ]

3. The   t

was in the field [ ]

4. My dad's   p

is full [ ]

Things That Go: Sentences

Directions: Draw a line from the first part of each sentence to the part that completes it. Put a period at the end of each sentence.

Example:

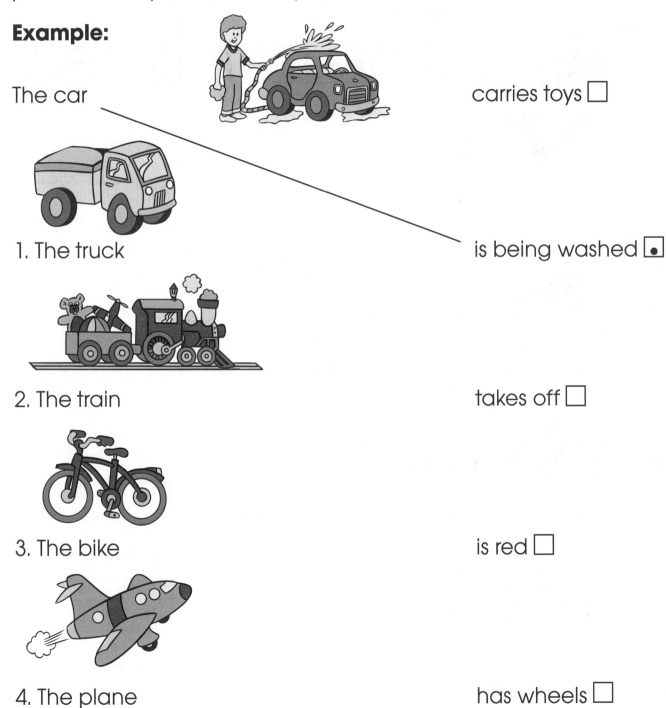

The car   carries toys ☐

1. The truck   is being washed ▪

2. The train   takes off ☐

3. The bike   is red ☐

4. The plane   has wheels ☐

Name _____

Review

Directions: Use the words in the pictures to write a sentence about each thing that goes. Put a period at the end of each sentence.

Example:

The is red ___The car is red.___

The  flies

_____

- - - - - - - - - - - - - - - - - - - -

The has apples

_____

- - - - - - - - - - - - - - - - - - - -

The  has wheels

_____

- - - - - - - - - - - - - - - - - - - -

The  goes fast

_____

- - - - - - - - - - - - - - - - - - - -

_____

Clothing Words

Directions: Trace the letters to write the name of each clothing word. Then, write each name again by yourself.

Example:

shirt   shirt

pants

jacket

socks

shoes

dress

hat

Clothing Words: Beginning Sounds

Directions: Circle the words that begin with the same sound as the first word in each row.

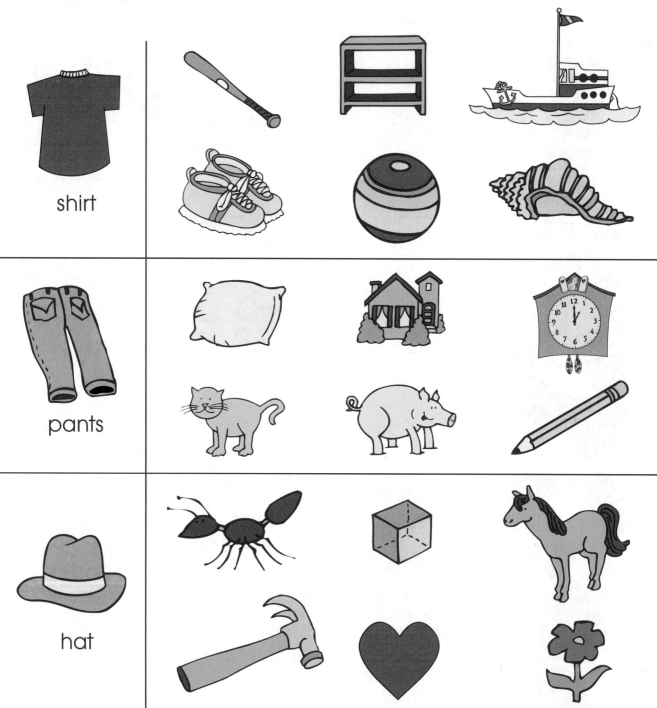

Clothing Words: Sentences

Directions: Some of these sentences tell a whole idea. Others have something missing. If something is missing, draw a line to the word that completes the sentence. Put a period at the end of each sentence.

Example:

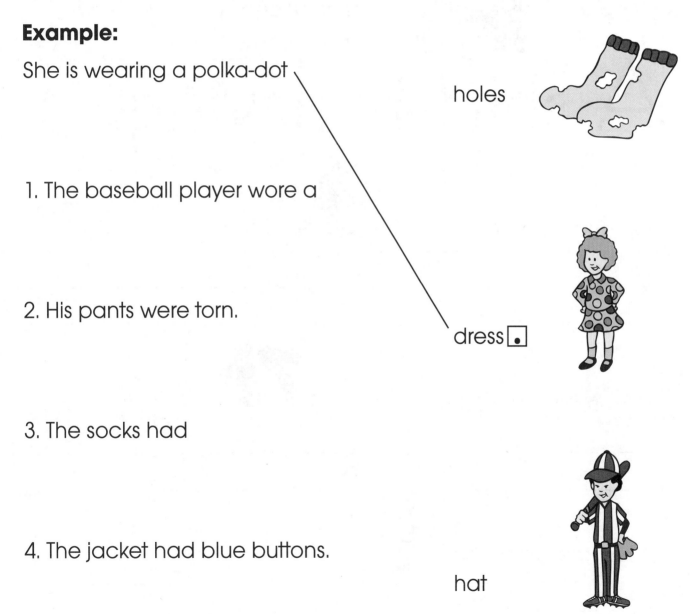

She is wearing a polka-dot

holes

1. The baseball player wore a

2. His pants were torn.

dress .

3. The socks had

4. The jacket had blue buttons.

hat

5. The shoes were brown.

Clothing Words: Sentences

Directions: The words by each picture are mixed up. Write them to make a sentence that tells about the picture. Begin each sentence with a capital letter, and end it with a period.

Example:  is shirt a drying

A shirt is drying.

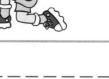

1. ties his shoes he

_____

_ _ _ _ _ _ _ _ _ _ _ _ _ _ _ _ _ _ _

_____

2. red wear I a jacket

_ _ _ _ _ _ _ _ _ _ _ _ _ _ _ _ _ _ _

_____

3. blue are pants his

_____

_ _ _ _ _ _ _ _ _ _ _ _ _ _ _ _ _ _ _

_____

Clothing Words: Sentences

Directions: Use the clothing words to complete these sentences. Then, put a period at the end.

Example:

Mike is wearing a  <u>hat.</u>

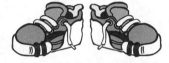

1. Put on your socks before your _____ ☐

2. When it's cold, wear a _____ ☐

3. The little girl liked to wear a pink _____ ☐

4. He wore jeans with the _____ ☐

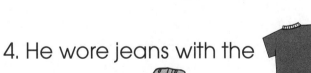

5. The man wore a suit coat and _____ ☐

6. The clown wore long, striped _____ ☐

Name _____

Review

Directions: Write three sentences that tell about this picture. Begin each sentence with a capital letter, and end it with a period.

1. _____

2. _____

3. _____

Food Names

Directions: Trace the letters to write each food word. Write each name again by yourself. Then, color the pictures.

Example:

bread bread

cookie cookie

apple apple

carrotcarrot

milk milk

egg egg egg

Food Names: Beginning Sounds

Directions: Write the food names that answer the questions.

egg	milk	ice cream	apple	cookie	cake

1. Which food words start with the same sounds as the pictures?

_____   _____

_____

2. Which food word ends with the same sound as the picture?

_____

3. Which food words have two letters together that are the same?

_____   _____   _____

_____   _____   _____

_____

Food Names: Asking Sentences

An **asking sentence** asks a question. Asking sentences end with a question mark.

Directions: Write each sentence on the line. Begin each sentence with a capital letter. Put a period at the end of the telling sentences and a question mark at the end of the asking sentences.

Example: do you like carrots

Do you like carrots?

1. the cup is full of milk

- -

2. is that cookie good

- -

3. she ate the apple

- -

Name _____

Food Names: Asking Sentences

Directions: Change each telling sentence into an asking sentence by moving the words. Put a question mark at the end of each question.

Example: The girl is eating.

Is the girl eating?

1. He is sharing.

_____

_____

2. He is drinking.

_____

_____

3. She is baking.

_____

_____

Food Names: Asking Sentences

Directions: Use the food names to answer each question.

1. Which one can you drink?

_____

2. Which one do you have to keep very cold?

_____

3. Which one grows on trees?

_____

4. Which one do you put birthday candles on?

_____

5. Which one do people sometimes eat in the morning?

_____

6. Which one do you like best?

_____

Food Names: Sentences

Directions: In each sentence, write a word in the first blank to tell who is doing something. Write one of the food names in the second blank. Then, draw a picture to go with each sentence.

The **mother** is making **a cake.**

1. The _____ is eating _____

2. The _____ is buying _____

Food Names: Completing a Story

Directions: Write the food names in the story.

Kim got up in the morning.

"Do you want an _____ ?" her mother asked.

"Yes, please," Kim said.

"May I have some _____ , too? Oh, and I

would love a piece of _____ ."

"Okay," her mother said.

She put an _____ in Kim's lunch.

"Do you want a _____ or some

_____ today?"

"Both!" Kim said.

Name _____

Review

Directions: Write two telling sentences and one asking sentence about this picture. Use the food, color, and animal words you know.

Two telling sentences:

1. _____

2. _____

One asking sentence:

3. _____

Number Words

Directions: Trace the letters to write the name of each number. Write the numbers again by yourself. Then, color the number pictures.

Example:

1 one one

2 two two

3 three three

4 four four

5 five five

6 six six

7 seven seven

8 eight eight

9 nine nine

10 ten ten

Number Words: Asking Sentences

Directions: Write each sentence on the line. Begin each sentence with a capital letter. Put a period at the end of the telling sentences and a question mark at the end of the asking sentences.

Example: may I eat two crackers

May I eat two crackers?

1. I see five flowers

I see five flowers

2. is one cat yellow

Is one cat yellow

3. are there six eggs

Are there sixeggs

Number Words: Asking Sentences

Directions: Use a number word to answer each question.

one	five	seven	three	eight

1. How many trees are there?

three

2. How many flowers are there?

seven

3. How many presents are there?

five

4. How many clocks are there?

one

5. How many forks are there?

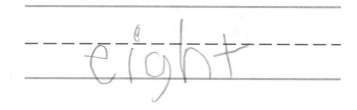
eight

Name _____

one two three four five six seven eight nine ten

Number Words: Asking Sentences

Directions: Use the number words to answer each question.

1. How many eyes do you have? ___ two

2. How many mouths do you have? ___ one

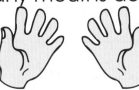

3. How many fingers do you have? ___ ten

4. How many wheels are on a car? ___ four

5. How many peas are in the pod? ___ three

6. How many cups do you see? ___ six

Name _____

Number Words: Asking Sentences

Directions: Change each telling sentence into an asking sentence by rearranging the words and adding new ones. Put a question mark at the end of each question.

Example: He ate one egg.

Is he eating one egg?

Does have

1. She has two dogs.

Does she have two dogs?

2. Three balls can bounce.

Did the three balls bounce?

3. One balloon is red.

is the balloon red?

SPELLING

Name _____

Review

Directions: Write two telling sentences and one asking sentence about this picture. Use the number words you know.

Two telling sentences:

_____

1. _____

_____

2. _____

One asking sentence:

_____

3. _____

Comprehensive Curriculum - Grade 1

290

Action Words

Action words tell things we can do.

Directions: Trace the letters to write each action word. Then, write the action word again by yourself.

Example:

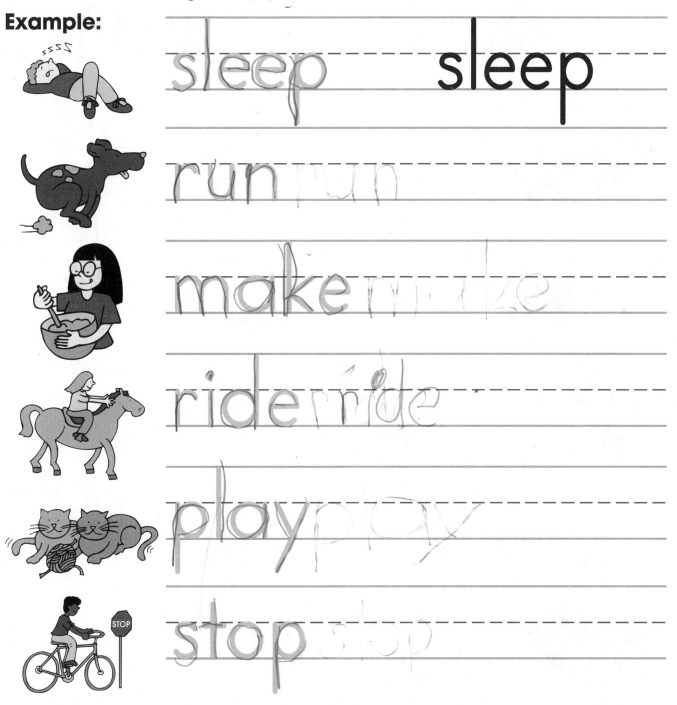

sleep   sleep

run run

make make

ride ride

play play

stop stop

Action Words

Directions: Circle the word that is spelled correctly. Then, write the correct spelling in the blank.

Example:

seep
(sleep)
slep

sleep

paly
pay
play

seee
cee
see

rum
run
runn

jump
jumb
junp

mack
maek
make

Action Words

Directions: Read each sentence, and write the correct words in the blanks.

Example:

go
sleep

I will _____ go _____ to bed and _____ sleep _____ all night.

1.
see
jump

The girls _____ the frogs _____ .

2.
sit
run

After the boys _____ , they _____ and rest.

3.
stop
play

They _____ at the park so they can _____ .

4.
ride
make

They will _____ a car to _____ in.

Action Words: Beginning and Ending Sounds

Directions: Write the action words that answer the questions.

| sit | run | make | see | jump | stop | play | ride |

1. Which words begin with the same sound as ☀ ?

_____   _____   _____

_____   _____   _____

2. Which words begin with the same sound as 🐰 ?

_____   _____

_____   _____

3. Which words begin with the same sound as each of these words?

_____   _____   _____

_____   _____   _____

4. Which words end with the same sound as these?

_____   _____   _____

_____   _____   _____

Name _____

Action Words: More Than One

To show more than one of something, add **s** to the end of the word.

Example: one cat    two cats

Directions: In each sentence, add **s** to show more than one. Then, write the action word that completes each sentence.

sit	jump	stop	ride

Example:

The frog __s__ __sleep__ in the sun.

1. The boy ____ _____ on the fence.

2. The car ____ _____ at the sign.

3. The girl ____ _____ in the water.

4. The dog ____ _____ in the wagon.

Action Words: Asking Sentences

Directions: Write an asking sentence about each picture. Begin each sentence with **can**. Add an action word. Begin each asking sentence with a capital letter, and end it with a question mark.

Example:

I with you can

Can I sit with you?

she can

_____

_ _

with you can I

_____

_ _

can she fast

_____

_ _

Review

Directions: Write three telling sentences and one asking sentence about this picture. Put an action word in each sentence.

Three telling sentences:

1. _____

_____

2. _____

_____

3. _____

One asking sentence:

_____

4. _____

Name _____

Sense Words

Directions: Circle the word that is spelled correctly. Then, write the correct spelling in the blank.

Example:

tast
(taste)
tste

touch
tuch
touh

smel
smll
smell

her
hear
har

see
se
sea

Sense Words: Sentences

Directions: Read each sentence, and write the correct words in the blanks.

Example:

taste
mouth

I can ___taste___ things with my ___mouth___.

touch
hands

1. I can _____ things with my _____.

nose
smell

2. I can _____ things with my _____.

hear
ears

3. I can _____ with my _____.

see
eyes

4. I can _____ things with my _____.

Sense Words: Beginning Sounds

Directions: Use the sense words in the box to answer each question.

smell	see	taste	hear	touch

1. Which word begins with the same sound as   ?

        _____

2. Which word begins with the same sound as   ?

        _____

3. Which words begin with the same sound as   ?

        _____   _____

4. Which word begins with the same sound as   ?

        _____

Sense Words: More Than One

Directions: In each sentence, add **s** to show more than one. Then, write the sense word that completes each sentence.

Example: The dog __s__ __taste__ the food.

| see | touch | smell | hear |

1. The flower _____ _____ good.

2. I can _____ five bird _____ .

3. The girl _____ _____ the bells ring.

4. The boy _____ wanted to _____ the cactus.

Sense Words: Asking Sentences

Directions: Write an asking sentence about each picture. Begin each sentence with **can**. Add a sense word. Begin each asking sentence with a capital letter, and end it with a question mark.

Example:  can rose I a

Can I smell a rose?

1.    can I the dog

_ _

2.    can I pie the

_ _

3.    can he car the

_ _

4.   he can bell the

_ _

Review

Directions: Write three telling sentences and one asking sentence about this picture. Use a sense word in each sentence.

Three telling sentences:

_____

1. _____

_____

2. _____

_____

3. _____

One asking sentence:

_____

_____

4. _____

Weather Words: Beginning Sounds

Directions: Say the sound of the letter at the beginning of each row. Find the pictures in each row that begin with the same letter. Write the letter under the pictures.

Example:

s   S   S

w

c

p

s

r

Weather Words: Sentences

Directions: Write the weather word that completes each sentence. Put a period at the end of the telling sentences and a question mark at the end of the asking sentences.

Example:

Do flowers grow in the ___**sun**___ ?

| rain | water | wet | hot |

1. The sun makes me _____ ☐

2. When it rains, the grass gets _____ ☐

3. Do you think it will _____ on our picnic ☐

4. Should you drink the _____ from the rain ☐

Name _____

Weather Words: Sentences

Directions: Read the sentence parts below. Draw a line from the first part of the sentence to the second part that completes it.

Example: When I'm cold,——— I put on my coat.

I take off my shoes.

1. When it rains,   we ride our bikes to the park.

we play games inside.

2. I like snow   because I can eat lunch.

because I can make a snowman.

3. When the sun comes out,   the grass grows fast.

the grass gets wet.

4. At night, the rain   makes ice on my windows.

helps me go to sleep.

Weather Words: Completing a Story

Directions: Write the missing words to complete the story. The first letter of each word is written for you.

"Please may I go outside?" I asked.

"It's too C _____," my father told

me. "Maybe later the sun will come

out." Later, the sun did come out. Then, it began to r _____

again. "May I go out now?" I asked again. Dad looked out the

window. "You will get W _____," he said. "But I want to

see if the r _____ helped our flowers grow," I said. "You

mean you want to play in the W _____," Dad said with

a smile. How did Dad know that?

Weather Words: Sentences

Directions: Read the two sentences on each line, and draw a line between them. Then, write each sentence again on the lines below. Begin each sentence with a capital letter, and end each one with a period or a question mark.

Example: will it rain | the sky is dark

Will it rain?
The sky is dark.

1. she fell in the pond she got wet

_____

_____

2. do you like my hat it is red

_____

_____

Review

Directions: Write a telling sentence about each of these pictures. Then, write an asking sentence about one of the pictures. Use the weather words and other words you know.

Telling sentences:

_____

1. _____

_____

2. _____

Asking sentence:

_____

3. _____

My World

Directions: Fill in the missing letters for each word.

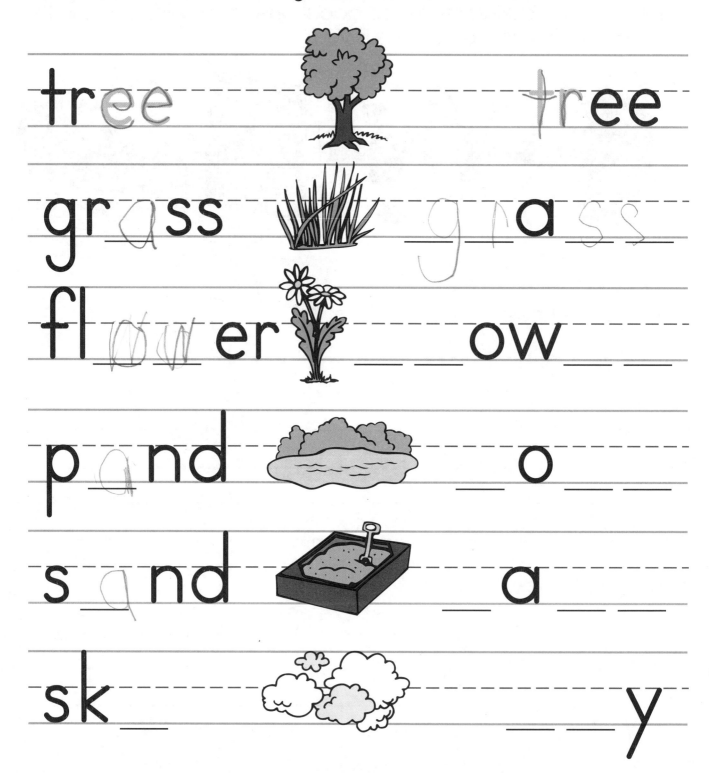

tree   tree

gr_a_ss   gr_a_ss

fl_ow_er   _ _ ow _ _

p_a_nd   _ _ o _

s_a_nd   _ a _ _

sk_ _   _ _ _ y

My World

Directions: The letters in the words below are mixed up. Unscramble the letters, and write each word correctly.

etre   free

srags   grass

loefwr   flower

dnop   pond

dnsa   sand

yks   sky

Name _____

My World: Beginning Sounds

Directions: Say the name of the first picture in each row. Write the beginning sound under its name. Find two pictures in each row that begin with the same sound as the first picture. Write the same first letter under them.

Example:

tree

t _____   t _____   _____   t _____   _____

 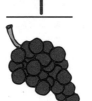 

_____   _____   _____   _____   _____

_____   _____   _____   _____   _____

_____   _____   _____   _____   _____

_____   _____   _____   _____   _____

My World: Sentences

Directions: Write the word that completes each sentence. Put a period at the end of the telling sentences and a question mark at the end of the asking sentences.

Example: Does the sun shine on the flowers ?

tree	grass	pond	sand	sky

1. The ___sky___ was full of dark clouds☑

2. Can you climb the ___tree___ ☐

3. Did you see the duck in the ___pond___ ☐

4. Is the child playing in the ___sand___ ☐

5. The ___grass___ in the yard was tall☐

My World: Sentences

Directions: Read the two sentences on each line, and draw a line between them. Then, write each sentence again on the lines below. Begin each sentence with a capital letter, and end each one with a period or a question mark.

Example: the tree has leaves|can we rake some

The tree has leaves.

Can we rake some?

1. the lake is fun we swim in it

_____

_____

_____

2. the sky is so blue isn't it pretty

_____

_____

_____

Review

Directions: Write three telling sentences about the picture. Then, write an asking sentence about the picture. Use the words that tell about your world and other words you know.

Telling sentences:

1. _____

_____

2. _____

_____

3. _____

Asking sentence:

_____

4. _____

Name _____

The Parts of My Body: Sentences

Directions: Write the word that completes each sentence. Put a period at the end of the telling sentences and a question mark at the end of the asking sentences.

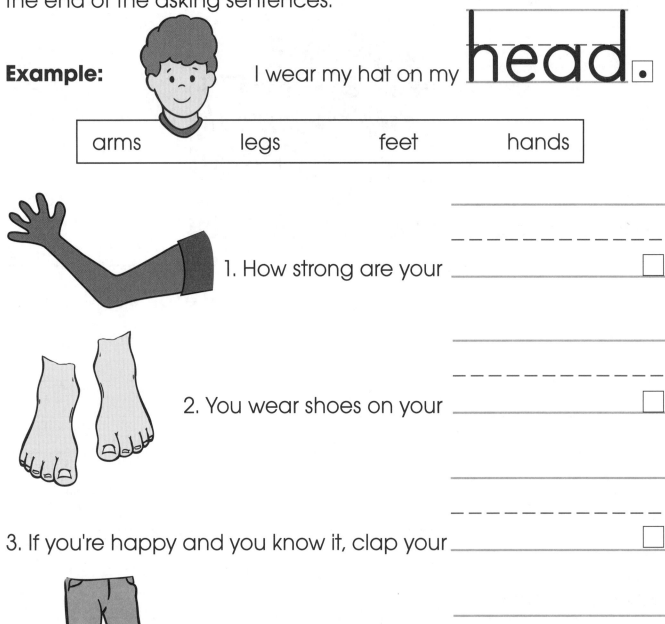

Example: I wear my hat on my **head.**

| arms | legs | feet | hands |

1. How strong are your _____ ☐

2. You wear shoes on your _____ ☐

3. If you're happy and you know it, clap your _____ ☐

4. My pants covered my _____ ☐

The Parts of My Body: Beginning Sounds

Directions: Say the sound of the letter at the beginning of each row. Find the pictures in each row that begin with the same letter. Write the letter under the pictures.

Example:

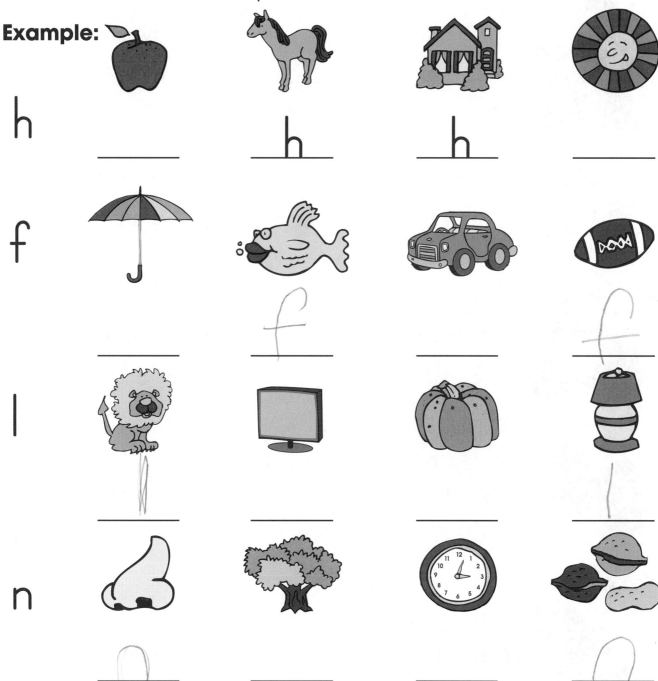

h

f

l

n

Name _____

The Parts of My Body: Sentences

Directions: Read the sentence parts below. Draw a line from the first part of the sentence to the second part that completes it.

1. I give big hugs   with my arms.

                            with my car.

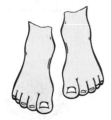

2. My feet   drive the car.

                            got wet in the rain.

3. I have a bump   on my head.

                            on my coat.

4. My mittens   keep my arms warm.

                            keep my hands warm.

5. I can jump high   using my legs.

                            using a spoon.

The Parts of My Body: Sentences

Directions: Read the two sentences on each line, and draw a line between them. Then, write each sentence again on the lines below. Begin each sentence with a capital letter, and end each one with a period or a question mark.

Example: wash your hands|they are dirty

Wash your hands.
They are dirty.

1. you have big arms are you very strong

_____

_____

2. I have two feet I can run fast

_____

_____

Review

Directions: Write a telling sentence about each of these pictures. Then, write an asking sentence about one of the pictures. Use the words that name the parts of your body and other words you know.

Telling sentences:

_____

_ _

1. _____

_____

_ _

2. _____

Asking sentence:

_____

_ _

3. _____

Opposite Words

Some words are opposites. **Opposites** are things that are different in every way. **Dark** and **light** are opposites.

Directions: Trace the letters to write each word. Then, write the word again by yourself.

Example:

new   new

old old

big big

little little

lost lost

found

Opposite Words

Directions: Circle one word in each sentence that is not spelled correctly. Then, write the word correctly.

| dark | found | old | first | lost |

Example:

The house is (litle).

little

1. Are those your olde shoes?

2. I fond your book.

3. She is frist in line.

4. She losst her lunch.

5. I am afraid of the drak.

Opposite Words: Beginning and Ending Sounds

Directions: Write the opposite words that answer the questions.

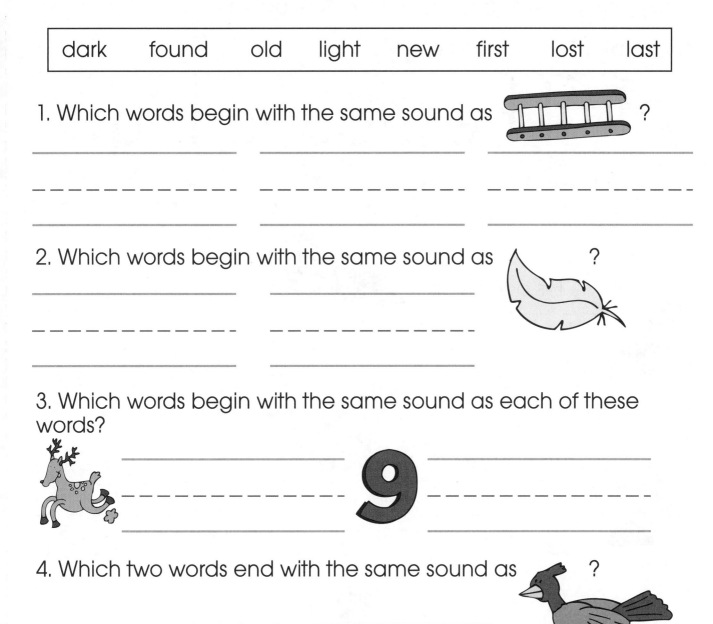

| dark | found | old | light | new | first | lost | last |

1. Which words begin with the same sound as ⬛⬛⬛ ?

_____   _____   _____

-- -- -- -- -- --   -- -- -- -- -- --   -- -- -- -- -- --

_____   _____   _____

2. Which words begin with the same sound as 🪶 ?

_____   _____

-- -- -- -- -- --   -- -- -- -- -- --

_____   _____

3. Which words begin with the same sound as each of these words?

_____ **9** _____

-- -- -- -- -- --   -- -- -- -- -- --

_____   _____

4. Which two words end with the same sound as 🐦 ?

_____   _____

-- -- -- -- -- --   -- -- -- -- -- --

_____   _____

Name _____

Opposite Words: Sentences

Directions: Read the sentence by the first picture. Then, look at the next picture. Write a sentence that tells about it.

Example: The dog is little.

The dog is big.

found	new	first	lost	old	last

1. His book is lost.

_____

_____

2. The dog eats first.

_____

_____

3. I like my old shirt.

_____

_____

Opposite Words: Sentences

Directions: Read the sentence about the first picture. Write another sentence about the second picture. Use the opposite words.

Example: This apple is little.

This apple is big.

| dark | old | first | new | light | last |

1. This coat is light.

_____

2. This woman is first.

_____

3. This car is old.

_____

Name _____

Opposite Words: Sentences

Directions: Write opposite words to complete these sentences.

Example:

The rain made my  flower grow  .

dark	first	found	last	light	lost

1. Jenna picked the red flowers _____

and the yellow flowers _____ .

2. All day John looked for his _____ shoe.

Then, his father called, "John, come here! I _____ your shoe."

3. When I get up, it is _____ outside. By the

time I go to school, it is _____ .

Review

Directions: Look at the pictures in each row. Write one sentence about the last picture in each row. Begin each sentence with a capital letter, and end it with a period.

_____

- -

_____

_____

- -

_____

More Action Words

Directions: Fill in the missing letters for each word.

Example:

paint   paint

c_tch   cat___

c_lor   col___

ea_____t

gr_____ow

fl_____y

More Action Words:
Beginning and Ending Sounds

Words that **rhyme** have the same ending sound.

Directions: Write the words that answer the questions.

catch	fly	eat	grow	buy	color

1. Which words begin with the same sound as  ?

_____   _____

_____   _____

_____   _____

2. Which word begins with the same sound as each of these
   pictures?

_____

_____   _____

3. Which words rhyme with  ?

_____   _____

_____   _____

4. Which word rhymes with these?

_____   _____

_____   _____

More Action Words: Sentences

Directions: Write a sentence that tells about the picture. Use the words next to the picture. Remember to begin each sentence with a capital letter, and end it with a period.

Example: likes boy to paint the

The boy likes to paint.

 1. boy see grow the

_____

_ _

_____

 2. bird the can fly

_____

_ _

_____

 3. she will color

_____

_ _

_____

More Action Words: Sentences

Directions: Put the two sentences together to make one new sentence.

Example: The ball is red. The ball is blue.

The ball is red and blue.

1. I eat apples. I eat cookies.

2. We buy milk. We buy eggs.

Name _____

Review

Directions: Use the action words you know to write sentences that tell about these pictures. Write a question about the last picture.

Example:

The flowers grow.

_____

- - - - - - - - - - - - - - - - - - - -

_____

- - - - - - - - - - - - - - - - - - - -

_____

Write a question about this picture.

_____

- - - - - - - - - - - - - - - - - - - -

_____

People Words

Directions: Trace the letters to write each word. Then, write the word again by yourself.

girl

boy

man

woman

people

children

People Words

Directions: Write a people word in each sentence to tell who is doing something.

1. The _____ was last in line at the toy store.

2. The _____ took a walk in the woods.

3. The _____ had to help her father.

4. The _____ had a surprise for the children.

5. Some _____ like to eat outside.

6. Something came out of the box when the _____ opened it.

People Words

Sometimes, we use other words in place of people names. For **boy** or **man**, we can use the word **he**. For **girl** or **woman**, we can use the word **she**. For two or more people, we can use the word **they**.

Directions: Write the words **he**, **she**, or **they** in these sentences.

Example: The boy likes soccer.

 likes soccer.

1. The girl is running fast.

_____ is running fast.

2. The man reads the paper.

_____ reads the paper.

3. The woman has a cold.

_____ has a cold.

4. Two children came to school.

_____ came to school.

Name _____

People Words: Sentences

Directions: Write the people word that completes each sentence.

people	man	girl	children	boy	woman

1. The _____ feeds the cat.

2. The _____ are buying dessert.

3. What is the _____ painting?

4. The _____ will grow corn.

5. The dog runs to the _____ .

6. There are long lines of _____ .

Name _____

Number Recognition

Directions: Write the numbers 1-10. Color the bear.

Number Recognition 1, 2, 3, 4, 5

Directions: Use the color codes to color the parrot.

Color:
1s red
2s blue
3s yellow
4s green
5s orange

Number Recognition 6, 7, 8, 9, 10

Directions: Use the code to color the carousel horse.

Color:
- **6**s purple
- **7**s yellow
- **8**s black
- **9**s pink
- **10**s brown

Number Recognition

Directions: Count the number of objects in each group. Draw a line to the correct number.

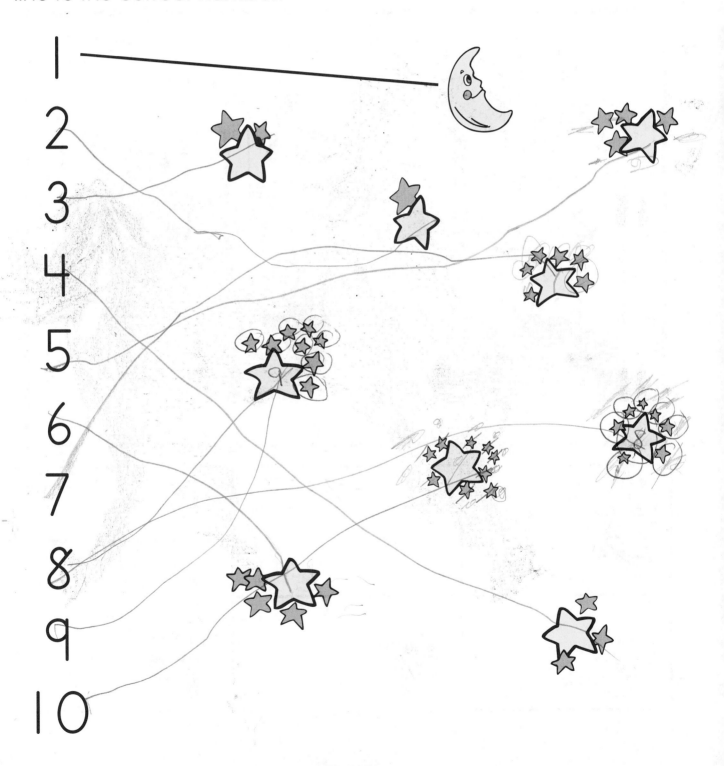

Name ______________________________

Counting

Directions: How many are there of each picture? Write the answers in the boxes. The first one is done for you.

 1		
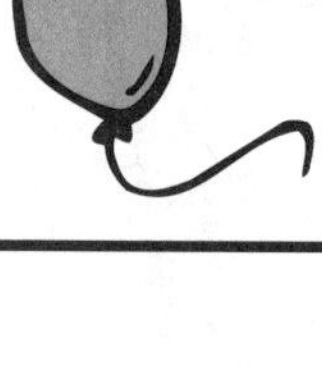		

Counting

Directions: How many are there of each picture? Write the answers in the boxes. The first one is done for you.

Review

Directions: Count the flowers, and write the answers.

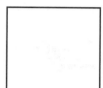

Directions: Fill in the missing numbers. Connect the dots to finish the picture.

2
1
10
4
6
7

Number Recognition

Directions: Cut out the pieces. Mix them up, and match the number with the picture.

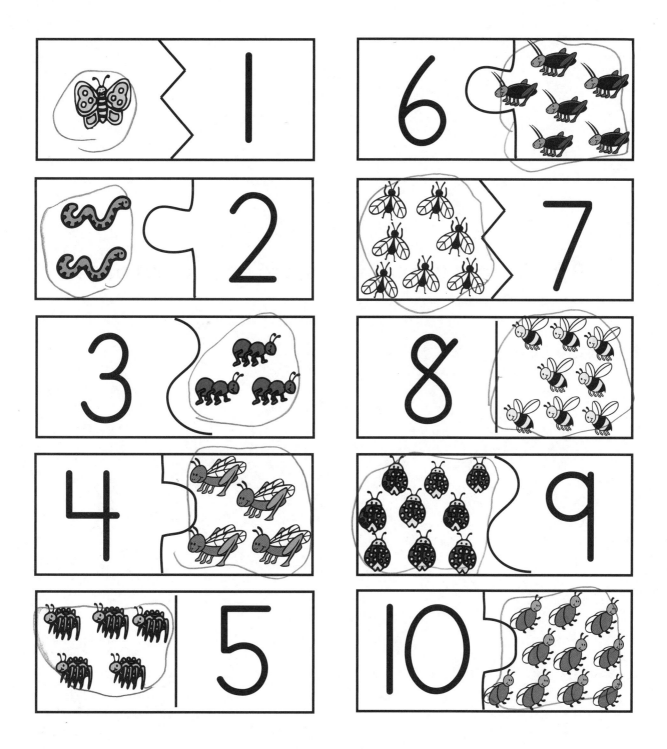

Page is blank for cutting exercise on previous page.

Number Word Find

Directions: Find the number words for 0 through 12 hidden in the box.

```
t  e  a  z  w  z  x  a  b  i  g  t  e  n
o  l  z  r  b  e  r  e  v  e  d  l  a  j
t  w  e  l  v  e  a  b  o  n  e  c  d  z
i  a  r  p  q  d  p  s  u  j  x  e  i  w
c  f  o  p  l  s  c  k  i  q  u  i  i  o
m  s  t  f  v  i  o  e  t  t  f  g  h  d
t  n  u  w  u  x  g  z  w  h  g  h  r  o
n  i  n  e  k  f  d  f  o  u  r  t  j  f
a  s  g  l  q  c  w  k  o  s  n  v  m  i
n  y  c  e  b  o  n  h  h  p  o  m  p  v
b  e  x  v  s  s  e  v  e  n  w  e  n  e
t  h  r  e  e  r  t  a  l  j  k  x  q  z
m  o  a  n  e  n  i  m  u  t  w  a  y  x
```

Words to find:

zero	four	eight	eleven
one	five	nine	twelve
two	six	ten	
three	seven		

Number Words

Directions: Number the buildings from one to six.

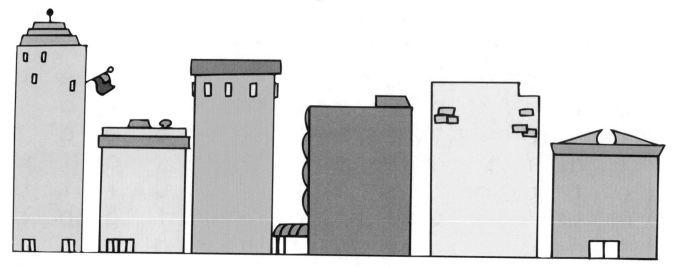

Directions: Draw a line from the word to the number.

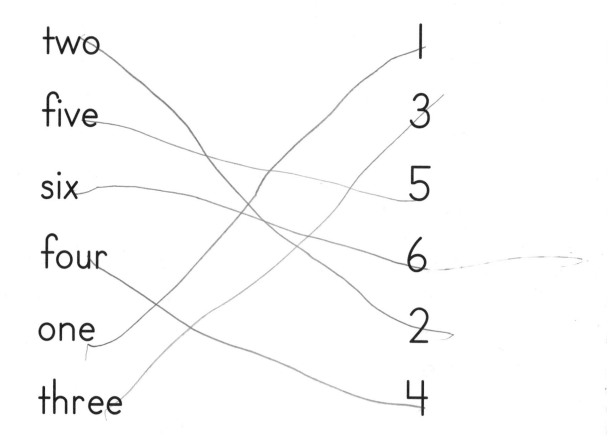

two

five

six

four

one

three

1

3

5

6

2

4

Number Words

Directions: Number the buildings from five to ten.

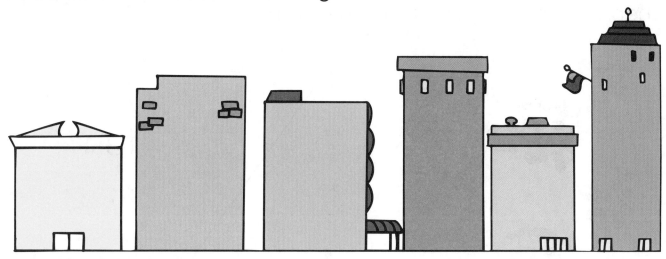

Directions: Draw a line from the word to the number.

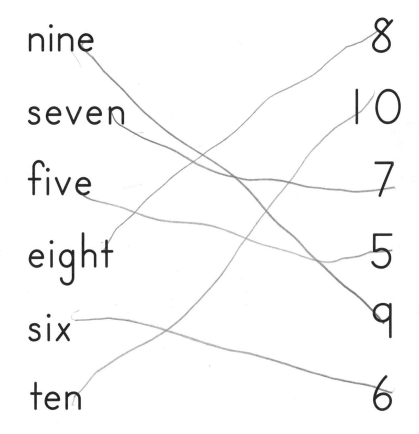

nine   8

seven   10

five   7

eight   5

six   q

ten   6

Number Recognition Review

Directions: Match the correct number of objects with the number. Then, match the number with the word.

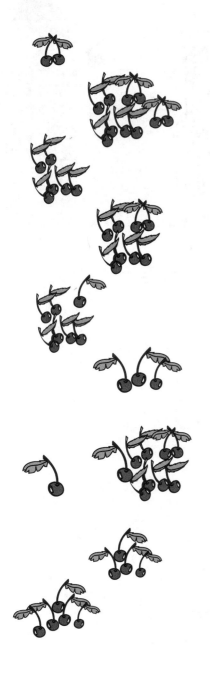

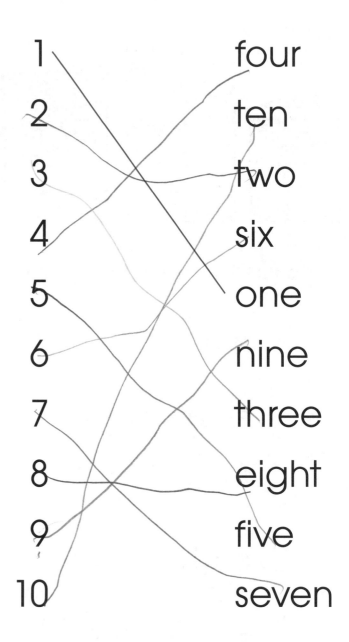

1   four

2   ten

3   two

4   six

5   one

6   nine

7   three

8   eight

9   five

10   seven

Number Match

Directions: Cut out the pictures and number words below. Mix them up, and match them again.

one		two	eight
		five	
	three		nine
four		seven	
	six		ten

1 2 3 4 5 6 7 8 9   10

B

12   2   2B   3   3

3   3   3   v

3 3 3 3 4 5 5 5 6 7 8

Page is blank for cutting exercise on previous page.

1   o   9 9 9

9 9

Sequencing Numbers

Sequencing is putting numbers in the correct order.

1, 2, 3, 4, 5, 6, 7, 8, 9, 10

Directions: Write the missing numbers.

Example: 4, ___5___ ,6

3, ___ ,5   7, ___ ,9   8, ___ ,10

6, ___ ,8   ___ ,3,4   ___ ,5,6

5, 6, ___   ___ ,6,7   ___ ,3,4

___ ,4,5   ___ ,7,8   5, ___ ,7

2, 3, ___   1, 2, ___   7, 8, ___

2, ___ ,4   ___ ,2,3   4, ___ ,6

6, 7, ___   3, 4, ___   1, ___ ,3

7, 8, ___   ___ ,3,4   ___ ,9,10

Name _____

Number Crossword Puzzle

Directions: Write the correct number word in the boxes provided.

Across
2. 4
3. 8
5. 2
7. 7
9. 10

Down
1. 0
2. 5
4. 3
6. 1
7. 6
8. 9

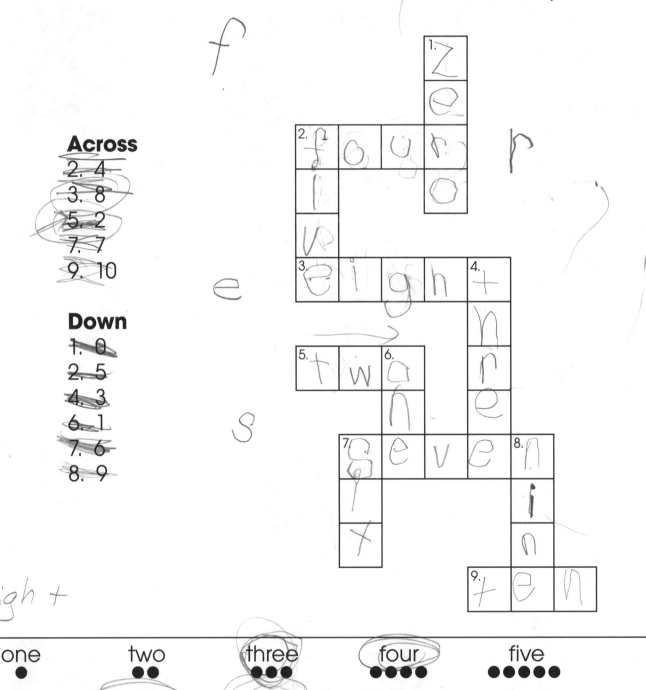

one	two	three	four	five
●	●●	●●●	●●●●	●●●●●
six	seven	eight	nine	ten	zero
●●● ●●●	●●●●● ●●	●●●● ●●●●	●●●●● ●●●●	●●●●● ●●●●●	

Review

Directions: Count the objects and write the number.

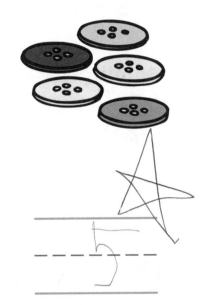

- - - - - - - - - -   - - - - - - - - - -   - - - - - - - - - -

Directions: Match the number to the word.

two   1

four   9

seven   2

three   3

one   4

nine   7

Ordinal Numbers

Ordinal numbers are used to indicate order in a series, such as **first**, **second**, or **third**.

Directions: Draw a line to the picture that corresponds to the ordinal number in the left column.

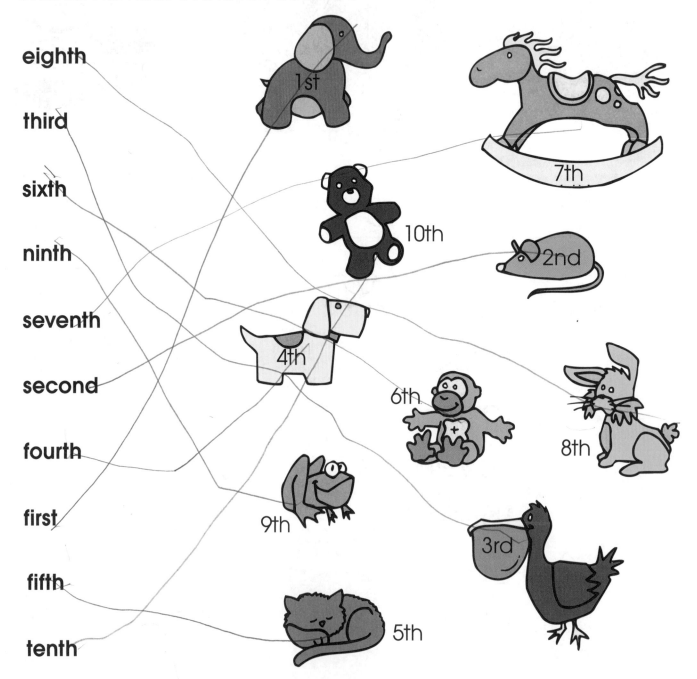

eighth

third

sixth

ninth

seventh

second

fourth

first

fifth

tenth

Name _____

Sequencing: At the Movies

Directions: The children are watching a movie. Read the sentences. Cut out the pictures below. Glue them where they belong in the picture.

1. The first child is eating popcorn.
2. The third child is eating candy.
3. The fourth child has a cup of fruit punch.
4. The second child is eating a big pretzel.

Comprehensive Curriculum - **Grade 1**

Page is blank for cutting exercise on previous page.

Sequencing: Standing in Line

Directions: These children are waiting to see a movie. Look at them and follow the instructions.

1. Color the person who is first in line yellow.

2. Color the person who is last in line orange.

3. Color the person who is second in line pink.

4. Circle the person who is at the end of the line.

Addition 1, 2

Addition means "putting together" or adding two or more numbers to find the sum. "+" is a plus sign. It means to add the 2 numbers. "=" is an equal sign. It tells how much they are together.

Directions: Count the objects and write the number.

 +  =  2

 +  =  3

 +  = 4

Addition

Directions: Count the shapes, and write the numbers below to tell how many in all.

 +  =

_____ _____ _____

_ _ _ _ _   _ _ _ _ _   _ _ _ _ _

_____ _____ _____

 + =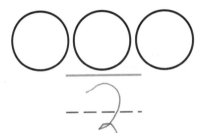

2   1   3

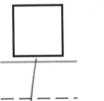 + 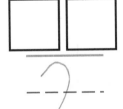 =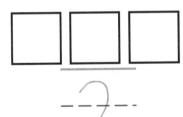

1   2   3

 + ☆ = ☆☆☆☆

3   1   4

Addition

Directions: Draw the correct number of dots next to the numbers in each problem. Add up the number of dots fo find your answer.

Example:

$$3$$
$$+2$$
$$\overline{5}$$

$$2 + 2 = \underline{4}$$

4 $+2$ $\overline{}$	$1 + 5 = \underline{}$
3 $+1$ $\overline{}$	$4 + 3 = \underline{}$
6 $+2$ $\overline{}$	$5 + 3 = \underline{}$

Addition 3, 4, 5, 6

Directions: Practice writing the numbers, and then add. Draw dots to help, if needed.

3

4

5

6

$$\begin{array}{r} 2 \\ +4 \\ \hline \end{array}$$

$$\begin{array}{r} 1 \\ +4 \\ \hline \end{array}$$

$$\begin{array}{r} 3 \\ +2 \\ \hline \end{array}$$

$$\begin{array}{r} 1 \\ +2 \\ \hline \end{array}$$

Addition 4, 5, 6, 7

Directions: Practice writing the numbers, and then add. Draw dots to help, if needed.

4 ------------------------

5 ------------------------

6 ------------------------

7 ------------------------

```
   2        3
  +5       +1
 ____     ____
```

```
   4        2
  +1       +4
 ____     ____
```

Addition 6, 7, 8

Directions: Practice writing the numbers, and then add. Draw dots to help, if needed.

6 – – – – – – – – – – – – – – – – –

7 – – – – – – – – – – – – – – – – –

8 – – – – – – – – – – – – – – – – –

$$\begin{array}{r} 3 \\ +4 \\ \hline \end{array}$$
$$\begin{array}{r} 5 \\ +1 \\ \hline \end{array}$$

$$\begin{array}{r} 2 \\ +6 \\ \hline \end{array}$$
$$\begin{array}{r} 4 \\ +4 \\ \hline \end{array}$$

Addition 7, 8, 9

Directions: Practice writing the numbers, and then add. Draw dots to help, if needed.

7 --------------

8 --------------

9 --------------

$$\begin{array}{r} 8 \\ +1 \\ \hline \end{array}$$
$$\begin{array}{r} 3 \\ +5 \\ \hline \end{array}$$

$$\begin{array}{r} 2 \\ +7 \\ \hline \end{array}$$
$$\begin{array}{r} 6 \\ +1 \\ \hline \end{array}$$

Addition Table

Directions: Add across and down with a friend. Fill in the spaces.

+	0	1	2	3	4	5
0	0					
1	1	2				
2			4			
3	3			6		
4						
5						10

Do you notice any number patterns in the addition table?

Subtraction 1, 2, 3

Subtraction means "taking away" or subtracting one number from another. "−" is a minus sign. It means to subtract the second number from the first.

Directions: Practice writing the numbers, and then subtract. Draw dots and cross them out, if needed.

1

2

3

$$3 \quad \quad 4$$
$$-1 \quad \quad -3$$
$$\overline{2}$$

$$2 \quad \quad 3$$
$$-1 \quad \quad -2$$

Subtraction 3, 4, 5, 6

Directions: Practice writing the numbers, and then subtract. Draw dots and cross them out, if needed.

3

4

5

6

$$\begin{array}{r} 5 \\ -2 \\ \hline \end{array}$$

$$\begin{array}{r} 6 \\ -1 \\ \hline \end{array}$$

$$\begin{array}{r} 6 \\ -3 \\ \hline \end{array}$$

$$\begin{array}{r} 5 \\ -1 \\ \hline \end{array}$$

Comprehensive Curriculum - **Grade 1**

Name _____

Subtraction

Directions: Draw the correct number of dots next to the numbers in each problem. Cross out the ones subtracted to find your answer.

Example:

$$5 \quad \bullet\bullet\bullet$$
$$\underline{-2} \quad \cancel{\bullet}\cancel{\bullet}$$
$$3$$

$$2 - 1 = 1$$
$$\bullet \qquad \cancel{\bullet}$$

$4 - 2 = \underline{}$	8 $\underline{-6}$
6 $\underline{-1}$	$3 - 1 = \underline{}$
$9 - 6 = \underline{}$	4 $\underline{-3}$

Name _____

Review

Directions: Trace the numbers. Solve the problems.

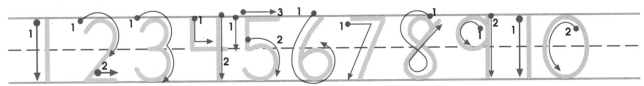

$$\begin{array}{r} 9 \\ -3 \\ \hline \end{array}$$

$$\begin{array}{r} 6 \\ +2 \\ \hline \end{array}$$

$$\begin{array}{r} 3 \\ +4 \\ \hline \end{array}$$

$$\begin{array}{r} 2 \\ -1 \\ \hline \end{array}$$

$$\begin{array}{r} 5 \\ +4 \\ \hline \end{array}$$

$$\begin{array}{r} 9 \\ -5 \\ \hline \end{array}$$

$$\begin{array}{r} 7 \\ +2 \\ \hline \end{array}$$

$$\begin{array}{r} 8 \\ -6 \\ \hline \end{array}$$

$$\begin{array}{r} 4 \\ -2 \\ \hline \end{array}$$

$$\begin{array}{r} 6 \\ +3 \\ \hline \end{array}$$

$$\begin{array}{r} 9 \\ -7 \\ \hline \end{array}$$

$$\begin{array}{r} 1 \\ +7 \\ \hline \end{array}$$

Comprehensive Curriculum - **Grade 1**

Name _____

Zero

Directions: Write the number that tells how many.

Example:

How many monkeys?

   3

How many monkeys?

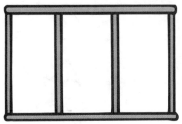   0

How many
kites?

_____

How many
kites?

_____

How many flowers?

_____

How many flowers?

_____

How many apples?

_____

How many apples?

_____

Zero

Directions: Write the number that tells how many.

How many sailboats?

_ _ _ _ _ _ _ _ _

How many sailboats?

_ _ _ _ _ _ _ _ _

How many eggs?

_ _ _ _ _ _ _ _ _

How many eggs?

_ _ _ _ _ _ _ _ _

How many flowers?

_ _ _ _ _ _ _ _ _

How many flowers?

_ _ _ _ _ _ _ _ _

How many candles?

_ _ _ _ _ _ _ _ _

How many candles?

_ _ _ _ _ _ _ _ _

Picture Problems: Addition

Directions: Solve the number problem under each picture.

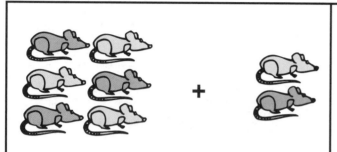

6 + 2 = 8

3 + 1 = 4

5 + 3 = 8

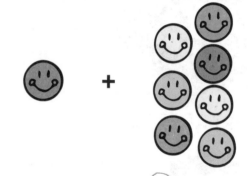

1 + 7 = 8

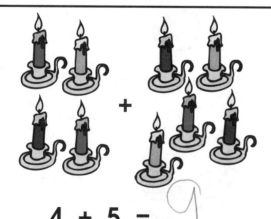

4 + 5 = 9

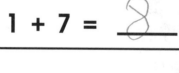

0 + 7 = 7

Picture Problems: Addition

Directions: Solve the number problem under each picture.

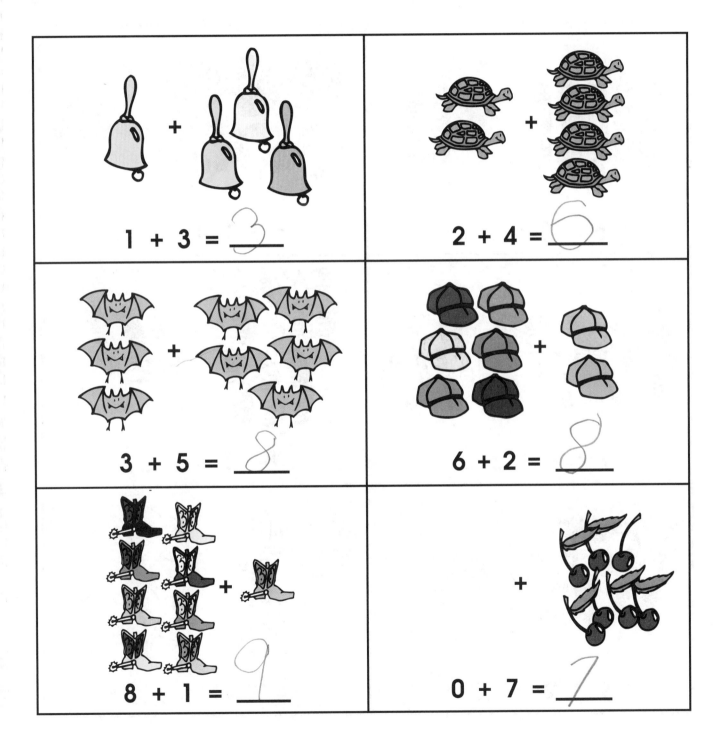

1 + 3 = 3

2 + 4 = 6

3 + 5 = 8

6 + 2 = 8

8 + 1 = 9

0 + 7 = 7

Picture Problems: Subtraction

Directions: Solve the number problem under each picture.

5 - 2 = _____

6 - 1 = _____

7 - 4 = _____

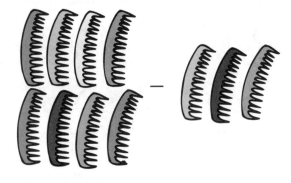

8 - 3 = _____

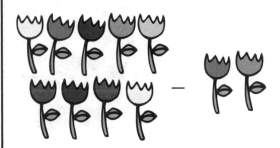

9 - 2 = _____

4 - 4 = _____

Picture Problems: Subtraction

Directions: Solve the number problem under each picture.

6 - 2 = _____

9 - 5 = _____

7 - 2 = _____

4 -1 = _____

8 - 1 = _____

4 - 0 = _____

Picture Problems: Addition and Subtraction

Directions: Solve the number problem under each picture.

7 - 4 = _____

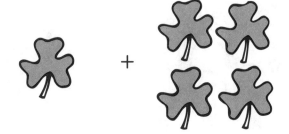

1 + 4 = _____

3 + 5 = _____

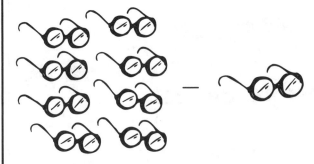

8 - 1 = _____

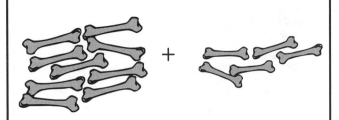

9 + 5 = _____

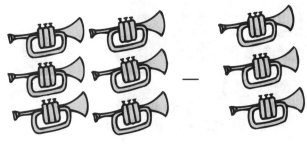

6 - 3 = _____

Picture Problems: Addition and Subtraction

Directions: Solve the number problem under each picture.
Write **+** or **−** to show if you should add or subtract.

How many s in all?

4 + 5 = _____

How many 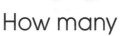s in all?

7   5 = _____

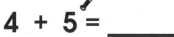 

How many s are left?

12   3 = _____

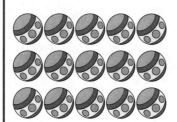 

How many s are left?

15   8 = _____

How many 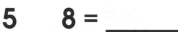s in all?

5   8 = _____

How many s are left?

11   4 = _____

MATH

Name _____

Picture Problems: Addition and Subtraction

Directions: Solve the number problem under each picture.
Write **+** or **−** to show if you should add or subtract.

How many s in all?

7 + 5 = ___12___

How many s are left?

8   3 = _____

How many s are left?

9   4 = _____

How many s in all?

14   1 = _____

How many s are left?

15   6 = _____

How many s in all?

9   5 = _____

Review: Addition and Subtraction

Directions: Solve the number problem under each picture.
Write **+** or **−** to show if you should add or subtract.

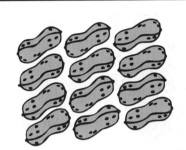

How many s are left?

12   4 = _____

How many s in all?

6   8 = _____

How many s are left?

4   4 = _____

How many s are left?

11   7 = _____

How many s in all?

9   3 = _____

How many s in all?

10   0 = _____

Addition 1-5

Directions: Count the tools in each tool box. Write your answers in the blanks. Circle the problem that matches your answer.

4

2   2
+2   +1

___

5   4
+0   +2

___

6   4
+2   +3

___

3   2
+1   +3

Addition 1-5

Directions: Look at the red numbers, and draw that many more flowers in the pot. Count them to get your total.

Example: 3 + 2 = __5__

1 + 4 = ___

1
+1
‾‾‾

2
+2
‾‾‾

3 + 1 = ___

Name _____

Addition 1-5

Directions: Add the numbers. Put your answers in the nests.

Example: $2 + 3 =$  5

$1 + 2 =$

$1 + 3 =$

$4 + 1 =$

$1 + 1 =$

Name _____

Addition 6-10

Directions: Add the numbers. Put your answers in the doghouses.

Example: $4 + 2 = 6$

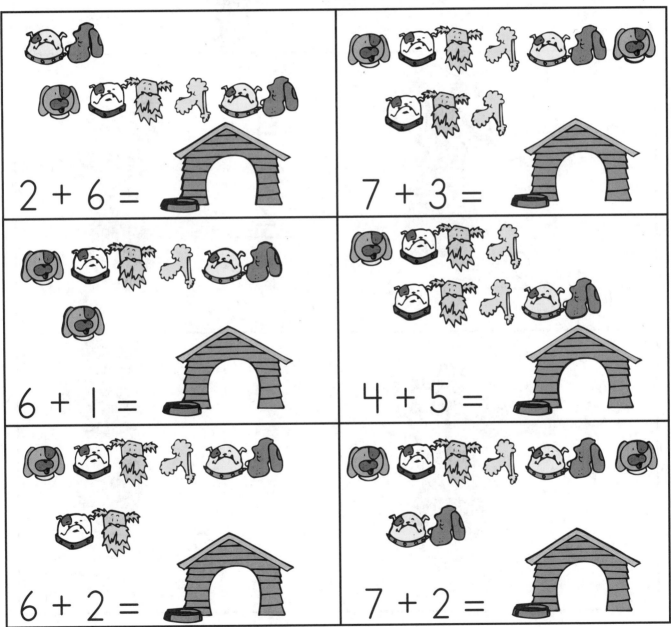

$2 + 6 =$

$7 + 3 =$

$6 + 1 =$

$4 + 5 =$

$6 + 2 =$

$7 + 2 =$

Comprehensive Curriculum - **Grade 1**

Name _____

Subtraction 1-5

Directions: Subtract the red numbers by crossing out that many flowers in the pot. Count the ones not crossed out to get the answer.

Example: 2 – 1 = __1__

5 – 2 = ___

$$\begin{array}{r} 4 \\ -\ 2 \\ \hline \end{array}$$

$$\begin{array}{r} 3 \\ -\ 1 \\ \hline \end{array}$$

4 – 3 = ___

Subtraction 1-5

Directions: Count the fruit in each bowl. Write your answers on the blanks. Circle the problem that matches your answer.

Subtraction 6-10

Directions: Count the flowers. Write your answer on the blank. Circle the problem that matches your answer.

Addition and Subtraction

Directions: Solve the problems. Remember, addition means "putting together" or adding two or more numbers to find the sum. Subtraction means "taking away" or subtracting one number from another.

$1 + 3 =$ _____ $4 - 3 =$ _____ $4 + 5 =$ _____

$6 + 1 =$ _____ $7 - 2 =$ _____ $8 - 4 =$ _____

$9 - 1 =$ _____ $10 - 3 =$ _____

 $5 - 2 =$ _____ $6 + 3 =$ _____

$8 + 2 =$ _____ $5 + 5 =$ _____

Name _____

Addition and Subtraction

Remember, addition means "putting together" or adding two or more numbers to find the sum. Subtraction means "taking away" or subtracting one number from another.

Directions: Solve the problems. From your answers, use the code to color the quilt.

Color:
6 = blue
7 = yellow
8 = green
9 = red
10 = orange

Place Value: Tens and Ones

The **place value** of a digit, or numeral is shown by where it is in the number. For example, in the number **23**, **2** has the place value of **tens**, and **3** is **ones**.

Directions: Count the groups of ten crayons, and write the number by the word **tens**. Count the other crayons, and write the number by the word **ones**.

Example:  + = _|_ ten + _|_ one

 + = ____ tens + ____ ones

 + = ____ tens + ____ ones

 + = ____ tens + ____ ones

---

6 tens + 3 ones = ____   5 tens + 1 one = ____

3 tens + 8 ones = ____   9 tens + 7 ones = ____

4 tens + 5 ones = ____   2 tens + 8 ones = ____

Name _____

Place Value: Tens and Ones

Directions: Count the groups of ten blocks, and write the number by the word **tens**. Count the other blocks, and write the number by the word **ones**.

Example:

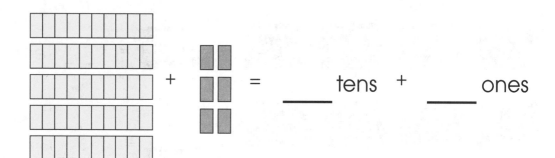

+ = ___1___ ten + ___2___ ones

+ = _____ tens + _____ ones

+ = _____ tens + _____ ones

+ = _____ tens + _____ ones

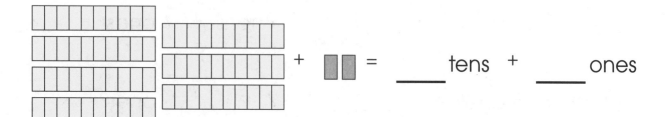

+ = _____ tens + _____ ones

Place Value: Tens and Ones

Directions: Write the answers in the correct spaces.

		tens	ones		
3 tens, 2 ones		3	2	=	32
3 tens, 7 ones		___	___	=	___
9 tens, 1 one		___	___	=	___
5 tens, 6 ones		___	___	=	___
6 tens, 5 ones		___	___	=	___
6 tens, 8 ones		___	___	=	___
2 tens, 8 ones		___	___	=	___
4 tens, 9 ones		___	___	=	___
1 ten, 4 ones		___	___	=	___
8 tens, 2 ones		___	___	=	___
4 tens, 2 ones		___	___	=	___

28 = ___ tens, ___ ones

64 = ___ tens, ___ ones

56 = ___ tens, ___ ones

72 = ___ tens, ___ ones

38 = ___ tens, ___ ones

17 = ___ ten, ___ ones

63 = ___ tens, ___ ones

12 = ___ ten, ___ ones

Review: Place Value

The place value of each digit or numeral is shown by where it is in the number. For example, in the number **123**, **1** has the place value of **hundreds**, **2** is **tens**, and **3** is **ones**.

Directions: Count the groups of crayons and add.

Example:

Hundreds	Tens	Ones
1	1	3

1 Hundred + 1 Ten + 3 Ones

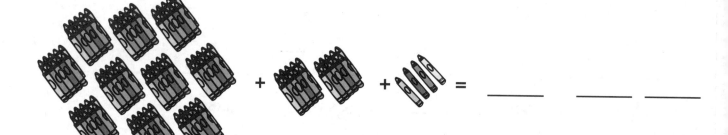

Counting by Fives

Directions: Count by fives to draw the path to the playground.

Counting by Fives

Directions: Use tally marks to count by fives. Write the number next to the tallies.

Example: A tally mark stands for one (1). Five tally marks look like this: ||||.

|||| _____

|||| |||| _____

|||| ||||
|||| _____

|||| ||||
|||| |||| _____

|||| |||| ||||
|||| |||| _____

|||| |||| ||||
|||| |||| |||| _____

|||| |||| ||||
|||| ||||
|||| |||| _____

|||| |||| ||||
|||| |||| ||||
|||| |||| _____

|||| |||| ||||
|||| |||| ||||
|||| |||| |||| _____

			_____

Counting by Tens

Directions: Count in order by tens to draw the path the boy takes to the store.

Counting by Tens

Directions: Use the groups of tens to count to 100.

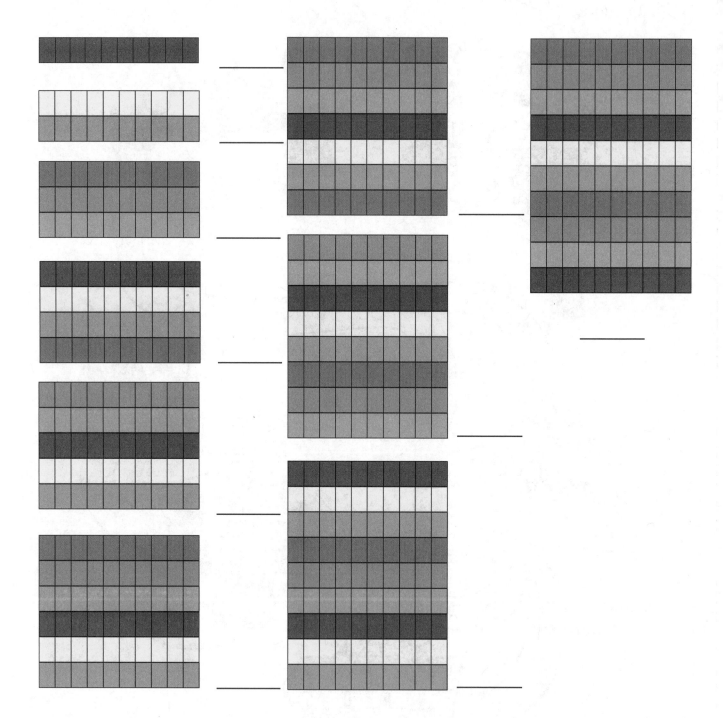

Name _____

Addition: 10-15

Directions: Count groups of ten crayons. Add the remaining ones to make the correct number.

		tens	ones
	+	3	9
	+	___	___
	+	___	___
	+	___	___
	+	___	___
	+	___	___

6 + 6 = ___   8 + 4 = ___   9 + 5 = ___

Comprehensive Curriculum - **Grade 1**

Subtraction: 10-15

Directions: Count the crayons in each group. Put an **X** through the number of crayons being subtracted. How many are left?

(crayons) (crayons with X)	-	5	=	_10_
(crayons) (crayons)	-	4	=	_____
(crayons) (crayons)	-	7	=	_____
(crayons) (crayons)	-	6	=	_____
(crayons) (crayons)	-	5	=	_____
(crayons) (crayons)	-	8	=	_____

13 - 8 = _____   11 - 5 = _____   12 - 9 = _____

14 - 7 = _____   10 - 7 = _____   13 - 3 = _____

15 - 9 = _____   11 - 8 = _____   12 - 10 = _____

Shapes: Square

A **square** is a figure with four corners and four sides of the same length. This is a square: ☐.

Directions: Find the squares, and circle them.

Directions: Trace the word. Write the word.

Shapes: Circle

A **circle** is a figure that is round. This is a circle: ○ .

Directions: Find the circles, and put a square around them.

Directions: Trace the word. Write the word.

circle

Shapes: Square and Circle

Directions: Practice drawing squares. Trace the samples, and make four of your own.

Directions: Practice drawing circles. Trace the samples, and make four of your own.

Name _____

Shapes: Triangle

A **triangle** is a figure with three corners and three sides. This is a triangle: △.

Directions: Find the triangles, and put a circle around them.

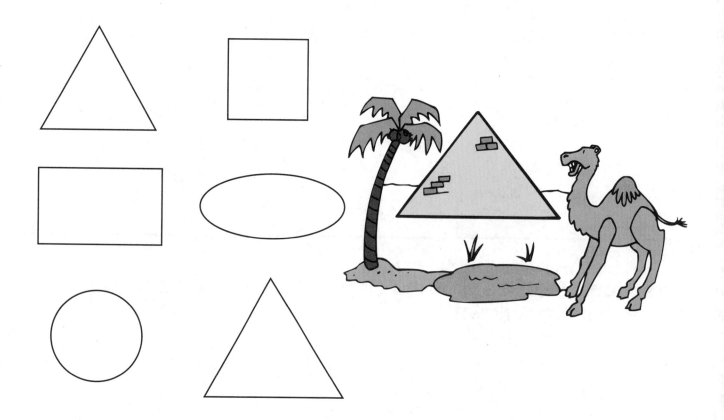

Directions: Trace the word. Write the word.

triangle _____

Shapes: Rectangle

A **rectangle** is a figure with four corners and four sides. Sides opposite each other are the same length. This is a rectangle: ☐.

Directions: Find the rectangles, and put a circle around them.

Directions: Trace the word. Write the word.

rectangle

Shapes: Triangle and Rectangle

Directions: Practice drawing triangles. Trace the samples, and make four of your own.

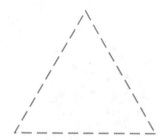

Directions: Practice drawing rectangles. Trace the samples, and make four of your own.

Patterns: Rectangles

Directions: In each picture, there is more than one rectangle. Trace each rectangle with a different color crayon. Under each picture, write how many rectangles you found.

_____rectangles

_____rectangles

Patterns: Triangles

Directions: In each picture, there is more than one triangle. Trace each triangle with a different color crayon. Under each picture, write how many triangles you found.

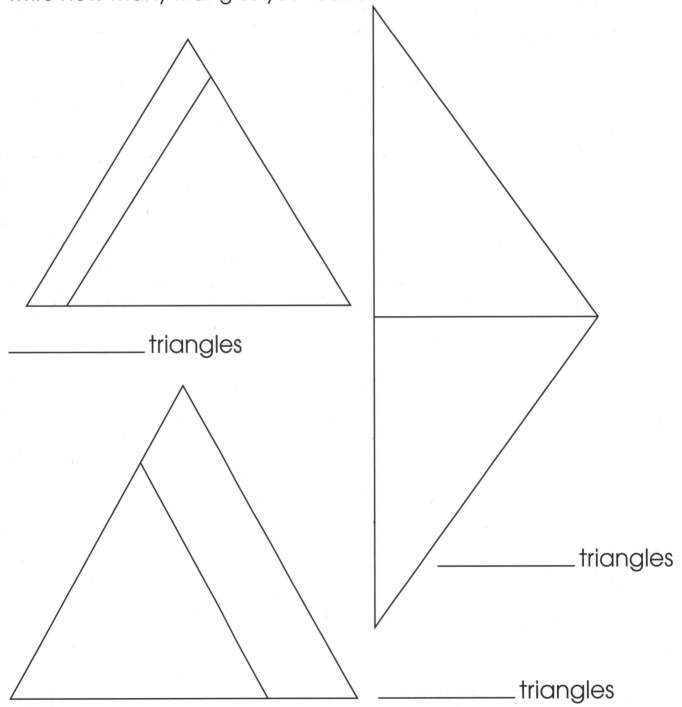

_____ triangles

_____ triangles

_____ triangles

Shapes: Oval and Rhombus

An **oval** is an egg-shaped figure. A rhombus is a figure with four sides of the same length. Its corners form points at the top, side, and bottom. This is an oval: ⬭. This is a rhombus: ◇.

Directions: Color the ovals red. Color the rhombuses blue.

Directions: Trace the word. Write the word.

oval -

rhombus -

Shapes: Oval and Rhombus

Directions: Practice drawing ovals. Trace the samples, and make four of your own.

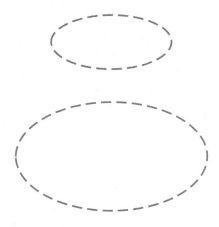

Directions: Practice drawing rhombuses. Trace the samples, and make four of your own.

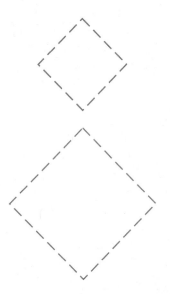

Following Directions: Shapes and Colors

Directions: Color the squares ☐ purple.

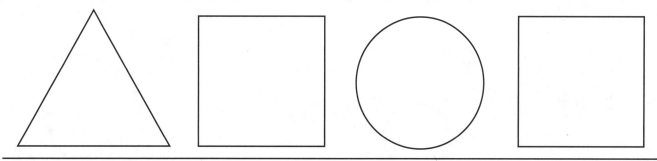

Directions: Color the heart ♡ blue.

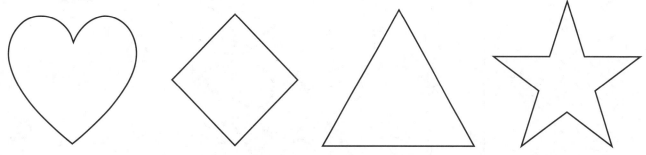

Directions: Color the rhombuses ◇ yellow.

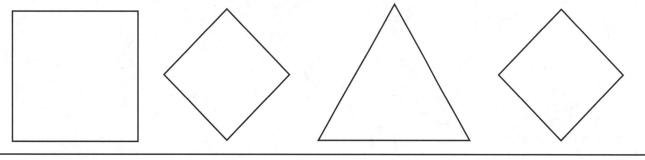

Directions: Color the star ☆ red.

Shape Review

Directions: Color the shapes in the picture as shown.

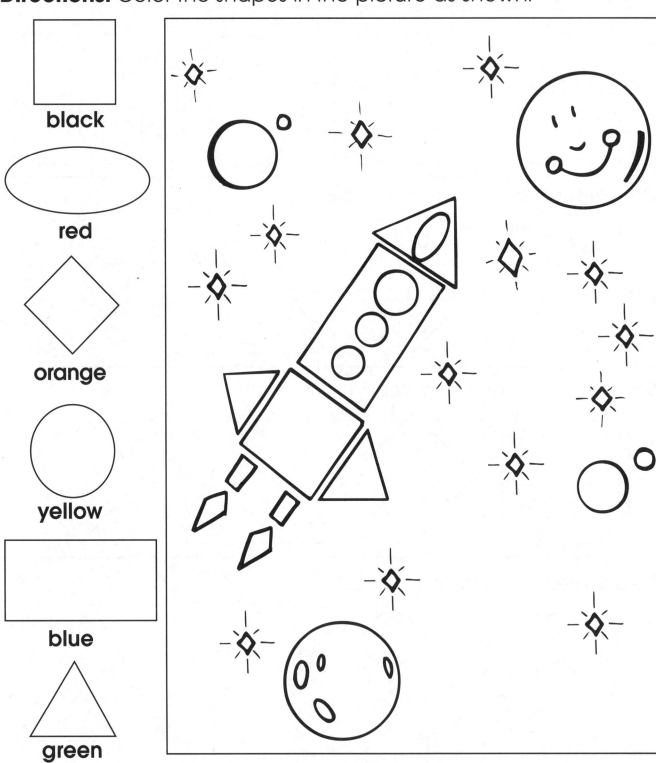

black

red

orange

yellow

blue

green

Shape Review

Directions: Trace the circles
Trace the squares
Trace the rectangles
Trace the triangles
Trace the ovals
Trace the rhombuses

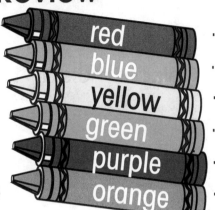

red
blue
yellow
green
purple
orange

Classifying: Stars

Help Connor find the stars.

Directions: Color all the stars blue.

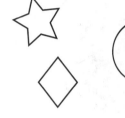

How many stars did you and Connor find? _____

Classifying: Shapes

Mary and Rudy are taking a trip into space. Help them find the stars, moons, circles, and rhombuses.

Directions: Color the shapes.

Use yellow for ☆s.   Use blue for ☾s.

Use red for Os.   Use purple for ◇s.

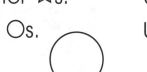

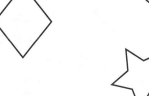

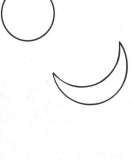

How many stars? _____   How many moons? _____

How many circles? _____   How many rhombuses? _____

Classifying: Shapes

Directions: Look at the shapes. Answer the questions.

1. How many all-white shapes? _____

2. How many all-blue shapes? _____

3. How many half-white shapes? _____

4. How many all-blue stars? _____

5. How many all-white circles? _____

6. How many half-blue shapes? _____

Same and Different: Shapes

Directions: Color the shape that looks the same as the first shape in each row.

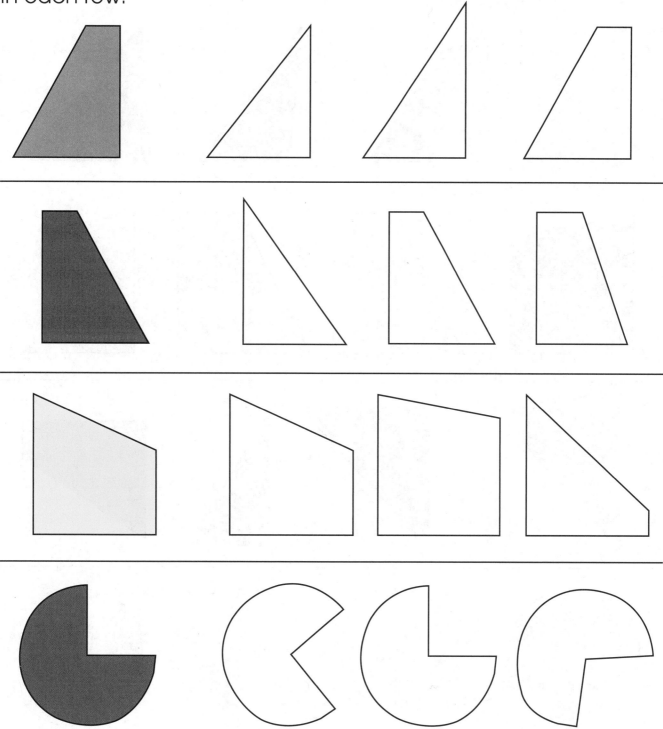

Same and Different: Shapes

Directions: Draw an **X** on the shapes in each row that do not match the first shape.

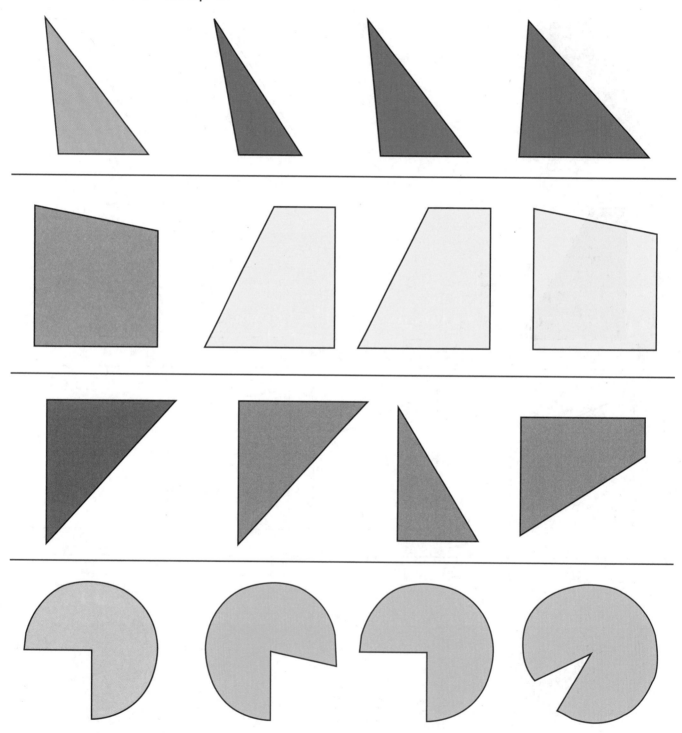

Copying: Shapes and Colors

Directions: Color your circle to look the same.

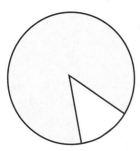 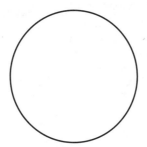

Directions: Color your square to look the same.

Directions: Trace the triangle. Color it to look the same.

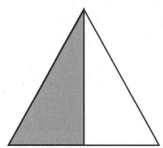 

Directions: Trace the star. Color it to look the same.

Copying: Shapes and Colors

Directions: Color the second shape the same as the first one. Then, draw and color the shape two more times.

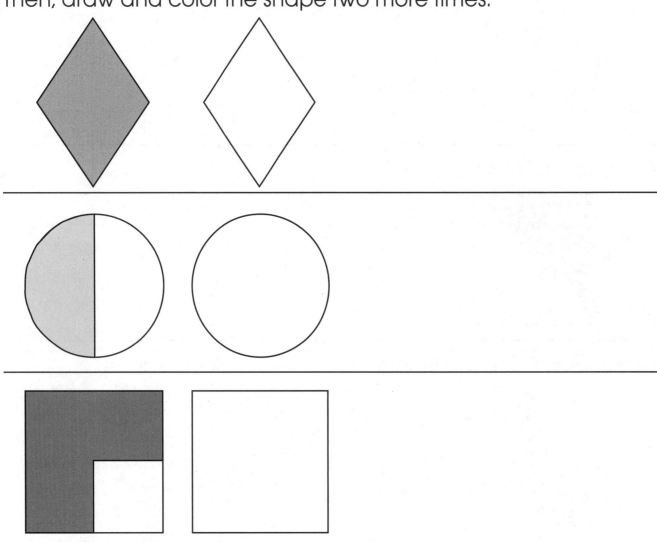

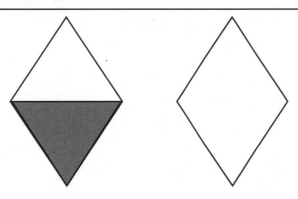

MATH

Patterns: Shapes

Directions: Draw a line from the box on the left to the box on the right with the same shape and color pattern.

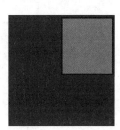

Comprehensive Curriculum - **Grade 1**

Patterns: Shapes

Directions: Draw a line from the box on the left to the box on the right with the same shape and color pattern.

  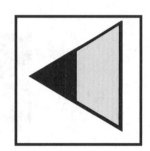 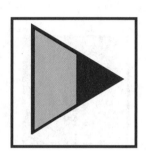

  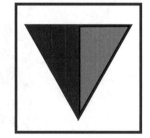 

Patterns: Find and Copy

Directions: Circle the shape in the middle box that matches the one on the left. Draw another shape with the same pattern in the box on the right.

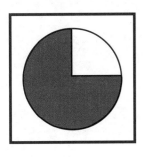 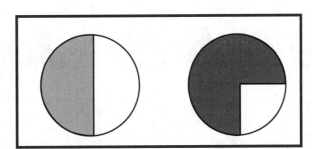 

 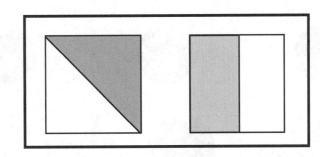 

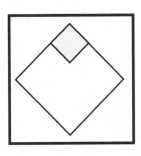 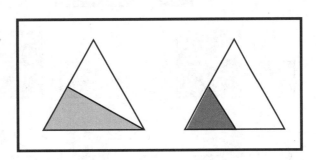 

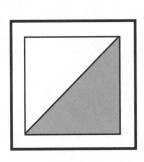 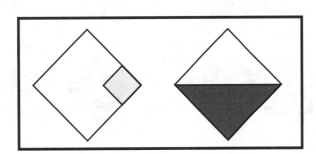

Patterns

Directions: Draw what comes next in each pattern.

Example:

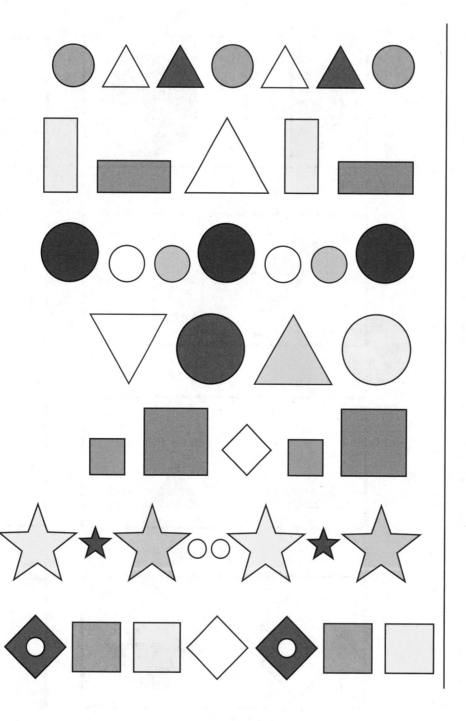

Patterns

Directions: Fill in the missing shape in each row. Then, color it.

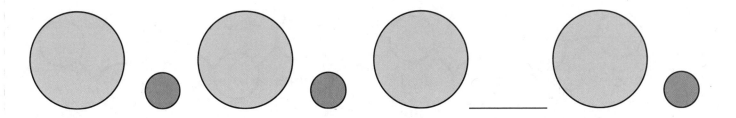

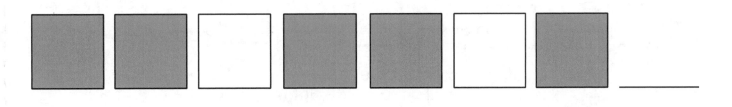

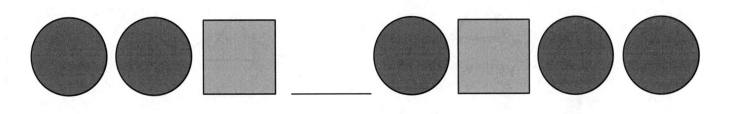

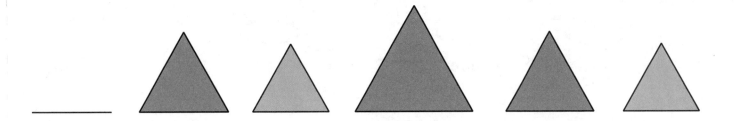

Patterns

Directions: Color to complete the patterns.

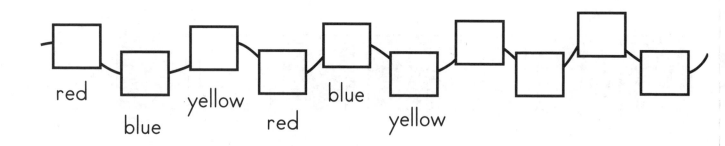

red blue blue red blue blue

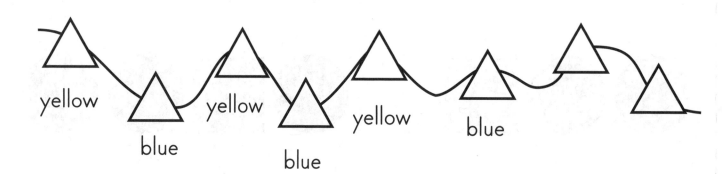

red blue yellow red blue yellow

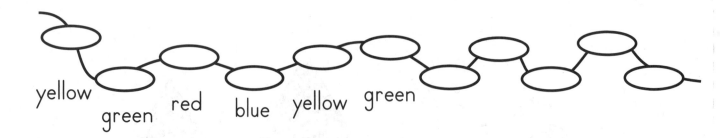

yellow blue yellow blue yellow blue

yellow green red blue yellow green

Fractions: Whole and Half

A **fraction** is a number that names part of a whole, such as $\frac{1}{2}$ or $\frac{3}{4}$.

Directions: Color half of each object.

Example:

whole apple

half an apple

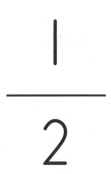

$$\frac{1}{2}$$

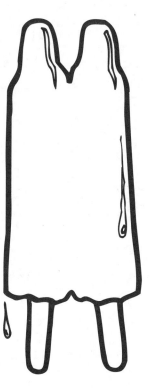

Fractions: Halves $\frac{1}{2}$

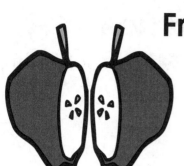

$\frac{1}{2}$ $\dfrac{\text{Part shaded or divided}}{\text{Number of equal parts}}$

Directions: Color only the shapes that show halves.

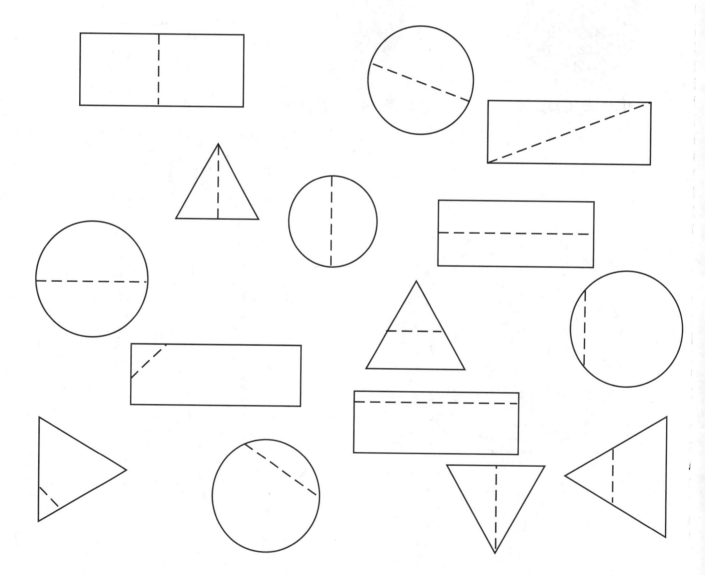

Fractions: Thirds $\frac{1}{3}$

Directions: Circle the objects that have 3 equal parts.

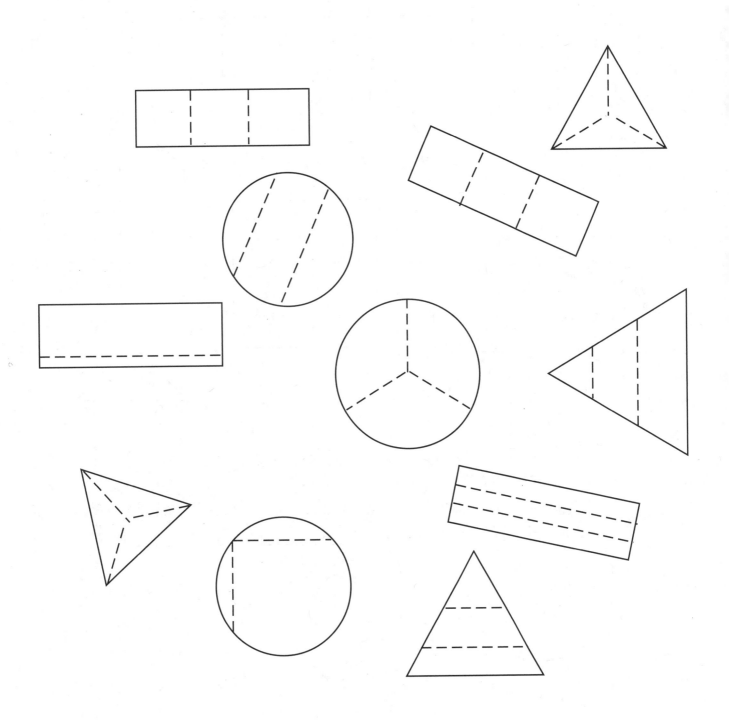

Fractions: Fourths $\frac{1}{4}$

Directions: Circle the objects that have 4 equal parts.

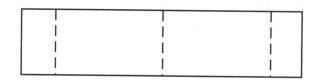

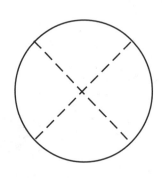
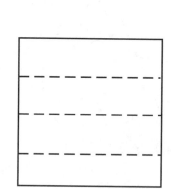
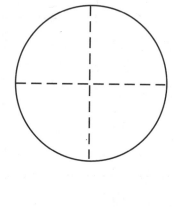

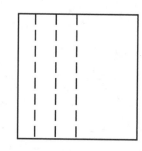
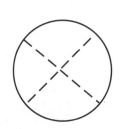

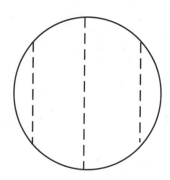
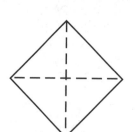
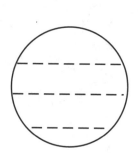

Fractions: Thirds and Fourths

Directions: Each object has 3 equal parts. Color one section.

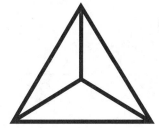  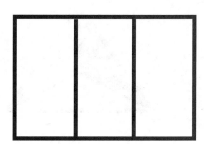

Directions: Each object has 4 equal parts. Color one section.

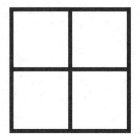 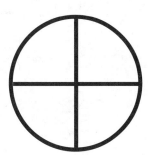 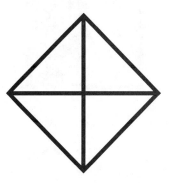

Review: Fractions

Directions: Count the equal parts, then write the fraction.

Example:

Shaded part = __1__   Write $\dfrac{1}{3}$

Equal parts = __3__

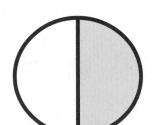

Shaded part = __1__   Write   ___

Equal parts = ____

Shaded part = __1__   Write   ___

Equal parts = ____

Shaded part = __1__   Write   ___

Equal parts = ____

Review

Directions: Write the missing numbers by counting by tens and fives.

_____ , 20, _____ , _____ , _____ , _____ , 70, _____ , _____ , 100

5, _____ , 15, _____ , _____ , 30, _____ , _____ , _____ , _____

Directions: Color the object with thirds red. Color the object with halves blue. Color the object with fourths green.

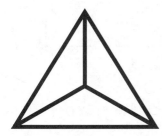 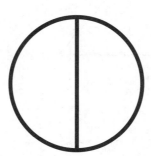 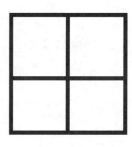

Directions: Draw a line to the correct equal part.

$\frac{1}{3}$

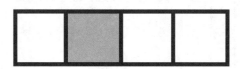

$\frac{1}{4}$

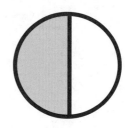

$\frac{1}{2}$

Name _____

Tracking: Straight Lines

Directions: Draw a straight line from A to B. Use a different color crayon for each line.

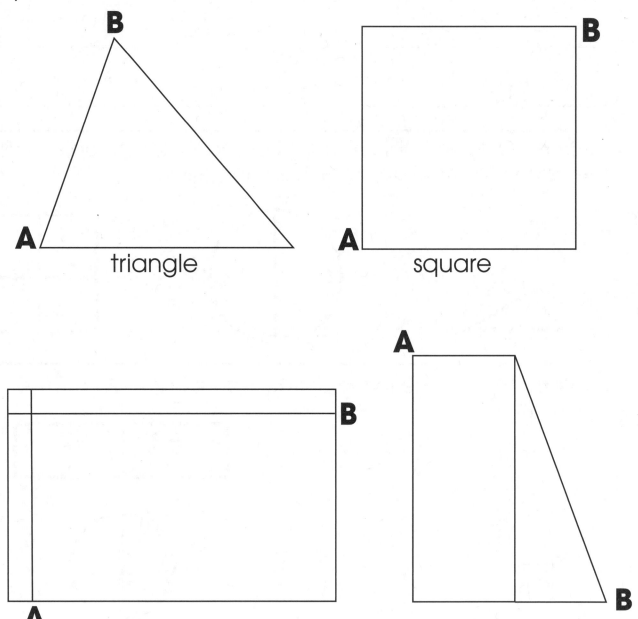

triangle

square

rectangle

odd shape

What shapes do you see hidden in these shapes? _____

Tracking: Different Paths

Directions: Trace three paths from A to B.

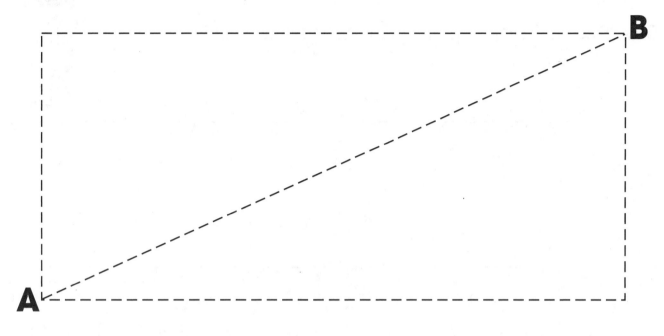

Directions: Trace the path from A to B.

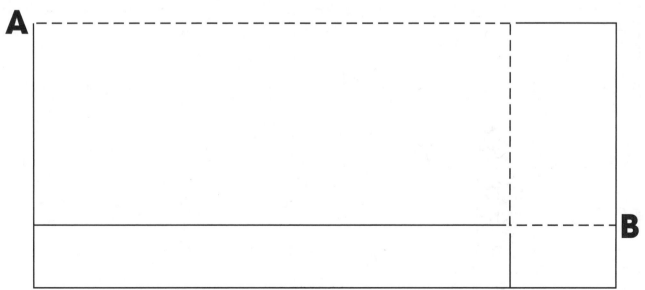

How many corners did you turn? _____

Tracking: Different Paths

Help Megan find Mark.

Directions: Trace a path from Megan to Mark.

How many different paths can she follow to reach him? _____

Tracking: Different Paths

Directions: Use different colors to trace three paths the bear could take to get the honey.

Time: Hour

The short hand of the clock tells the hour. The long hand tells how many minutes after the hour. When the minute hand is on the **12**, it is the beginning of the hour.

Directions: Look at each clock. Write the time.

Example:

___3__ o'clock

____ o'clock

____ o'clock

____ o'clock

____ o'clock

____ o'clock

____ o'clock

____ o'clock

____ o'clock

Time: Hour, Half-Hour

The short hand of the clock tells the hour. The long hand tells how many minutes after the hour. When the minute hand is on the **6**, it is on the half-hour. A half-hour is thirty minutes. It is written **:30**, such as **5:30**.

Directions: Look at each clock. Write the time.

Example:

hour   half-hour

$\underline{}\,1\,\underline{}$: $\underline{}\,30\,\underline{}$

___ : ___   ___ : ___   ___ : ___   ___ : ___

___ : ___   ___ : ___   ___ : ___   ___ : ___

Comprehensive Curriculum - Grade 1

Time: Hour, Half-Hour

Directions: Draw the hands on each clock to show the correct time.

2:30

9:00

7:00

4:30

3:00

1:30

Time: Counting by Fives

Directions: Fill in the numbers on the clock face. Count by fives around the clock.

60

5

55

10

50

15

45

20

40

25

35

30

There are 60 minutes in one hour.

Time: Review

Directions: Look at the time on the digital clocks and draw the hands on the clocks.

Directions: Look at each clock. Write the time.

 _____o'clock

 _____o'clock

Directions: Look at each clock. Write the time.

____:____   ____:____   ____:____

Review: Time

Directions: Tell what time it is on the clocks.

 _____

 _____

 _____

 _____

 _____

 _____

Review: Time

Directions: Match the time on the clock with the digital time.

10:00

5:00

3:00

9:00

2:00

Money: Penny and Nickel

A penny is worth one cent. It is written **1¢** or **$.01**. A nickel is worth five cents. It is written **5¢** or **$.05**.

Directions: Count the money, and write the answers.

penny   1 penny = 1¢

nickel   1 nickel = 5¢

   = ___3___ ¢

   = ___15___ ¢

   = _____ ¢

   = _____ ¢

   = _____ ¢

   = _____ ¢

Money: Penny, Nickel, Dime

A penny is worth one cent. It is written **I ¢** or **$.01**. A nickel is worth five cents. It is written **5¢** or **$.05**. A dime is worth ten cents. It is written **10¢** or **$.10**.

Directions: Add the coins pictured, and write the total amounts in the blanks.

Example:

dime   **nickel**   **nickel**   **pennies**

10¢ =   5¢   +   5¢   =   10¢

10¢   +   1¢   =   _____ ¢   10¢ + _____ ¢ = _____ ¢

_____ ¢ +   _____ ¢ +   _____ ¢   =   _____ ¢

_____ ¢ + _____ ¢   =   _____ ¢

Name _____

Money

Directions: Match the amounts in each purse to the price tags.

Money: Penny, Nickel, Dime

Directions: Match the correct amount of money with the price of the object.

Review

Directions: What time is it?

_____ o'clock

Directions: Draw the hands on each clock.

2:30

7:30

11:00

Directions: How much money?

= _____ ¢

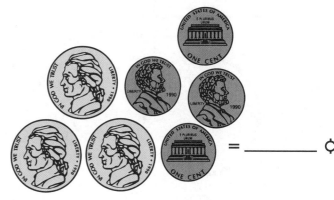
= _____ ¢

Directions: Add or subtract.

9 + 3 = _____   6 + 8 = _____   15 - 9 = _____

12 - 8 = _____   12 + 2 = _____   7 + 6 = _____

Review

Directions: Follow the instructions.

1. How much money?

_____ ¢

2. **Tens**   **Ones**   **Hundreds** **Tens** **Ones**

57 = _____   _____   128 = _____ _____ _____

3. What is this shape? Circle the answer.

Square

Triangle

Circle

What is this shape? _____

4.    Shaded part = _____   Write _____

Equal parts = _____

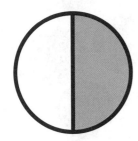   Shaded part = _____   Write _____

Equal parts = _____

5.   12 + 3 = _____   9 + 6 = _____   15 - 7 = _____

Measurement

An inch is a unit of length in the standard measurement system.

Directions: Cut out the ruler at the bottom of the page. Measure the objects to the nearest inch.

The screwdriver is _____ inches long.

The pencil is _____ inches long.

The pen is _____ inches long.

The fork is _____ inches long.

Cut ✂ –

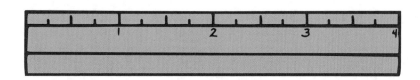

Comprehensive Curriculum - **Grade 1**

Page is blank for cutting exercise on previous page.

Abbreviation: A short way of writing words. Examples: Mon., Tues., etc.

Addition: "Putting together" or adding two or more numbers to find the sum.

Alphabetical (ABC) Order: Putting letters or words in the order in which they appear in the alphabet.

Antonyms: Words that are opposites. Example: *big* and *small.*

Asking Sentences: Sentences that ask a question. An asking sentence begins with a capital letter and ends with a question mark.

Beginning Consonants: Consonant sounds that come at the beginning of words.

Beginning Sounds: The sounds you hear first in a word.

Capital Letters: Letters that are used at the beginning of names of people, places, days, months, and holidays. Capital letters are also used at the beginning of sentences. These letters (*A, B, C, D, E, F, G, H, I, J, K, L, M, N, O, P, Q, R, S, T, U, V, W, X, Y,* and *Z*) are sometimes called uppercase or "big" letters.

Circle: A figure that is round. It looks like this: ○.

Classifying: Putting objects, words, or ideas that are alike into categories.

Compound Words: Two words that are put together to make one new word. Example: *house* + *boat* = *houseboat*

Comprehension: Understanding what is seen, heard, or read.

Consonant Blends or Teams: Two consonant sounds put together.

Consonants: The letters *b, c, d, f, g, h, j, k, l, m, n, p, q, r, s, t, v, w, x, y,* and *z.* Consonants are all the letters except *a, e, i, o,* and *u.*

Describing Words: Words that tell more about a person, place, or thing.

Digits: The symbols used to write numbers: 0, 1, 2, 3, 4, 5, 6, 7, 8, and 9.

Dime: Ten cents. It is written 10¢ or $.10.

Directions: To show or tell someone how to do something.

Ending Consonants: Consonant sounds that come at the end of words.

Ending Sounds: The sounds made by the last letters of words.

Fraction: A number that names part of a whole, such as $\frac{1}{2}$ or $\frac{2}{3}$.

Half-Hour: Thirty minutes. When the long hand of the clock is pointing to the six, the time is on the half-hour. It is written :30, such as 5:30.

Homophones: Words that sound the same but are spelled differently and mean different things. Example: *blue* and *blew*

Hour: Sixty minutes. The short hand of a clock tells the hour. It is written 2:00.

Long Vowels: The letters *a*, *e*, *i*, *o*, and *u*, which say the "long" or letter name sound. Long *a* is the sound you hear in *hay*. Long *e* is the sound you hear in *me*. Long *i* is the sound you hear in *pie*. Long *o* is the sound you hear in *no*. Long *u* is the sound you hear in *cute*.

Making Inferences: Using logic to figure out what is unspoken but known to be true.

Nickel: Five cents. It is written 5¢ or $.05.

Noun: Name of a person, place, or thing.

Opposites: Things that are different in every way.

Ordinal Numbers: Numbers that indicate order in a series, such as *first*, *second*, or *third*.

Oval: A figure that is egg-shaped. It looks like this: ⬭.

Pattern: A repeated arrangement of pictures, letters, or shapes.

Penny: One cent. It is written 1¢ or $.01.

Period: Tells you when to stop reading and is found at the end of sentences. It looks like this: .

Picture Clues: Looking at the pictures to figure out meaning.

Place Value: The value of a digit, or numeral, shown by where it is in the number. For example, in the number 23, 2 has the place value of tens and 3 is ones.

Predicting: Telling what is likely to happen based on available facts.

Rectangle: A figure with four corners and four sides. Sides opposite each other are the same length. It looks like this: ☐.

Rhombus: A figure with four sides of the same length. Its corners form points at the top, sides, and bottom. It looks like this: ◇.

Rhymes: Words with the same ending sounds.

Rhyming Words: Words that sound alike at the end of the word. Example: *cat* and *rat*

Same and Different: Being able to tell how things are alike and not alike.

Sentence: A group of words that tells a complete idea.

Sequencing: Putting numbers in the correct order, such as 7, 8, 9.

Short Vowels: The letters *a*, *e*, *i*, *o*, and *u*, which say the short sound. Short *a* is the sound you hear in *ant*. Short *e* is the sound you hear in *elephant*. Short *i* is the sound you hear in *igloo*. Short *o* is the sound you hear in *octopus*. Short *u* is the sound you hear in *umbrella*.

Similar: Things that are almost the same.

Square: A figure with four corners and four sides of the same length. It looks like this: ☐.

Subtraction: "Taking away" or subtracting one number from another. For example: $10 - 3 = 7$

Super Silent E: The *e* that is added to some words that changes the short vowel sound to a long vowel sound. Example: *rip + e = ripe*

Synonyms: Words that mean the same thing. Example: *small* and *little*

Telling Sentences: Sentences that tell something. A telling sentence begins with a capital letter and ends with a period.

Tracking: Following a path.

Triangle: A figure with three corners and three sides. It looks like this: △ .

Verbs: Words that tell what a person or thing can do.

Vowels: The letters *a*, *e*, *i*, *o*, *u*, and sometimes *y*.

Name, Address, Phone Number
Answers will vary.

This book belongs to

_____

I live at

_____

The city I live in is

_____

The state I live in is

_____

My phone number is

_____

Page 6

Review the Alphabet
Directions: Practice writing the letters.   Child will write letters as shown.

Aa Aa Aa Aa Aa Aa
Bb Bb Bb Bb Bb Bb
Cc Cc Cc Cc Cc
Dd Dd Dd Dd Dd Dd
Ee Ee Ee Ee Ee Ee
Ff Ff Ff Ff Ff Ff
Gg Gg Gg Gg Gg
Hh Hh Hh Hh Hh Hh
Ii Ii Ii Ii Ii Ii Ii Ii Ii

Page 7

Review the Alphabet
Directions: Practice writing the letters.   Child will write letters as shown.

Jj Jj Jj Jj Jj Jj
Kk Kk Kk Kk Kk Kk
Ll Ll Ll Ll Ll Ll
Mm Mm Mm Mm Mm
Nn Nn Nn Nn Nn Nn
Oo Oo Oo Oo Oo
Pp Pp Pp Pp Pp Pp
Qq Qq Qq Qq Qq
Rr Rr Rr Rr Rr Rr

Page 8

Review the Alphabet
Directions: Practice writing the letters.   Child will write letters as shown.

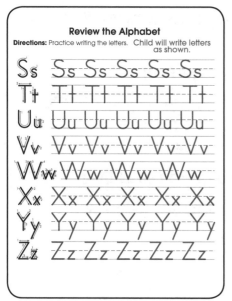

Ss Ss Ss Ss Ss Ss
Tt Tt Tt Tt Tt Tt
Uu Uu Uu Uu Uu Uu
Vv Vv Vv Vv Vv Vv
Ww Ww Ww Ww Ww
Xx Xx Xx Xx Xx Xx
Yy Yy Yy Yy Yy Yy
Zz Zz Zz Zz Zz Zz

Page 9

Letter Recognition
Directions: In each set, match the lowercase letter to the uppercase letter.

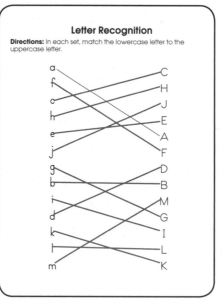

Page 10

Letter Recognition
Directions: In each set, match the lowercase letter to the uppercase letter.

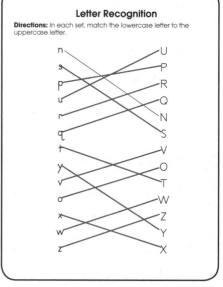

Page 11

Beginning Consonants: Bb, Cc, Dd, Ff

Beginning consonants are the sounds that come at the beginning of words. Consonants are the letters **b, c, d, f, g, h, j, k, l, m, n, p, q, r, s, t, v, w, x, y,** and **z.**
Directions: Say the name of each letter. Say the sound each letter makes. Circle the letters that make the beginning sound for each picture.

Page 12

Beginning Consonants: Bb, Cc, Dd, Ff

Directions: Say the name of each letter. Say the sound each letter makes. Draw a line from each letter to the picture that begins with that sound.

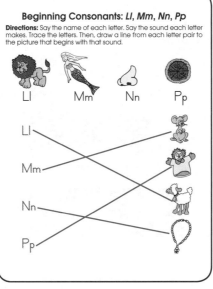

Page 13

Beginning Consonants: Gg, Hh, Jj, Kk

Directions: Say the name of each letter. Say the sound each letter makes. Trace the letter pair that makes the beginning sound in each picture.

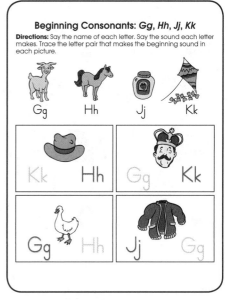

Page 14

Beginning Consonants: Gg, Hh, Jj, Kk

Directions: Say the name of each letter. Say the sound each letter makes. Draw a line from each letter pair to the picture that begins with that sound.

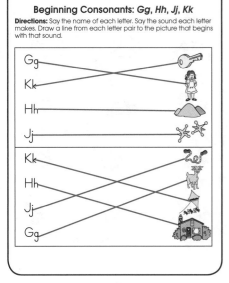

Page 15

Beginning Consonants: Ll, Mm, Nn, Pp

Directions: Say the name of each letter. Say the sound each letter makes. Trace the letters. Then, draw a line from each letter pair to the picture that begins with that sound.

Page 16

Beginning Consonants: Ll, Mm, Nn, Pp

Directions: Say the name of each letter. Say the sound each letter makes. Trace the letter pair that makes the beginning sound in each picture.

Page 17

Comprehensive Curriculum - **Grade 1**

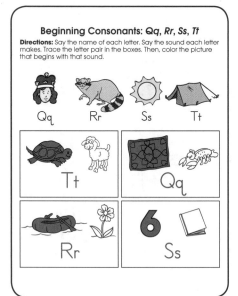

Beginning Consonants: *Qq, Rr, Ss, Tt*

Directions: Say the name of each letter. Say the sound each letter makes. Trace the letter pair in the boxes. Then, color the picture that begins with that sound.

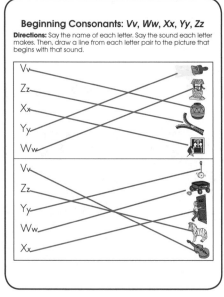

Page 18

Beginning Consonants: *Qq, Rr, Ss, Tt*

Directions: Say the name of each letter. Say the sound each letter makes. Draw a line from each letter pair to the picture that begins with that sound.

Page 19

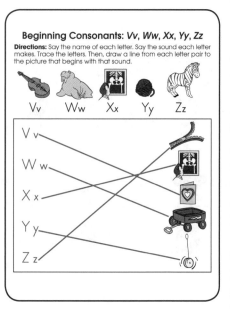

Beginning Consonants: *Vv, Ww, Xx, Yy, Zz*

Directions: Say the name of each letter. Say the sound each letter makes. Trace the letters. Then, draw a line from each letter pair to the picture that begins with that sound.

Page 20

Beginning Consonants: *Vv, Ww, Xx, Yy, Zz*

Directions: Say the name of each letter. Say the sound each letter makes. Then, draw a line from each letter pair to the picture that begins with that sound.

Page 21

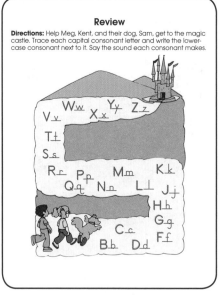

Review

Directions: Help Meg, Kent, and their dog, Sam, get to the magic castle. Trace each capital consonant letter and write the lower-case consonant next to it. Say the sound each letter makes.

Page 22

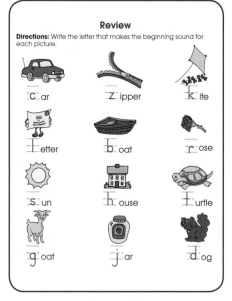

Review

Directions: Write the letter that makes the beginning sound for each picture.

Car Zipper Kite
Letter boat rose
Sun house turtle
goat jar dog

Page 23

Ending Consonants: *B*, *D*, and *F*

Ending consonants are the sounds that come at the ends of words.
Directions: Say the name of each picture. Then, write the letter that makes the **ending** sound for each picture.

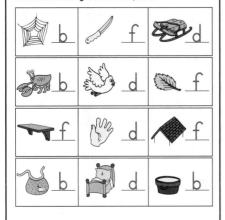

Page 24

Ending Consonants: *G*, *M*, and *N*

Directions: Say the name of each picture. Draw a line from each letter to the pictures that end with that sound.

Page 25

Ending Consonants: *K*, *L*, and *P*

Directions: Trace the letter in each row. Say the name of each picture. Then, color the pictures in each row that end with that sound.

k

l

p

Page 26

Ending Consonants: *R*, *S*, *T*, and *X*

Directions: Say the name of each picture. Then, circle the ending sound for each picture.

(r)s t x   r (s) t x

(r)s t x   r s (t) x

r s (t) x   r (s) t x

r s t (x)   r s (t) x

Page 27

Beginning and Ending Consonants

Directions: Say the name of each picture. Draw a **blue** circle around the picture if it **begins** with the sound of the letter below it. Draw a **green** triangle around the picture if it **ends** with the sound of the letter below it.

w   l   m

k   n   v

t   s   z

Page 28

Beginning and Ending Consonants

Directions: Say the name of each picture. Draw a triangle around the letter that makes the **beginning** sound. Draw a square around the letter that makes the **ending** sound. Color the pictures.

o (r) [t]   f d (m)   v [t] (b)

x (c) [r]   [t] g (a)   (a) a [k]

[l] m (n)   x (g) [r]   p [t] (n)

Page 29

Comprehensive Curriculum - **Grade 1**

ANSWER KEY

Beginning and Ending Consonants

Directions: Say the name of each picture. Write the beginning and ending sounds for each picture.

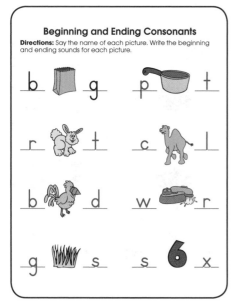

Page 30

Short Vowels

Vowels are the letters **a, e, i, o,** and **u.** Short **a** is the sound you hear in **ant.** Short **e** is the sound you hear in **elephant.** Short **i** is the sound you hear in **igloo.** Short **o** is the sound you hear in **octopus.** Short **u** is the sound you hear in **umbrella.**

Directions: Say the short vowel sound at the beginning of each row. Say the name of each picture. Then, color the pictures that have the same short vowel sound as that letter.

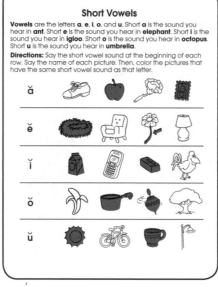

Page 31

Short Vowel Sounds

Directions: There are three pictures in each box. The words that name the pictures have missing letters. Write **a, e, i, o,** or **u** to finish the words.

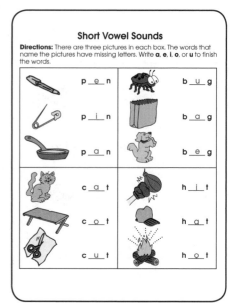

Page 32

Long Vowels

Vowels are the letters **a, e, i, o,** and **u.** Long vowel sounds say their own names. Long **a** is the sound you hear in **hay.** Long **e** is the sound you hear in **me.** Long **i** is the sound you hear in **pie.** Long **o** is the sound you hear in **no.** Long **u** is the sound you hear in **cute.**

Directions: Say the long vowel sound at the beginning of each row. Say the name of each picture. Color the pictures in each row that have the same long vowel sound as that letter.

Page 33

Long Vowel Sounds

Directions: Write **a, e, i, o,** or **u** in each blank to finish the word. Draw a line from the word to the picture.

Page 34

Words with A

Directions: Each train has a group of pictures. Write the word that names the pictures. Read your rhyming words.

These trains use the short **a** sound, as in the word **cat:**

These trains use the long **a** sound, as in the word **lake:**

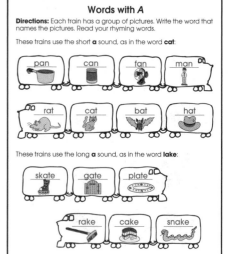

Page 35

Short and Long *Aa*

Directions: Say the name of each picture. If it has the short **a** sound, color it **red**. If it has the long **a** sound, color it **yellow**.

Page 36

Words with *E*

Directions: Short **e** sounds like the **e** in **hen**. Long **e** sounds like the **e** in **bee**. Look at the pictures. If the word has a short **e** sound, draw a line to the **hen** with your **red** crayon. If the word has a long **e** sound, draw a line to the **bee** with your **green** crayon.

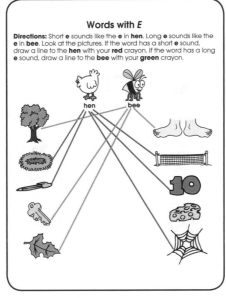

Page 37

Short and Long *Ee*

Directions: Say the name of each picture. Circle the pictures that have the short **e** sound. Draw a triangle around the pictures that have the long **e** sound.

Page 38

Words with *I*

Directions: Short **i** sounds like the **i** in **pig**. Long **i** sounds like the **i** in **kite**. Draw a circle around the words with the short **i** sound. Draw an **X** on the words with the long **i** sound.

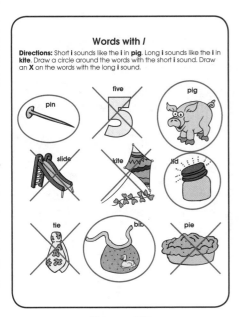

Page 39

Short and Long *Ii*

Directions: Say the name of each picture. If it has the short **i** sound, color it **yellow**. If it has the long **i** sound, color it **red**.

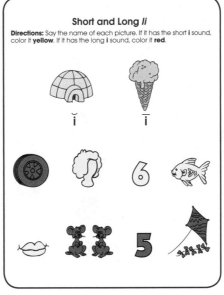

Page 40

Words with *O*

Directions: The short **o** sounds like the **o** in **dog**. Long **o** sounds like the **o** in **rope**. Draw a line from the picture to the word that names it. Draw a circle around the word if it has a short **o** sound.

hot dog

fox

blocks

rose

boat

Page 41

Short and Long Oo

Directions: Say the name of each picture. If the picture has the long **o** sound, write a **green L** on the blank. If the picture has the short **o** sound, write a **red S** on the blank.

Page 42

Words with U

Directions: The short **u** sounds like the **u** in **bug**. The long **u** sounds like the **u** in **blue**. Draw a circle around the words with short **u**. Draw an **X** on the words with long **u**.

Page 43

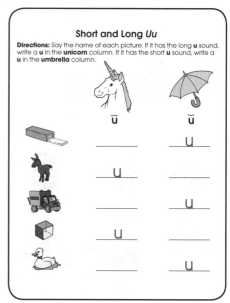

Short and Long Uu

Directions: Say the name of each picture. If it has the long **u** sound, write a **u** in the **unicorn** column. If it has the short **u** sound, write a **u** in the **umbrella** column.

Page 44

Super Silent E

When you add an **e** to the end of some words, the vowel changes from a short vowel sound to a long vowel sound. The **e** is silent.

Example: rip + **e** = ripe

Directions: Say the word under the first picture in each pair. Then, add an **e** to the word under the next picture. Say the new word.

pet — Pete — tub — tube
man — mane — kit — kite
pin — pine — cap — cape

Page 45

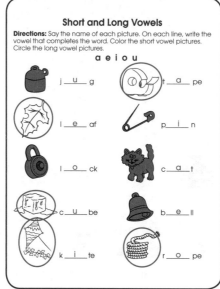

Short and Long Vowels

Directions: Say the name of each picture. On each line, write the vowel that completes the word. Color the short vowel pictures. Circle the long vowel pictures.

a e i o u

j u g   t a pe
l e af   p i n
l o ck   c a t
c u be   b e ll
k i te   r o pe

Page 46

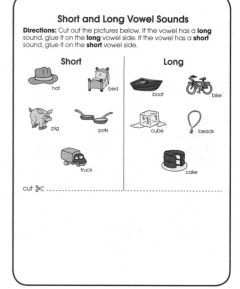

Short and Long Vowel Sounds

Directions: Cut out the pictures below. If the vowel has a **long** sound, glue it on the **long** vowel side. If the vowel has a **short** sound, glue it on the **short** vowel side.

Short	Long
hat, bed	boat, bike
pig, pots	cube, beads
truck	cake

cut ✂ - - - - - - - - - - - - - - - - -

Page 47

Review

Directions: Color all of the vowels black to discover something hidden in the puzzle.

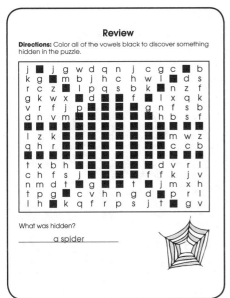

What was hidden?

_____a spider_____

Page 49

Review

Directions: Circle the word if it has a long vowel sound.

Remember: A long vowel says its name.

feet snake cup
hose tie hat
dog rake bug
bone bib net

Page 50

Review

Directions: On each line, write the vowel that completes the word.

a   e   i   o   u

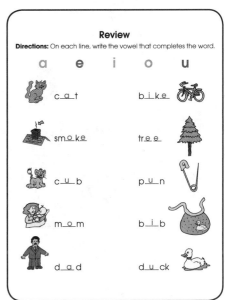

c_a_t   b_i_ke
sm_o_ke   tr_e_e
c_u_b   p_u_n
m_o_m   b_i_b
d_a_d   d_u_ck

Page 51

Review

Directions: Circle the **long vowel** words with a **red** crayon. Underline the **short vowel** words with a **blue** crayon.

Remember: The vowel is long if:
• There are two vowels in the word. The first vowel is the sound you hear.
• There is a "super silent e" at the end.

cub   red   (coat)
(bite)   (cube)   (cage)
cat   (mean)   (rake)
bit   cot   hen
(leaf)   (feet)   key
pen   web   (bee)
nest   (boat)   fox
(rose)   dog   pig

Page 52

My Vowel List

Keep this list handy, and add more words to it.
Answers will vary.

short a
(ă as in **cat**)
_____

short e
(ĕ as in **get**)
_____

short i
(ĭ as in **pin**)
_____

short o
(ŏ as in **cot**)
_____

short u
(ŭ as in **cut**)
_____

long a
(ā as in **train**)
_____

long e
(ē as in **tree**)
_____

long i
(ī as in **ice**)
_____

long o
(ō as in **boat**)
_____

long u
(ū as in **cube**)
_____

Page 53

Consonant Blends

Consonant blends are two or more consonant sounds together in a word. The blend is made by combining the consonant sounds.

Example: floor

Directions: The name of each picture begins with a **blend**. Circle the beginning blend for each picture.

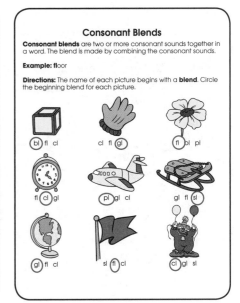

bl (fl) cl   cl fl (gl)   fl bl (pl)
fl (cl) gl   (pl) gl cl   gl fl (sl)
(gl) fl cl   sl (fl) cl   (cl) gl sl

Page 55

Consonant Blends

Directions: The beginning blend for each word is missing. Fill in the correct blend to finish the word. Draw a line from the word to the picture.

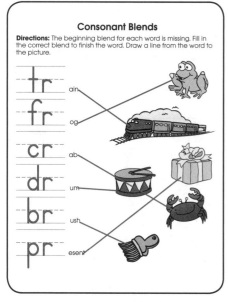

tr ___ain
fr ___og
cr ___ab
dr ___um
br ___ush
pr ___esent

Page 56

Consonant Blends

Directions: Draw a line from the picture to the blend that begins its name.

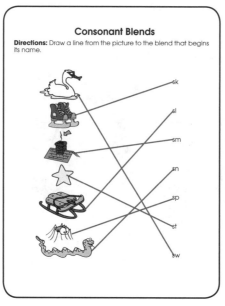

sk
sl
sm
sn
sp
st
sw

Page 57

Consonant Teams

Consonant teams are two or more consonant letters that have a single sound.

Examples: sh and **ch**

Directions: Look at the first picture in each row. Circle the pictures in the row that begin with the same sound.

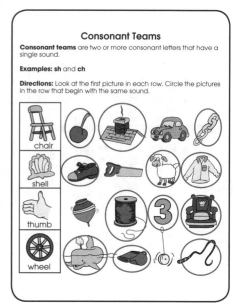

chair
shell
thumb
wheel

Page 58

Beginning Blends and Teams

Directions: Say the blend for each word as you search for it.

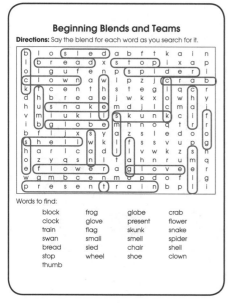

Words to find:

block, clock, train, swan, bread, stop, thumb
frog, glove, flag, small, sled, wheel
globe, present, skunk, smell, chair, shoe
crab, flower, snake, spider, shell, clown

Page 59

Ending Consonant Blends

Directions: Write **lt** or **ft** to complete the words.

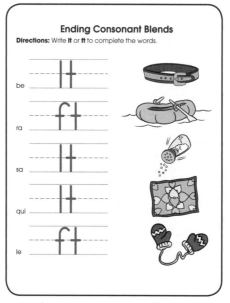

be__lt__
ra__ft__
sa__lt__
qui__lt__
le__ft__

Page 60

Ending Consonant Blends

Directions: Draw a line from the picture to the blend that ends the word.

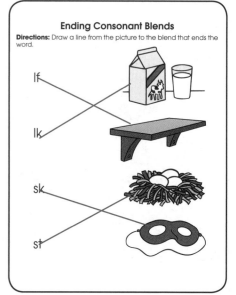

lf
lk
sk
st

Page 61

Ending Consonant Blends

Directions: Every jukebox has a word ending and a list of letters. Add each of the letters to the word ending to make rhyming words.

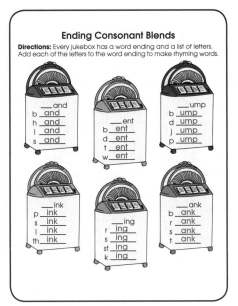

b __and__
h __and__
l __and__
s __and__

__ump__
b __ump__
d __ump__
j __ump__
p __ump__

__ent__
b __ent__
d __ent__
t __ent__
w __ent__

__ink__
p __ink__
s __ink__
l __ink__
th __ink__

__ing__
r __ing__
s __ing__
st __ing__
k __ing__

__ank__
b __ank__
r __ank__
s __ank__
t __ank__

Page 62

Ending Consonant Blends and Teams

Directions: Say the blend for each word as you search for it.

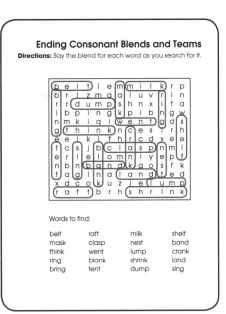

Words to find:

belt	raft	milk	shelf
mask	clasp	nest	band
think	went	lump	crank
ring	blank	shrink	land
bring	tent	dump	sing

Page 63

Review

Directions: Finish each sentence with a word from the word box.

sting	shelf	drank	plant	stamp

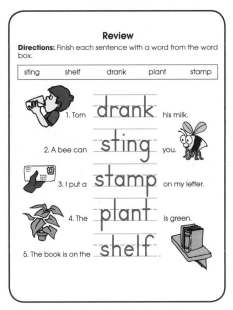

1. Tom __drank__ his milk.

2. A bee can __sting__ you.

3. I put a __stamp__ on my letter.

4. The __plant__ is green.

5. The book is on the __shelf__.

Page 64

Rhyming Words

Rhyming words are words that sound alike at the end of the word. **Cat** and **hat** rhyme.

Directions: Draw a circle around each word pair that rhymes. Draw an **X** on each pair that does not rhyme.

Example:

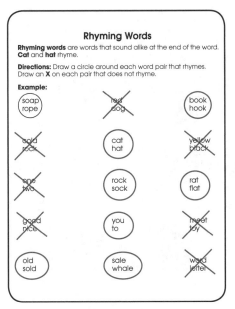

soap rope

red dog

book hook

gold rock

cat hat

yellow black

one two

rock sock

rat flat

good nice

you to

meet toy

old sold

sale whale

word letter

Page 65

Rhyming Words

Rhyming words are words that sound alike at the end of the word.

Directions: Draw a line to match the pictures that rhyme. Write two of your rhyming word pairs below.

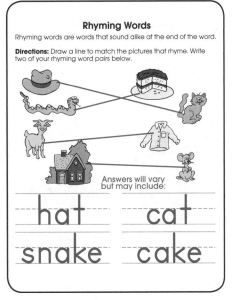

Answers will vary but may include:

__hat__   __cat__
__snake__   __cake__

Page 66

ABC Order

Directions: **ABC** order is the order in which letters come in the alphabet. Draw a line to connect the dots. Follow the letters in ABC order. Then, color the picture.

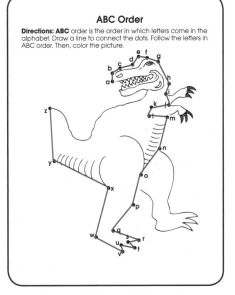

Page 67

ABC Order

Directions: Draw a line to connect the dots. Follow the letters in ABC order. Then, color the picture.

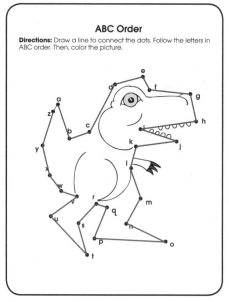

Page 68

ABC Order

Directions: Circle the first letter of each word. Then, put each pair of words in ABC order.

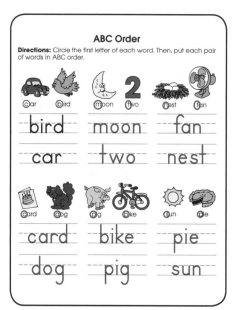

Page 69

ABC Order

Directions: Look at the words in each box. Circle the word that comes first in ABC order.

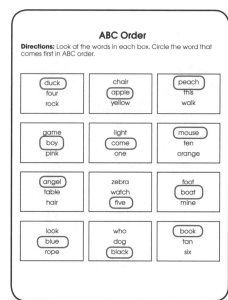

(duck) four rock	chair (apple) yellow	(peach) this walk
game (boy) pink	light (come) one	(mouse) ten orange
(angel) table hair	zebra watch (five)	foot (boat) mine
look (blue) rope	who dog (black)	(book) tan six

Page 70

ABC Order

Directions: Cut out the foods Mom wants to buy when she goes shopping. Glue the words in ABC order on the shopping list.

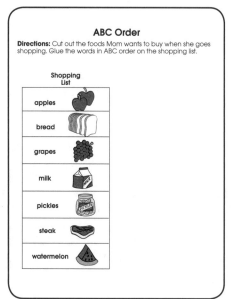

Shopping List

apples
bread
grapes
milk
pickles
steak
watermelon

Page 71

Sequencing: ABC Order

Directions: Put each group of words in ABC order by numbering them 1, 2, 3.

Example:

cold 1   **w**arm 3   **h**ot 2

small 3   **b**ig 1   **c**ute 2

doll 2
truck 3   **b**all 1

baby 1
sister 3   family 2

man 3
boy 1   **g**randma 2

Page 73

ABC Order

Directions: Put the words in ABC order. Circle the first letter of each word. Then, write 1, 2, 3, 4, 5, or 6 on the line next to each animal's name.

(s)kunk 4   (d)og 2

(b)utterfly 1   (z)ebra 6

(t)iger 5   (f)ish 3

Page 74

Compound Words

Compound words are two words that are put together to make one new word.

Directions: Look at the pictures and the two words that are next to each other. Put the words together to make a new word. Write the new word.

Example:

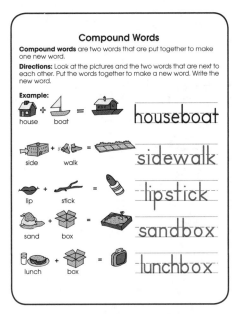

house ÷ boat = houseboat

side + walk = sidewalk

lip + stick = lipstick

sand + box = sandbox

lunch + box = lunchbox

Page 75

Compound Words

Directions: Circle the compound word that completes each sentence. Write each word on the line.

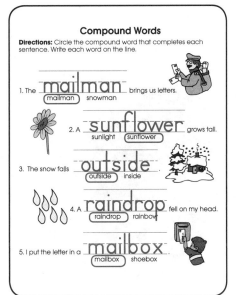

1. The **mailman** brings us letters.
   mailman / snowman

2. A **sunflower** grows tall.
   sunlight / sunflower

3. The snow falls **outside**.
   outside / inside

4. A **raindrop** fell on my head.
   raindrop / rainbow

5. I put the letter in a **mailbox**.
   mailbox / shoebox

Page 76

Compound Words

Directions: Cut out the pictures and words at the bottom of the page. Put two words together to make a compound word. Write the new word.

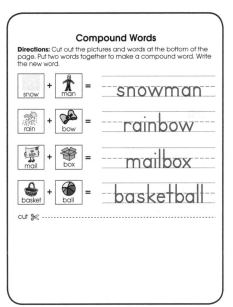

snow + man = snowman

rain + bow = rainbow

mail + box = mailbox

basket + ball = basketball

cut ✂ -

Page 77

Names

Your name begins with a capital letter. People's names always begin with a capital letter.

Directions: Write your name. Did you remember to use a capital letter?

Answers will vary.
- -

Directions: Write each person's name. Use a capital letter at the beginning.

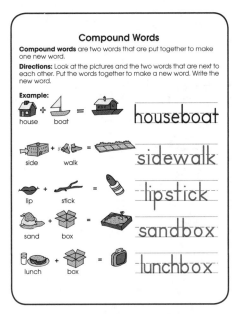

Zola — Zola

Katie — Katie

Marco — Marco

Jake — Jake

Write a friend's name. Use a capital letter at the beginning.

Answers will vary.
- - - - - - - - - - -

Page 81

Names: Days of the Week

The days of the week begin with capital letters.

Directions: Write the days of the week in the spaces below. Put them in order. Be sure to start with capital letters.

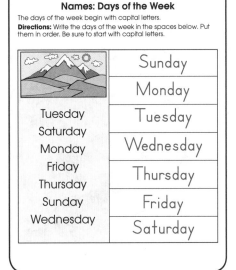

Tuesday	Sunday
Saturday	Monday
Monday	Tuesday
Friday	Wednesday
Thursday	Thursday
Sunday	Friday
Wednesday	Saturday

Page 82

Names: Months of the Year

The months of the year begin with capital letters.

Directions: Write the months of the year in order on the calendar below. Be sure to use capital letters.

| January | December | April | May | October | June |
| September | February | July | March | November | August |

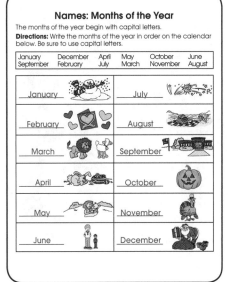

January	July
February	August
March	September
April	October
May	November
June	December

Page 83

More Than One

Directions: An **s** at the end of a word often means there is more than one. Look at each picture. Circle the correct word. Write the word on the line.

two
dog (dogs)

four
flower (flowers)

one
bikes (bike)

dogs   flowers   bike

three
(toys) toy

a
(lamb) lambs

two
cat (cats)

toys   lamb   cats

Page 84

More Than One

Directions: Read the nouns under the pictures. Then, write each noun under **One** or **More Than One**.

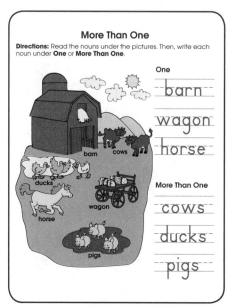

One

barn

wagon

horse

More Than One

cows

ducks

pigs

Page 85

More Than One

Directions: Circle the correct word to complete each sentence.

Remember: An **s** at the end of a word can mean more than one.

I have two (apple, (apples)).

I can eat one (hot dogs, (hot dog)).

My dad has five ((hats), hat).

You can read four (book, (books)).

Six (letter, (letters)) are in the mailbox.

One (plants, (plant)) needs water.

Three (rabbit, (rabbits)) were pulled from the magician's hat.

Page 86

More Than One

Directions: Choose the word that completes each sentence. Write each word on the line.

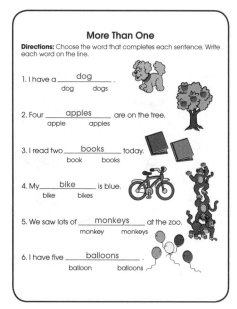

1. I have a ___dog___ .
   dog   dogs

2. Four ___apples___ are on the tree.
   apple   apples

3. I read two ___books___ today.
   book   books

4. My ___bike___ is blue.
   bike   bikes

5. We saw lots of ___monkeys___ at the zoo.
   monkey   monkeys

6. I have five ___balloons___ .
   balloon   balloons

Page 88

Riddles

Directions: Read the word. Trace and write it on the line. Then, draw a line from the riddle to the animal it tells about.

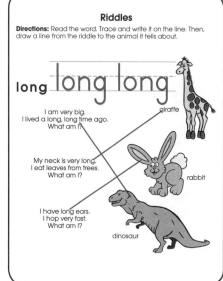

long   long long

I am very big.
I lived a long, long time ago.
What am I?

giraffe

My neck is very long.
I eat leaves from trees.
What am I?

rabbit

I have long ears.
I hop very fast.
What am I?

dinosaur

Page 89

Riddles

Directions: Read the word, and write it on the line. Then, read each riddle and draw a line to the picture and word that tells about it.

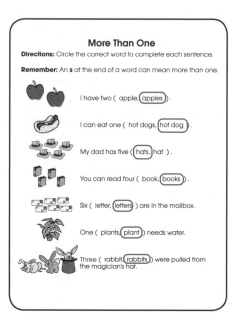

house

house

kitten

kitten

flower

flower

pony

pony

I like to play.
I am little. I am soft.
What am I?

house

I am big.
People live in me.
What am I?

kitten

I am pretty.
I am green and yellow.
What am I?

flower

I can jump. I can run.
I am brown.
What am I?

pony

Page 90

Riddles

Directions: Write a word from the box to answer each riddle.

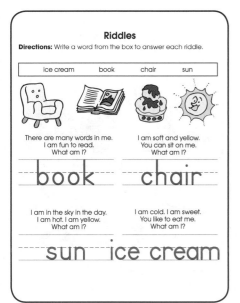

| ice cream | book | chair | sun |

There are many words in me. I am fun to read. What am I?

book

I am soft and yellow. You can sit on me. What am I?

chair

I am in the sky in the day. I am hot. I am yellow. What am I?

sun

I am cold. I am sweet. You like to eat me. What am I?

ice cream

Page 91

Picture Clues

Directions: Read the sentence. Circle the word that makes sense. Use the picture clues to help you. Then, write the word.

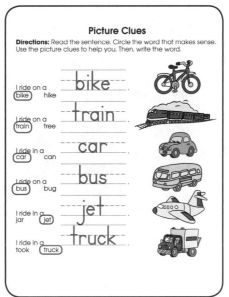

I ride on a (bike) hike — **bike**
I ride on a (train) tree — **train**
I ride in a (car) can — **car**
I ride on a (bus) bug — **bus**
I ride in a jar (jet) — **jet**
I ride in a took (truck) — **truck**

Page 92

Picture Clues

Directions: Read the sentence. Circle the word that makes sense. Use the picture clues to help you. Then, write the word.

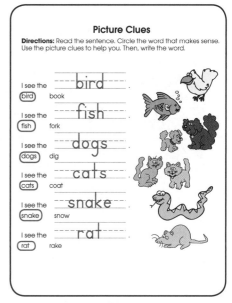

I see the (bird) book — **bird**
I see the (fish) fork — **fish**
I see the (dogs) dig — **dogs**
I see the (cats) coat — **cats**
I see the (snake) snow — **snake**
I see the (rat) rake — **rat**

Page 93

Picture Clues

Directions: Draw a line from the picture to its sentence.

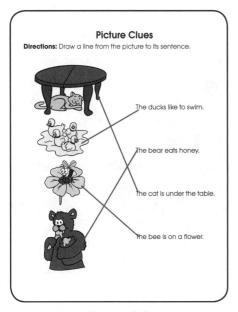

The ducks like to swim.
The bear eats honey.
The cat is under the table.
The bee is on a flower.

Page 94

Picture Clues

Directions: Cut out the pictures below. Glue them next to the sentences.

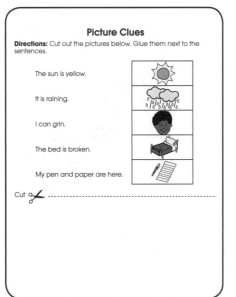

The sun is yellow.
It is raining.
I can grin.
The bed is broken.
My pen and paper are here.

Cut ✂ --------

Page 95

Comprehension

Directions: Look at the picture. Write the words from the box to finish the sentences.

| frog | log | bird | fish | ducks |

The **frog** can jump.
The turtle is on a **log**.
A **bird** is in the tree.
The boy wants a **fish**.
I see three **ducks**.

Page 97

Comprehension

Directions: Read the poem. Write the correct words in the blanks.

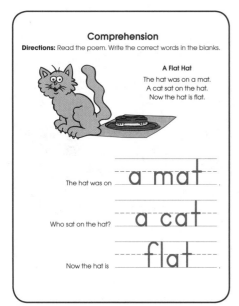

A Flat Hat

The hat was on a mat.
A cat sat on the hat.
Now the hat is flat.

The hat was on a mat

Who sat on the hat? a cat

Now the hat is flat

Page 98

Following Directions: Color the Path

Directions: Color the path the girl should take to go home. Use the sentences to help you.

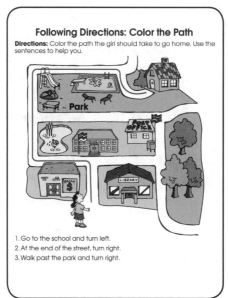

1. Go to the school and turn left.
2. At the end of the street, turn right.
3. Walk past the park and turn right.

Page 99

Following Directions

Directions: Look at the pictures. Follow the directions in each box.

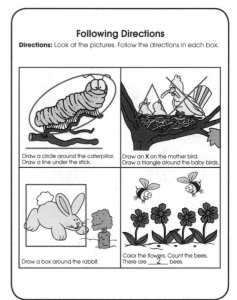

Draw a circle around the caterpillar.
Draw a line under the stick.

Draw an **X** on the mother bird.
Draw a triangle around the baby birds.

Draw a box around the rabbit.

Color the flowers. Count the bees.
There are ___2___ bees.

Page 100

Classifying

Directions: Classifying is sorting things into groups. Draw a circle around the pictures that answer the question.

What Can Swim?

What Can Fly?

Page 101

Classifying: These Keep Me Warm

Directions: Color the things that keep you warm.

socks
apple
lunchbox
earmuffs
cookie
coat
hat
umbrella
gloves
book

Page 102

Classifying: Objects

Help Dan clean up the park.

Directions: Circle the litter. Underline the coins. Draw a box around the balls.

Page 103

Page 104

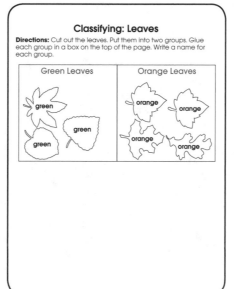

Page 105

Page 107

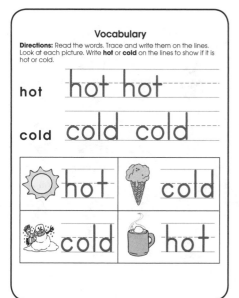

Page 108

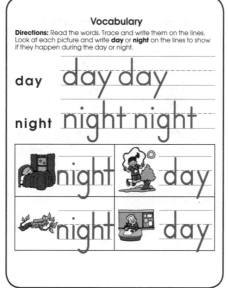

Page 109

Classifying: Night and Day

Directions: Write the words from the box under the pictures they describe.

stars   sun   moon   rays   dark   light   night   day

stars	sun
moon	rays
dark	light
night	day

Page 110

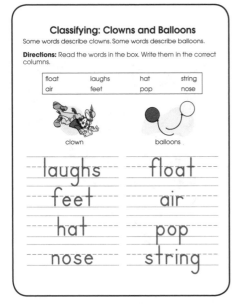

Classifying: Clowns and Balloons

Some words describe clowns. Some words describe balloons.

Directions: Read the words in the box. Write them in the correct columns.

float	laughs	hat	string
air	feet	pop	nose

clown   balloons

laughs	float
feet	air
hat	pop
nose	string

Page 111

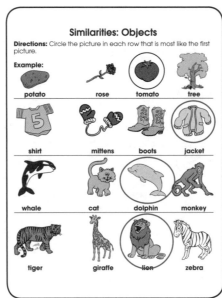

Similarities: Objects

Directions: Circle the picture in each row that is most like the first picture.

Example:

potato   rose   (tomato)   tree

shirt   mittens   boots   (jacket)

whale   cat   (dolphin)   monkey

tiger   giraffe   (lion)   zebra

Page 112

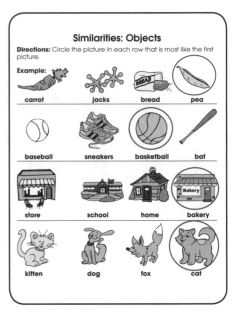

Similarities: Objects

Directions: Circle the picture in each row that is most like the first picture.

Example:

carrot   jacks   bread   (pea)

baseball   sneakers   (basketball)   bat

store   school   home   (bakery)

kitten   dog   fox   (cat)

Page 113

Classifying: Food Groups

Directions: Color the meats and eggs brown. Color the fruits and vegetables green. Color the breads tan. Color the dairy foods (like milk and cheese) yellow.

fish   bread   apple   cheese

crackers   carrot   orange   eggs

steaks   pear   milk   yogurt

ice cream   chicken   potato   pretzel

Page 114

Same and Different: These Don't Belong

Directions: Circle the pictures in each row that go together.

Row 1   cookies   cake   beans   ice cream

Row 2   apple   banana   orange   cookies

Row 3   kite   dice   checkers   chess

Directions: Write the names of the things that do not belong.

Row 1   beans

Row 2   cookies

Row 3   kite

Page 115

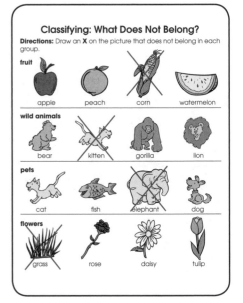

Classifying: What Does Not Belong?

Directions: Draw an **X** on the picture that does not belong in each group.

fruit

apple   peach   corn   watermelon

wild animals

bear   kitten   gorilla   lion

pets

cat   fish   elephant   dog

flowers

grass   rose   daisy   tulip

Page 116

Classifying: What Does Not Belong?

Directions: Draw an **X** on the word in each row that does not belong.

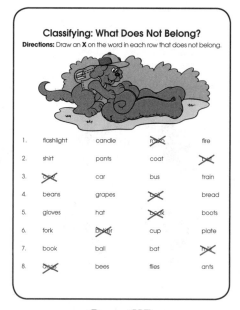

1.	flashlight	candle	~~radio~~	fire
2.	shirt	pants	coat	~~sock~~
3.	~~sea~~	car	bus	train
4.	beans	grapes	~~bed~~	bread
5.	gloves	hat	~~book~~	boots
6.	fork	~~butter~~	cup	plate
7.	book	ball	bat	~~milk~~
8.	~~dogs~~	bees	flies	ants

Page 117

Classifying: Objects

Directions: Write each word in the correct row at the bottom of the page.

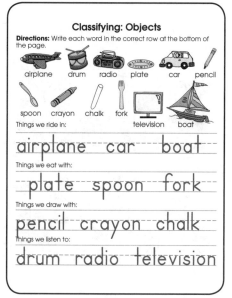

airplane   drum   radio   plate   car   pencil

spoon   crayon   chalk   fork   television   boat

Things we ride in:

airplane   car   boat

Things we eat with:

plate   spoon   fork

Things we draw with:

pencil   crayon   chalk

Things we listen to:

drum   radio   television

Page 118

Classifying: Names, Numbers, Animals, Colors

Directions: Write the words from the box next to the kinds of words they are.

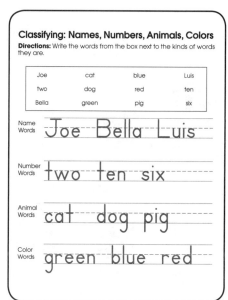

Joe	cat	blue	Luis
two	dog	red	ten
Bella	green	pig	six

Name Words: Joe Bella Luis

Number Words: two ten six

Animal Words: cat dog pig

Color Words: green blue red

Page 119

Classifying: Things That Belong Together

Directions: Circle the pictures in each row that belong together.

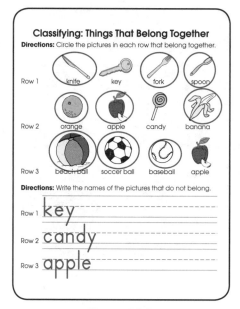

Row 1: knife   key   fork   spoon

Row 2: orange   apple   candy   banana

Row 3: beach ball   soccer ball   baseball   apple

Directions: Write the names of the pictures that do not belong.

Row 1: key

Row 2: candy

Row 3: apple

Page 120

Classifying: Why They Are Different

Directions: Look at your answers on page 120. Write why each object does not belong.

Row 1: It is not used for eating.

Row 2: It is not a fruit.

Row 3: It is not a ball.

Directions: For each object, draw a group of pictures that belong with it.

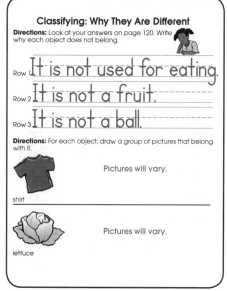

Pictures will vary.

shirt

Pictures will vary.

lettuce

Page 121

Classifying: What Does Not Belong?

Directions: Circle the two things that do not belong in the picture. Write why they do not belong.

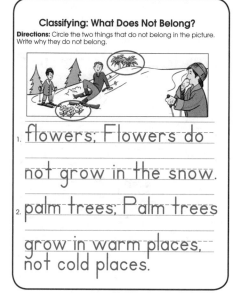

1. flowers; Flowers do not grow in the snow.

2. palm trees; Palm trees grow in warm places, not cold places.

Page 122

Sequencing: Fill the Glasses

Directions: Follow the instructions to fill each glass. Use crayons to draw your favorite drink in the ones that are full and half-full.

full   half-full   empty

empty   half-full   full

Page 123

Sequencing: Raking Leaves

Directions: Write a number in each box to show the order of the story.

Page 124

Sequencing: Make a Snowman!

Directions: Write the number of the sentence that goes with each picture in the box.

1. Roll a large snowball for the snowman's bottom.
2. Make another snowball, and put it on top of the first.
3. Put the last snowball on top.
4. Dress the snowman.

Page 125

Sequencing: A Recipe

Directions: Look at the recipe below. Put each step in order. Write 1, 2, 3, or 4 in the box.

HOW TO MAKE BREAD BUDDIES

| 3 | 1 |
Roll dough into balls and shapes. Connect pieces with a drop of water. / Mix 1 cup of water, 1 cup of salt, and 3 cups of flour.
Knead the dough. | 2 | | 4 |
Have an adult bake your bread buddy for 2-3 hours at 300°. Let it cool. Then, paint it!

Answers will vary.
What kind of bread buddy did you make?

Page 126

Sequencing: How Flowers Grow

Directions: Read the story. Then, write the steps to grow a flower.

First, find a sunny spot. Then, plant the seed. Water it. The flower will start to grow. Pull the weeds around it. Remember to keep giving the flower water. Enjoy your flower.

1. Find a sunny spot
2. Plant the seed
3. Water it
4. Pull the weeds around it
5. Keep giving the flower

Page 127

Sequencing: Make an Ice-Cream Cone

Directions: Number the boxes in order to show how to make an ice-cream cone.

Page 128

Sequencing: Eating a Cone

What if a person never ate an ice-cream cone? Could you tell them how to eat it? Think about what you do when you eat an ice-cream cone.

Directions: Write directions to teach someone how to eat an ice-cream cone.

How to Eat an Ice-Cream Cone

Answers will vary.

1. _____
2. _____
3. _____
4. _____

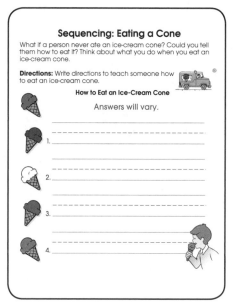

Page 129

Comprehension: Apples

Directions: Read about apples. Then, write the answers.

I like [apple]. Do you?   Some [apples] are red.

Some [apple] are green.   Some [apple] are yellow.

1. How many kinds of apples does the story tell about?

three

2. Name the kinds of apples.

red   green   yellow

3. What kind of apple do you like best?   Answers will vary.

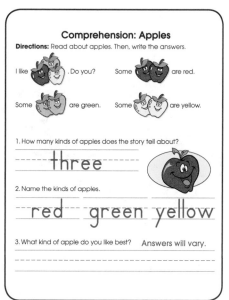

Page 130

Comprehension: Crayons

Directions: Read about crayons. Then, write your answers.

Crayons come in many colors.
Some crayons are dark colors.
Some crayons are light colors.
All crayons have wax in them.

1. How many colors of crayons are there?   (many)   few

2. Crayons come in   dark   colors
   and   light   colors.

3. What do all crayons have in them?

wax

Page 131

Comprehension

Directions: Read the story. Write the words from the story that complete each sentence.

Jane and Will like to play in the rain. They take off their shoes and socks. They splash in the puddles. It feels cold! It is fun to splash!

Jane and Will like to   play in the rain.

They take off their   shoes and socks.

They splash in   the puddles.

Do you like to splash in puddles?   Yes   No
Answers will vary.

Page 132

Comprehension

Directions: Read the story. Write the words from the story that complete each sentence.

Ben and Eva have a bug. It is red with black spots. They call it Spot. Spot likes to eat green leaves and grass. The children keep Spot in a box.

Ben and Eva have a   bug

It is   red   with black spots.

The bug's name is   Spot

The bug eats   green leaves and grass

Page 133

Comprehension: Snow Is Cold!

Directions: Read about snow. Circle the answers.

When you play in the snow, dress warmly. Wear a coat. Wear a hat. Wear gloves. Do you wear these when you play in the snow?

1. Snow is   warm.
   (cold.)

2. When you play in the snow, dress   (warmly.)
   quickly.

Directions: List three things to wear when you play in the snow.

a coat
a hat
gloves

Page 134

Comprehension: Growing Flowers

Directions: Read about flowers. Then, write the answers.

Some flowers grow in pots. Many flowers grow in flower beds. Others grow beside the road. Flowers begin from seeds. They grow into small buds. Then, they open wide and bloom. Flowers are pretty!

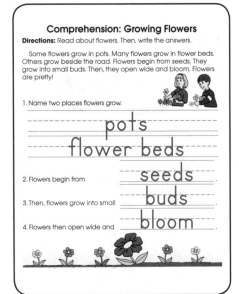

1. Name two places flowers grow.

pots

flower beds

2. Flowers begin from
seeds

3. Then, flowers grow into small
buds

4. Flowers then open wide and
bloom

Page 135

Comprehension: Raking Leaves

Directions: Read about raking leaves. Then, answer the questions.

I like to rake leaves. Do you? Leaves die each year. They get brown and dry. They fall from the trees. Then, we rake them up.

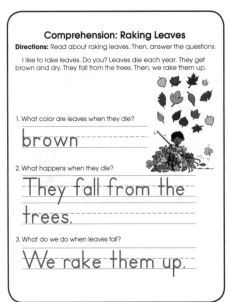

1. What color are leaves when they die?

brown

2. What happens when they die?

They fall from the trees.

3. What do we do when leaves fall?

We rake them up.

Page 136

Comprehension: Clocks

Directions: Read about clocks. Then, answer the questions.

Ticking Clocks

Many clocks make two sounds. The sounds are tick and tock. Big clocks often make loud tick-tocks. Little clocks often make quiet tick-tocks. Sometimes, people put little clocks in a box with a new puppy. The puppy likes the sound. The tick-tock makes the puppy feel safe.

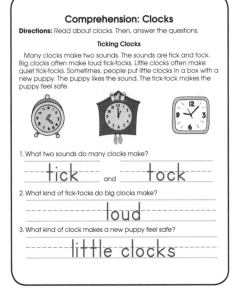

1. What two sounds do many clocks make?

tick   and   tock

2. What kind of tick-tocks do big clocks make?

loud

3. What kind of clock makes a new puppy feel safe?

little clocks

Page 137

Comprehension: Soup

Directions: Read about soup. Then, write the answers.

I Like Soup

Soup is good! It is good for you, too. We eat most kinds of soup hot. Some people eat cold soup in the summer. Carrots and beans are in some soups. Do you like crackers with soup?

1. Name two ways people eat soup.

cold   hot

2. Name two things that are in some soups.

carrots   beans

3. Name the kind of soup you like best.
Answers will vary.

Page 138

Review

Directions: Read about cookies. Then, write your answers.

Cookies are made with many things. All cookies are made with flour. Some cookies have nuts in them. Some cookies do not. Some cookies have chocolate chips. Some do not. Cookbooks give directions on how to make cookies.

First, turn on the oven. Then, get out all the things that go in the cookies. Mix them together. Roll them out, and cut the cookies. Bake the cookies. Now, eat them!

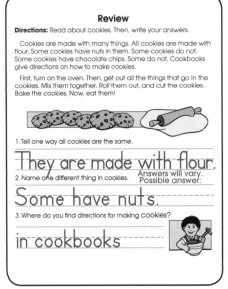

1. Tell one way all cookies are the same.

They are made with flour.

2. Name one different thing in cookies. Answers will vary.
Possible answer:
Some have nuts.

3. Where do you find directions for making cookies?

in cookbooks

Page 139

Review

Directions: Read the story. Then, circle the pictures of things that are wet.

Some things used in baking are dry. Some things used in baking are wet. To bake muffins, first mix the salt, sugar, and flour. Then, add the egg. Now, add the milk. Stir. Put the muffins in the oven.

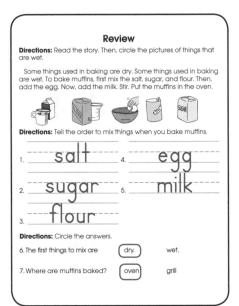

Directions: Tell the order to mix things when you bake muffins.

1. salt   4. egg

2. sugar   5. milk

3. flour

Directions: Circle the answers.

6. The first things to mix are   (dry.)   wet.

7. Where are muffins baked?   (oven)   grill

Page 140

Review

Directions: Read how to make energy balls. Then, answer the questions.

This snack is tasty and easy to make. You do not need to cook it. You will need a large bowl for mixing. You will need five things to make this snack.

Energy Balls
$\frac{1}{2}$ cup peanut butter
$\frac{2}{3}$ cup honey
$1\frac{1}{2}$ cups oatmeal
$\frac{1}{2}$ cup raisins
$\frac{1}{2}$ cup coconut flakes
Mix everything in the bowl. Roll the mix into small balls. If it is too sticky, get your hands damp.

1. What is third on the list of things needed?

oatmeal

2. How can you keep the mix from sticking to your hands?

Get your hands damp.

Directions: Write what to do to make energy balls.

3. First, mix everything in a bowl. Then,

roll the mix into small balls.

Page 141

Comprehension: The Teddy Bear Song

Do you know the Teddy Bear Song? It is very old!

Directions: Read the Teddy Bear Song. Then, answer the questions.

Teddy bear, teddy bear, turn around.
Teddy bear, teddy bear, touch the ground.
Teddy bear, teddy bear, climb upstairs.
Teddy bear, teddy bear, say your prayers.
Teddy bear, teddy bear, turn out the light.
Teddy bear, teddy bear, say, "Good night!"

1. What is the first thing the teddy bear does?

turns around

2. What is the last thing the teddy bear does?

says "good night"

3. What would you name a teddy bear?

Answers will vary.

Page 142

Sequencing: Put Teddy Bear to Bed

Directions: Read the song about the teddy bear again. Write a number in each box to show the order of the story.

Page 143

Comprehension: A New Teddy Bear Song

Directions: Write words to make a new teddy bear song. Act out your new song with your teddy bear as you read it.

Answers will vary.

Teddy bear, teddy bear, turn _____,

Teddy bear, teddy bear, touch the _____,

Teddy bear, teddy bear, climb _____,

Teddy bear, teddy bear, turn out _____,

Teddy bear, teddy bear, say, _____,

Page 144

Comprehension: Balloons

Directions: Read the story. Then, answer the questions.

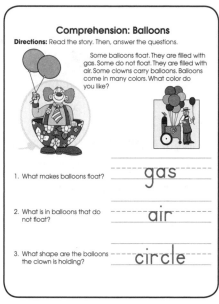

Some balloons float. They are filled with gas. Some do not float. They are filled with air. Some clowns carry balloons. Balloons come in many colors. What color do you like?

1. What makes balloons float?

gas

2. What is in balloons that do not float?

air

3. What shape are the balloons the clown is holding?

circle

Page 145

Comprehension: Balloons

Directions: Read the story about balloons again. Draw a picture for the sentence in each box.

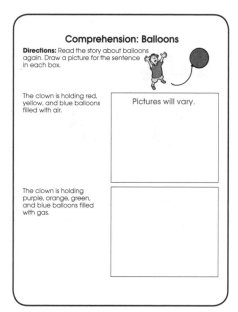

The clown is holding red, yellow, and blue balloons filled with air.

Pictures will vary.

The clown is holding purple, orange, green, and blue balloons filled with gas.

Page 146

Sequencing: Petting a Cat

Directions: Read the story. Then, write the answers.

Do you like cats? I do. To pet a cat, move slowly. Hold out your hand. The cat will come to you. Then, pet its head. Do not grab a cat! It will run away.

To pet a cat . . .

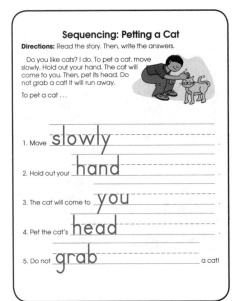

1. Move **slowly**
2. Hold out your **hand**
3. The cat will come to **you**
4. Pet the cat's **head**
5. Do not **grab** a cat!

Page 147

Comprehension: Cats

Directions: Read the story about cats again. Then, write the answers.

1. What is a good title for the story? **Answers will vary.**
2. The story tells you how to **pet a cat**
3. What part of your body should you pet a cat with? **your hand**
4. Why should you move slowly to pet a cat? **so the cat will not run away**
5. Why do you think a cat will run away if you grab it? **It will feel scared**

Page 148

Comprehension: Cats

Directions: Look at the pictures, and read about four cats. Then, write the correct name beside each cat.

Fluffy, Blackie, and Tiger are playing. Tom is sleeping. Blackie has spots. Tiger has stripes.

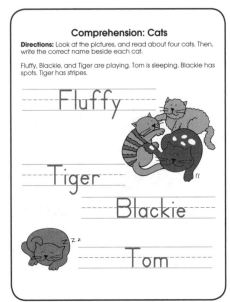

Fluffy
Tiger
Blackie
Tom

Page 149

Same and Different: Cats

Directions: Compare the picture of the cats on page 149 to this picture. Write a word from the box to tell what is different about each cat.

| purple ball | green bow | blue brush | red collar |

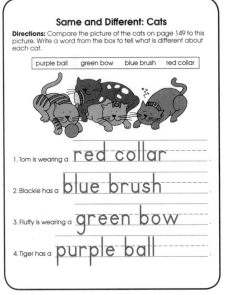

1. Tom is wearing a **red collar**
2. Blackie has a **blue brush**
3. Fluffy is wearing a **green bow**
4. Tiger has a **purple ball**

Page 150

Comprehension: Tigers

Directions: Read about tigers. Then, write the answers.

Tigers sleep during the day. They hunt at night. Tigers eat meat. They hunt deer. They like to eat wild pigs. If they cannot find meat, tigers will eat fish.

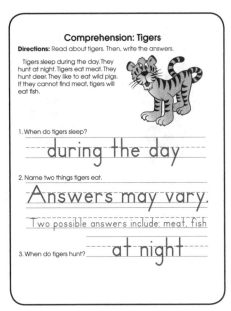

1. When do tigers sleep? **during the day**
2. Name two things tigers eat. **Answers may vary.** Two possible answers include: meat, fish
3. When do tigers hunt? **at night**

Page 151

Following Directions: Tiger Puzzle

Directions: Read the story about tigers again. Then, complete the puzzle.

1. f i s h
2. (l e e)
3. m e a t
4. p i g

Across:
1. When tigers cannot get meat, they eat _____
3. The food tigers like best is _____
4. Tigers like to eat this meat: wild _____

Down:
2. Tigers do this during the day.

Page 152

Following Directions: Draw a Tiger

Directions: Follow directions to complete the picture of the tiger.

1. Draw black stripes on the tiger's body and tail.
2. Color the tiger's tongue red.
3. Draw claws on the feet.
4. Draw a black nose and two black eyes on the tiger's face.
5. Color the rest of the tiger orange.
6. Draw tall green grass for the tiger to sleep in.

Page 153

Comprehension: How We Eat

Directions: Read the story. Use words from the box to answer the questions.

People eat with spoons and forks. They use a spoon to eat soup and ice cream. They use a fork to eat potatoes. They use a knife to cut their meat. They say, "Thank you. It was good!" when they finish.

| a fork | ice cream | a knife | soup |

1. What do we use to cut food?

   a knife

2. What are two things you can eat with a spoon?

   ice cream   soup

3. What do we use to eat meat and potatoes?

   a fork

Page 154

Classifying: Foods

Directions: Read the questions under each plate. Draw three foods on each plate to answer the questions.

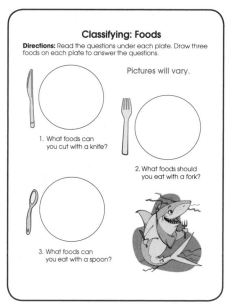

Pictures will vary.

1. What foods can you cut with a knife?
2. What foods should you eat with a fork?
3. What foods can you eat with a spoon?

Page 155

Comprehension: Write a Party Invitation

Directions: Read about the party. Then, complete the invitation.

The party will be at Dog's house. The party will start at 1:00 P.M. It will last 2 hours. Write your birthday for the date of the party.

Party Invitation

Where: Dog's house

Date: Answers will vary.

Time It Begins: 1:00 P.M.

Time It Ends: 3:00 P.M.

Answers will vary.

Directions: On the last line, write something else about the party.

Page 156

Sequencing: Pig Gets Ready

Directions: Number the pictures of Pig getting ready for the party to show the order of the story.

What kind of party do you think Pig is going to? a birthday party

Page 157

Comprehension: An Animal Party

Directions: Use the picture for clues. Write words from the box to answer the questions.

bear	cat
dog	elephant
giraffe	hippo
pig	tiger

1. Which animals have bow ties?

   cat   tiger

2. Which animal has a hat?

   bear

3. Which animal has a striped shirt?

   pig

Page 158

Classifying: Party Items

Directions: Draw a ☐ around objects that are food for the party. Draw a △ around the party guests. Draw a ○ around the objects used for fun at the party.

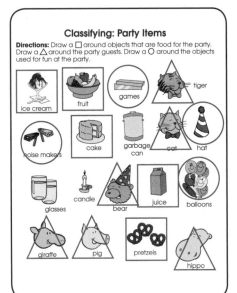

Comprehension: Play Simon Says

Directions: Read how to play Simon Says. Then, answer the questions.

SIMON SAYS, CLAP YOUR HANDS!

Simon Says

Here is how to play Simon Says: One kid is Simon. Simon is the leader. Everyone must do what Simon says and does but only if the leader says, "Simon says" first. Let's try it. "Simon says, 'Pat your head.'" "Simon says, 'Pat your nose. Pat your toes.'" Oops! Did you pat your toes? I did not say, "Simon says," first. If you patted your toes, you are out!

1. Who is the leader in this game? **Simon**

2. What must the leader say first each time? **Simon says**

3. What happens if you do something and the leader did not say, "Simon says"? **You are out.**

Page 160

Comprehension: Play Simon Says

Directions: Read each sentence. Look at the picture next to it. Circle the picture if the person is playing Simon Says correctly.

1. Simon says, "Put your hands on your hips."
2. Simon says, "Stand on one leg."
3. Simon says, "Put your hands on your head."
4. Simon says, "Ride a bike."
5. Simon says, "Jump up and down."
6. Simon says, "Pet a dog."
7. Simon says, "Make a big smile."

Page 161

Following Directions: Play Simon Says

Directions: Read the sentences. If Simon tells you to do something, follow the directions. If Simon does not tell you to do something, go to the next sentence.

1. Simon says: Cross out all the numbers 2 through 9.
2. Simon says: Cross out the vowel that is in the word **sun**.
3. Cross out the letter **B**.
4. Cross out the vowels **A** and **E**.
5. Simon says: Cross out the consonants in the word **cup**.
6. Cross out the letter **Z**.
7. Simon says: Cross out all the **K**s.
8. Simon says: Read your message.

Answer: Great job

Page 162

Comprehension: Rhymes

Directions: Read about words that rhyme. Then, circle the answers.

Words that rhyme have the same end sounds. **Wing** and **sing** rhyme. **Boy** and **toy** rhyme. **Dime** and **time** rhyme. Can you think of other words that rhyme?

1. Words that rhyme have the same (end sounds.) end letters.

2. **Time** rhymes with **tree**. (dime.)

Directions: Write one rhyme for each word. Answers will vary.

wing _____
boy _____
dime _____
pink _____

Page 163

Rhyming Words

Many poems have rhyming words. The rhyming words are usually at the end of the line.

Directions: Complete the poem with words from the box.

My Glue

I spilled my **glue**
I felt **blue**.
What could I **do**?
Hey! I have a **clue**!
I'll make it **clean**
The cleanest you've **seen**.
No one will **scream**
Wouldn't that be **mean**?

| blue | clue | scream | seen |
| glue | do | clean | mean |

Page 164

Classifying: Rhymes

Directions: Cut out the pieces. Read the words. Find two words that rhyme. Put the words together.

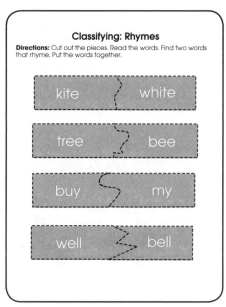

kite — white

tree — bee

buy — my

well — bell

Page 165

Classifying: Rhymes

Directions: Circle the pictures that rhyme in each row.

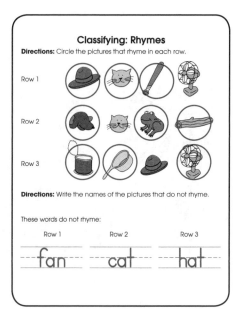

Row 1

Row 2

Row 3

Directions: Write the names of the pictures that do not rhyme.

These words do not rhyme:

Row 1	Row 2	Row 3
fan	cat	hat

Page 167

Comprehension: Babies

Directions: Read about babies. Then, write the answers.

Babies are small. Some babies cry a lot. They cry when they are wet. They cry when they are hungry. They smile when they are dry. They smile when they are fed.

1. Name two reasons babies cry.

wet   hungry

2. Name two reasons babies smile.

dry   fed

3. Write a baby's name you like.

Answers will vary.

Page 168

Comprehension: Babies

Directions: Read each sentence. Draw a picture of a baby's face in the box to show if she would cry or smile.

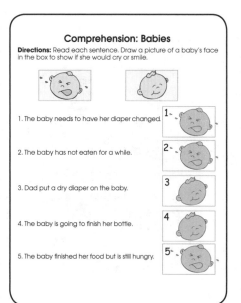

1. The baby needs to have her diaper changed.

2. The baby has not eaten for a while.

3. Dad put a dry diaper on the baby.

4. The baby is going to finish her bottle.

5. The baby finished her food but is still hungry.

Page 169

Sequencing: Feeding Baby

Directions: Read the sentences. Write a number in each box to show the order of the story.

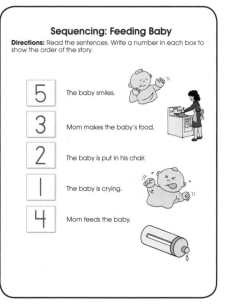

5 The baby smiles.

3 Mom makes the baby's food.

2 The baby is put in his chair.

1 The baby is crying.

4 Mom feeds the baby.

Page 170

Same and Different: Compare the Twins

Directions: Read the story. Then, use the words in the box and the picture to write your answers.

Ben and Ann are twin babies. They were born at the same time. They have the same mother. Ben is a boy baby. Ann is a girl baby.

mother	bow	boy	girl	hat	twins

1. Tell one way Ann and Ben are the same.   mother

2. Ann and Ben are   twins

3. Tell two ways Ann and Ben are different.

Ann is a   girl   . Ben is a   boy

Ann is wearing a   bow   . Ben is wearing a   hat

Page 171

Comprehensive Curriculum - **Grade 1**

Comprehension: Hats

Directions: Read about hats. Then, write your answers.

There are many kinds of hats. Some baseball hats have brims. Some fancy hats have feathers. Some knit hats pull down over your ears. Some hats are made of straw. Do you like hats?

1. Name four kinds of hats.

baseball   fancy

knit   straw

Directions: Circle the correct answers.

2. What kind of hats pull down over your ears?

straw hats

(knit hats)

3. What are some hats made of?

(straw)

mud

Page 172

Sequencing: Choosing a Hat

Directions: Write a number in each box to show the order of the story.

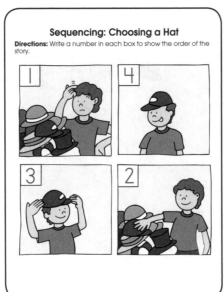

Page 173

Following Directions: Draw Hats

Directions: Draw a hat on each person. Read the sentences to know what kind of hat to draw.

1. The first girl is wearing a purple hat with feathers.

2. The boy next to the girl with the purple hat is wearing a red baseball hat.

3. The first boy is wearing a yellow knit hat.

4. The last boy is wearing a brown top hat.

5. The girl next to the boy with the red hat is wearing a blue straw hat.

Page 174

Classifying: Mr. Lincoln's Hat

Abraham Lincoln wore a tall hat. He liked to keep things in his hat so he would not lose them.

Directions: Cut out the pictures of things Mr. Lincoln could have kept in his hat. Glue those pictures on the hat.

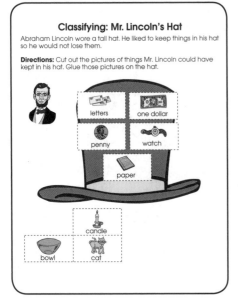

Page 175

Comprehension: Boats

Directions: Read about boats. Then, answer the questions.

See the boats! They float on water. Some boats have sails. The wind moves the sails. It makes the boats go. Many people name their sailboats. They paint the name on the side of the boat.

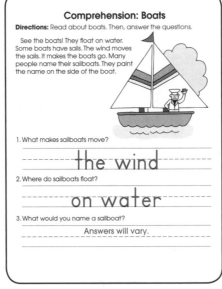

1. What makes sailboats move?

the wind

2. Where do sailboats float?

on water

3. What would you name a sailboat?

Answers will vary.

Page 177

Same and Different: Color the Boats

Directions: Find the three boats that are alike. Color them all the same. One boat is different. Color it differently.

Page 178

Comprehension: A Boat Ride

Directions: Write a sentence under each picture to tell what is happening. Read the story you wrote.

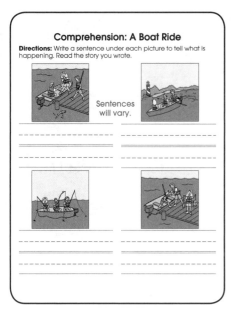

Sentences will vary.

Page 179

Comprehension: Travel

Directions: Read the story. Then, answer the questions.

Let's Take a Trip!

Pack your bag. Shall we go by car, plane, or train? Let's go to the sea. When we get there, let's ride in a sailboat.

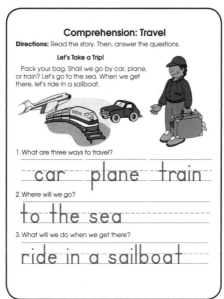

1. What are three ways to travel?

car plane train

2. Where will we go?

to the sea

3. What will we do when we get there?

ride in a sailboat

Page 180

Predicting: Words and Pictures

Directions: Complete each story by choosing the correct picture. Draw a line from the story to the picture.

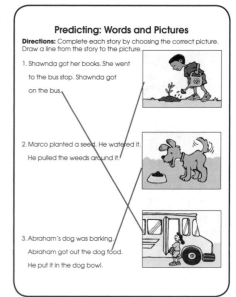

1. Shawnda got her books. She went to the bus stop. Shawnda got on the bus.

2. Marco planted a seed. He watered it. He pulled the weeds around it.

3. Abraham's dog was barking. Abraham got out the dog food. He put it in the dog bowl.

Page 181

Predicting: Story Ending

Directions: Read the story. Draw a picture in the last box to complete the story.

That's my ball.   I got it first.

Pictures will vary.

It's mine!

Page 182

Predicting: Story Ending

Directions: Read the story. Draw a picture in the last box to complete the story.

Marco likes to paint.   He likes to help his dad.

Pictures will vary.

He is tired when he's finished.

Page 183

Predicting: Story Ending

Directions: Read each story. Circle the sentence that tells how the story will end.

Ann was riding her bike. She saw a dog in the park. She stopped to pet it. Ann left to go home.

The dog went swimming.

The dog followed Ann.

The dog went home with a cat.

Antonio went to a baseball game. A baseball player hit a ball toward him. He reached out his hands.

The player caught the ball.

The ball bounced on a car.

Antonio caught the ball.

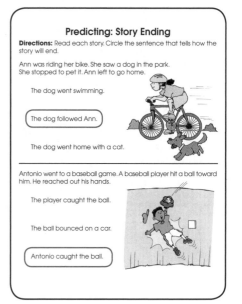

Page 184

Making Inferences: Baseball

Tess likes baseball. She likes to win. Tess's team does not win.

Directions: Circle the correct answers.

1. Tess likes

football. soccer. **baseball.**

2. Tess likes to

win. lose.

3. Tess uses a bat.

Yes No

4. Tess is

happy. **sad.**

Page 185

Making Inferences: The Stars

Layla looks at the stars. She sings a song about them. She makes a wish on them. The stars help Layla sleep.

Directions: Circle the correct answers.

1. Layla likes the

moon. sun. **stars.**

2. What song do you think she sings?

Row, Row, Row Your Boat

Twinkle, Twinkle Little Star

Happy Birthday to You

3. What does Layla "make" on the stars?

a wish a spaceship lunch

Page 186

Making Inferences: Feelings

Directions: Read each story. Choose a word from the box to show how each person feels.

happy	excited	sad	mad

1. Andy and Sam were best friends. Sam and his family moved far away. How does Sam feel?

sad

2. Deana could not sleep. It was the night before her birthday party. How does Deana feel?

excited

3. Jacob let his baby brother play with his teddy bear. His brother lost the bear. How does Jacob feel?

mad

4. Kia picked flowers for her mom. Her mom smiled when she got them. How does Kia feel?

happy

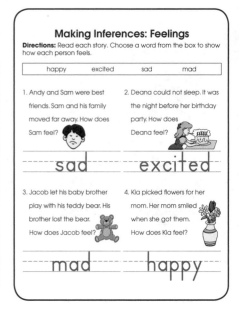

Page 187

Comprehension: Eating Ice Cream

Directions: Read the story. Write two things Sam could have done so he could have enjoyed eating his ice-cream cone.

It was a hot day. Sam went to the store and got an ice-cream cone. He sat at a table in the sun. Sam watched some friends play ball. Suddenly, his ice cream fell on the sidewalk.

Answers will vary.

1. _____

2. _____

Page 188

Review

Directions: Write a sentence to complete this story.

1. Evan's dog runs away.
2. Evan chases it.
3. The dog runs into a store.
4. _____

Answers will vary.

Directions: Read this story. Answer the questions.

Lea plays games with her little sister. Sometimes, Lea hides from her sister. Her sister calls her name over and over. Lea does not answer. Lea thinks it is funny.

1. Is Lea being nice or mean to her sister? **mean**

2. Do you think her sister likes Lea to hide? **no**

3. What would you do if you were Lea's sister?
Answers will vary.

Page 189

Books

Directions: What do you know about books? Use the words in the box below to complete the sentences.

title	book	author
illustrator	pages	left to right
fun	library	glossary

The name of the book is the **title**.

Left to right is the direction we read.

The person who wrote the words is the **author**.

Reading is **fun**!

There are many books in the **library**.

The person who draws the pictures is the **illustrator**.

The **glossary** is a kind of dictionary in the book to help you find the meanings of words.

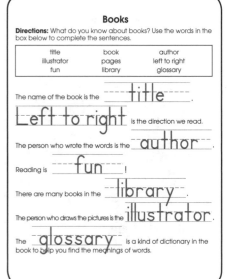

Page 190

Nouns

A **noun** is a word that names a person, place, or thing. When you read a sentence, the noun is what the sentence is about.

Directions: Complete each sentence with a noun.

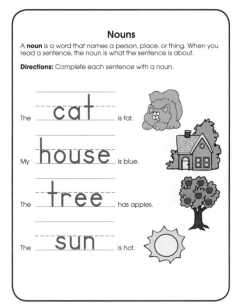

The ___cat___ is fat.

My ___house___ is blue.

The ___tree___ has apples.

The ___sun___ is hot.

Page 192

Nouns

Directions: Write these naming words in the correct box.

| store | zoo | child | baby | teacher | table |
| cat | park | gym | woman | sock | horse |

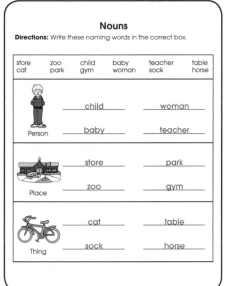

Person	___child___	___woman___
	___baby___	___teacher___
Place	___store___	___park___
	___zoo___	___gym___
Thing	___cat___	___table___
	___sock___	___horse___

Page 193

Things That Go Together

Some nouns name things that go together.

Directions: Draw a line to match the nouns on the left with the matching nouns on the right.

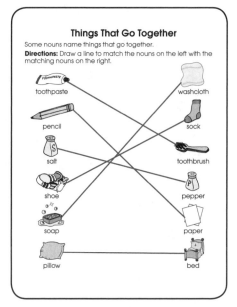

toothpaste   washcloth

pencil   sock

salt   toothbrush

shoe   pepper

soap   paper

pillow   bed

Page 194

Things That Go Together

Directions: Draw a line to connect the objects that go together.

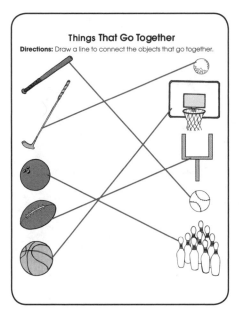

Page 195

Verbs

Verbs are words that tell what a person or a thing can do.

Example: The girl pats the dog.
The word **pats** is the verb. It shows action.

Directions: Draw a line between the verbs and the pictures that show the action.

eat

run

sleep

swim

sing

hop

Page 196

Verbs

Directions:
Look at the picture and read the words. Write an action word in each sentence below.

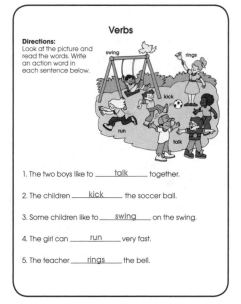

1. The two boys like to ___talk___ together.

2. The children ___kick___ the soccer ball.

3. Some children like to ___swing___ on the swing.

4. The girl can ___run___ very fast.

5. The teacher ___rings___ the bell.

Page 197

Comprehensive Curriculum - Grade 1

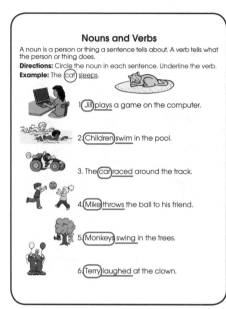

Nouns and Verbs

A noun is a person or thing a sentence tells about. A verb tells what the person or thing does.
Directions: Circle the noun in each sentence. Underline the verb.
Example: The (cat) sleeps.

1. (Jill) plays a game on the computer.
2. (Children) swim in the pool.
3. The (car) raced around the track.
4. (Mike) throws the ball to his friend.
5. (Monkeys) swing in the trees.
6. (Terry) laughed at the clown.

Page 198

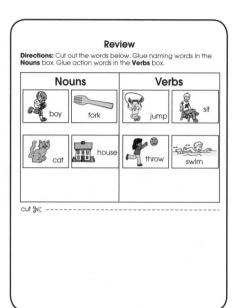

Review

Directions: Cut out the words below. Glue naming words in the **Nouns** box. Glue action words in the **Verbs** box.

Nouns	Verbs
boy fork	jump sit
cat house	throw swim

cut ✂ ------------------------------

Page 199

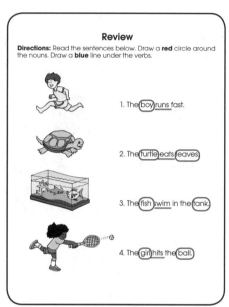

Review

Directions: Read the sentences below. Draw a **red** circle around the nouns. Draw a **blue** line under the verbs.

1. The (boy) runs fast.
2. The (turtle) eats (leaves).
3. The (fish) swim in the (tank).
4. The (girl) hits the (ball).

Page 201

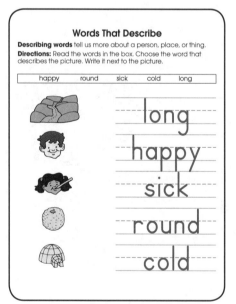

Words That Describe

Describing words tell us more about a person, place, or thing.
Directions: Read the words in the box. Choose the word that describes the picture. Write it next to the picture.

| happy | round | sick | cold | long |

long
happy
sick
round
cold

Page 202

Words That Describe

Directions: Read the words in the box. Choose the word that describes the picture. Write it next to the picture.

| wet | round | funny | soft | sad | tall |

soft tall
funny sad
round wet

Page 203

Words That Describe

Directions: Circle the describing word in each sentence. Draw a line from the sentence to the picture.

1. The (hungry) dog is eating.
2. The (tiny) bird is flying.
3. Horses have (long) legs.
4. She is a (fast) runner.
5. The (little) boy was lost.

Page 204

Words That Describe: Colors and Numbers

Colors and numbers can describe nouns.

Directions: Underline the describing word in each sentence. Draw a picture to go with each sentence.

A yellow moon was in the sky.

Pictures will vary.

Two worms are on the road.

The tree had red apples.

The girl wore a blue dress.

Page 205

Sequencing: Comparative Adjectives

Directions: Look at each group of pictures. Write 1, 2, or 3 under the picture to show where it should be.

Example:

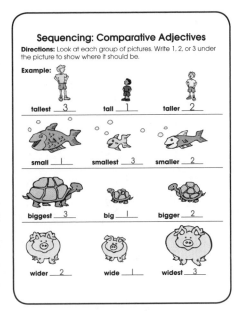

tallest __3__   tall __1__   taller __2__

small __1__   smallest __3__   smaller __2__

biggest __3__   big __1__   bigger __2__

wider __2__   wide __1__   widest __3__

Page 206

Sequencing: Comparative Adjectives

Directions: Look at the pictures in each row. Write 1, 2, or 3 under the picture to show where it should be.

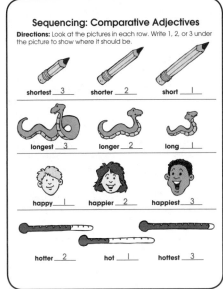

shortest __3__   shorter __2__   short __1__

longest __3__   longer __2__   long __1__

happy __1__   happier __2__   happiest __3__

hotter __2__   hot __1__   hottest __3__

Page 207

Synonyms

Synonyms are words that mean almost the same thing. **Start** and **begin** are synonyms.

Directions: Find the synonyms that describe each picture. Write the words in the boxes below the picture.

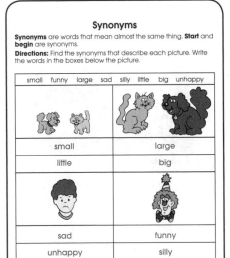

small funny large sad silly little big unhappy	
small	large
little	big
sad	funny
unhappy	silly

Page 208

Synonyms

Synonyms are words that mean almost the same thing.

Directions: Read the word in the center of each flower. Find a synonym for each word on a bee at the bottom of the page. Cut out and glue each bee on its matching flower.

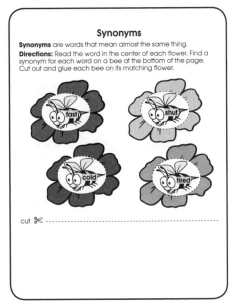

fast   shut

cold   tired

cut ✂ -

Page 209

Similarities: Synonyms

Directions: Circle the word in each row that is most like the first word in the row.

Example:

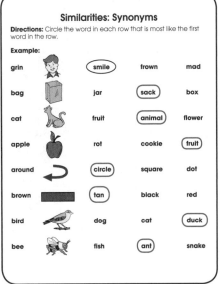

grin		smile	frown	mad
bag		jar	sack	box
cat		fruit	animal	flower
apple		rot	cookie	fruit
around		circle	square	dot
brown		tan	black	red
bird		dog	cat	duck
bee		fish	ant	snake

Page 211

Synonyms

Synonyms are words that have the same meaning.

Directions: Read each sentence, and look at the underlined word. Circle the word that means the same thing. Write the new words.

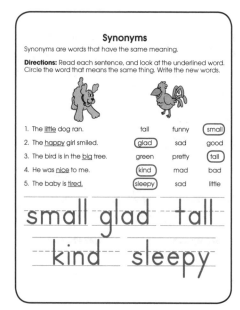

1. The little dog ran.	tall	funny	(small)
2. The happy girl smiled.	(glad)	sad	good
3. The bird is in the big tree.	green	pretty	(tall)
4. He was nice to me.	(kind)	mad	bad
5. The baby is tired.	(sleepy)	sad	little

small glad tall
kind sleepy

Page 212

Synonyms

Directions: Read each sentence, and look at the underlined word. Circle the word that means the same thing. Write the new words.

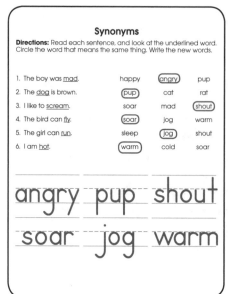

1. The boy was mad.	happy	(angry)	pup
2. The dog is brown.	(pup)	cat	rat
3. I like to scream.	soar	mad	(shout)
4. The bird can fly.	(soar)	jog	warm
5. The girl can run.	sleep	(jog)	shout
6. I am hot.	(warm)	cold	soar

angry pup shout
soar jog warm

Page 213

Similarities: Synonyms

Directions: Read each sentence. Read the word after the sentence. Find the word that is most like it in the sentence, and circle it.

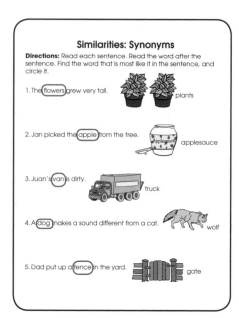

1. The (flowers) grew very tall.   plants

2. Jan picked the (apple) from the tree.   applesauce

3. Juan's (van) is dirty.   truck

4. A (dog) makes a sound different from a cat.   wolf

5. Dad put up a (fence) in the yard.   gate

Page 214

Similarities: Synonyms

Directions: Read the story. Write a word on the line that means almost the same as the word under the line.

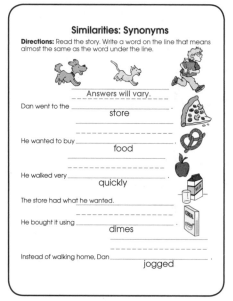

Answers will vary.

Dan went to the _____.
store

He wanted to buy _____,
food

He walked very _____.
quickly

The store had what he wanted.

He bought it using _____.
dimes

Instead of walking home, Dan _____.
jogged

Page 215

Antonyms

Antonyms are words that are opposites. **Hot** and **cold** are antonyms.

Directions: Draw a line between the antonyms.

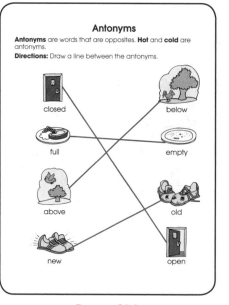

closed   below
full   empty
above   old
new   open

Page 216

Opposites

Directions: Draw lines to connect the words that are opposites.

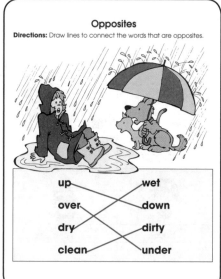

up   wet
over   down
dry   dirty
clean   under

Page 217

Opposites

Opposites are things that are different in every way.

Directions: Draw a line between the opposites.

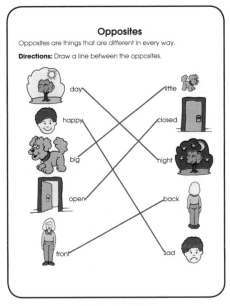

Antonyms

Directions: Find the two words that are opposites. Cut out the balloon basket, and glue it on the proper balloon.

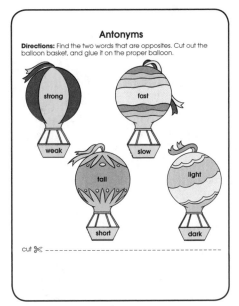

cut ✂ -

Opposites

Directions: Circle the picture in each row that is the opposite of the first picture.

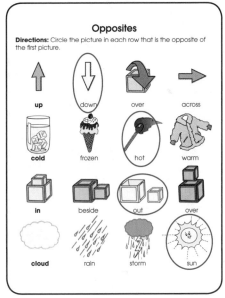

Page 218

Page 219

Page 221

Opposites

Directions: Read each clue. Write the answers in the puzzle.

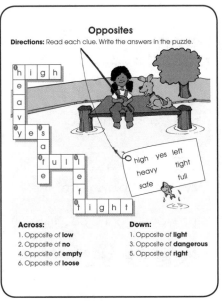

Across:
1. Opposite of **low**
2. Opposite of **no**
4. Opposite of **empty**
6. Opposite of **loose**

Down:
1. Opposite of **light**
3. Opposite of **dangerous**
5. Opposite of **right**

Opposites

Directions: Cut out the pieces. Read the words. Find the pairs of words that are opposites, and put the pieces together. On the blank pieces, write your own pair of opposites.

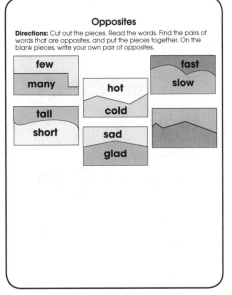

Opposites

Directions: Circle the two words in each sentence that are opposites.

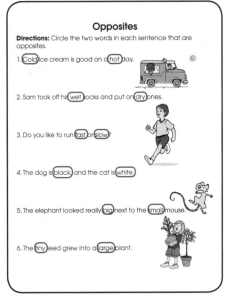

1. Cold ice cream is good on a hot day.

2. Sam took off his wet socks and put on dry ones.

3. Do you like to run fast or slow?

4. The dog is black and the cat is white.

5. The elephant looked really big next to the small mouse.

6. The tiny seed grew into a large plant.

Page 222

Page 223

Page 225

Homophones

Homophones are words that **sound** the same but are spelled differently and mean something different. **Blew** and **blue** are homophones.

Directions: Look at the word pairs. Choose the word that describes the picture. Write the word on the line next to the picture.

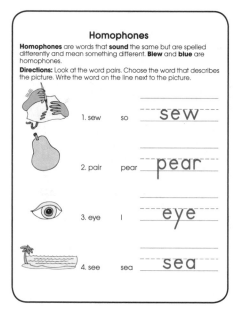

1. sew   so   sew
2. pair   pear pear
3. eye   I   eye
4. see   sea   sea

Page 226

Homophones

Directions: Read each sentence. Underline the two words that sound the same but are spelled differently and mean something different.

1. Ian <u>ate</u> <u>eight</u> grapes.

2. Kylie <u>read</u> Little <u>Red</u> Riding Hood.

3. I went <u>to</u> buy <u>two</u> dolls.

4. Five <u>blue</u> feathers <u>blew</u> in the wind.

5. <u>Would</u> you get <u>wood</u> for the fire?

Page 227

Following Directions: Days of the Week

Calendars show the days of the week in order. Sunday comes first. Saturday comes last. There are five days in between. An **abbreviation** is a short way of writing words. The abbreviations for the days of the week are usually the first three or four letters of the word followed by a period.

Example: Sunday — Sun.

Directions: Write the days of the week in order on the calendar. Use the abbreviations.

Day 1	Day 2	Day 3
Sunday	Monday	Tuesday
Sun.	Mon.	Tues.
Day 4	Day 5	Day 6
Wednesday	Thursday	Friday
Wed.	Thurs.	Fri.
	Day 7	
	Saturday	
	Sat.	

Page 228

Sentences

Sentences begin with capital letters.

Directions: Read the sentences, and write them below. Begin each sentence with a capital letter.

Example: the cat is fat.

The cat is fat.

my dog is big.

My dog is big.

the boy is sad.

The boy is sad.

bikes are fun!

Bikes are fun!

dad can bake.

Dad can bake.

Page 229

Word Order

If you change the order of the words in a sentence, you can change the meaning of the sentence.

Directions: Read the sentences. Draw a circle around the sentence that describes the picture.

Example:

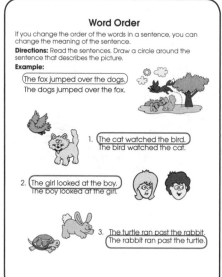

The fox jumped over the dogs.
The dogs jumped over the fox.

1. The cat watched the bird.
   The bird watched the cat.

2. The girl looked at the boy.
   The boy looked at the girl.

3. The turtle ran past the rabbit.
   The rabbit ran past the turtle.

Page 230

Word Order

Word order is the way words are arranged in a sentence so that they make sense.

Directions: Cut out the words, and put them in the correct order. Glue each sentence on another sheet of paper.

I like to ride my bike.

It is sunny and hot.

I can drink water.

My mom plays with me.

The dog can do tricks.

Can you go to the store?

Page 231

Word Order

Directions: Look at the picture. Put the words in order. Write the sentences on the lines below.

1. We made lemonade. some
2. good. It was
3. We the sold lemonade.
4. cost It five cents.
5. fun. We had

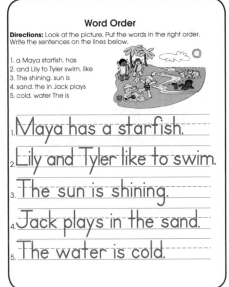

1. We made some lemonade.
2. It was good.
3. We sold the lemonade.
4. It cost five cents.
5. We had fun.

Page 233

Word Order

Directions: Look at the picture. Put the words in the right order. Write the sentences on the lines below.

1. a Maya starfish. has
2. and Lily to Tyler swim. like
3. The shining. sun is
4. sand. the in Jack plays
5. cold. water The is

1. Maya has a starfish.
2. Lily and Tyler like to swim.
3. The sun is shining.
4. Jack plays in the sand.
5. The water is cold.

Page 234

Review

Directions: Put the words in the right order to make a sentence. Write the sentences on the lines below.

1. a gerbil. has Ann
2. is The Mike. named gerbil
3. likes eat. Mike to
4. play. to Mike likes
5. happy a is gerbil. Mike

1. Ann has a gerbil.
2. The gerbil is named Mike.
3. Mike likes to eat.
4. Mike likes to play.
5. Mike is a happy gerbil.

Page 235

Telling Sentences

Directions: Read the sentences, and write them below. Begin each sentence with a capital letter. End each sentence with a period.

1. most children like pets
2. some children like dogs
3. some children like cats
4. some children like snakes
5. some children like all animals

1. Most children like pets.
2. Some children like dogs.
3. Some children like cats.
4. Some children like snakes.
5. Some children like all animals.

Page 236

Telling Sentences

Directions: Read the sentences, and write them below. Begin each sentence with a capital letter. End each sentence with a period.

1. i like to go to the store with Mom
2. we go on Friday
3. i get to push the cart
4. i get to buy the cereal
5. i like to help Mom

1. I like to go to the store with Mom.
2. We go on Friday.
3. I get to push the cart.
4. I get to buy the cereal.
5. I like to help Mom.

Page 237

Asking Sentences

Directions: Write the first word of each asking sentence. Be sure to begin each question with a capital letter. End each question with a question mark.

1. Do you like the zoo? do
2. How much does it cost? how
3. Can you feed the ducks? can
4. Will you see the monkeys? will
5. What time will you eat lunch? what

Page 238

Asking Sentences

Directions: Read the asking sentences. Write the sentences below. Begin each sentence with a capital letter. End each sentence with a question mark.

1. what game will we play
2. do you like to read
3. how old are you
4. who is your best friend
5. can you tie your shoes

1. What game will we play?
2. Do you like to read?
3. How old are you?
4. Who is your best friend?
5. Can you tie your shoes?

Page 239

Periods and Question Marks

Directions: Put a period or a question mark at the end of each sentence below.

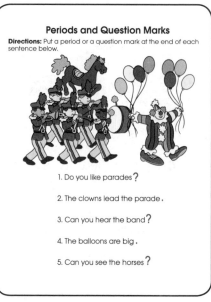

1. Do you like parades?
2. The clowns lead the parade.
3. Can you hear the band?
4. The balloons are big.
5. Can you see the horses?

Page 240

Review

Directions: Look at the picture. In the space below, write one telling sentence about the picture. Then, write one asking sentence about the picture.

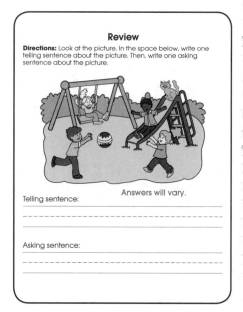

Answers will vary.

Telling sentence: _____

Asking sentence: _____

Page 241

Is and Are

Use **is** in sentences about one person or one thing. Use **are** in sentences about more than one person or thing.

Example: The dog **is** barking.
The dogs **are** barking.

Directions: Write **is** or **are** in the sentences below.

1. Jim ___is___ playing baseball.
2. Eli and Sam ___are___ good friends.
3. Cupcakes ___are___ my favorite treat.
4. Amina ___is___ a good soccer player.

Page 242

Is and Are

Directions: Write **is** or **are** in the sentences below.
Example: Lexi _is_ sleeping.

1. Cats and dogs ___are___ good pets.
2. Luke ___is___ my best friend.
3. Apples ___are___ good to eat.
4. We ___are___ going to the zoo.
5. Pedro ___is___ coming to my house.
6. When ___are___ you all going to the zoo?

Page 243

Vocabulary

Directions: Read the words. Trace and write them on the lines. Circle the word which completes each sentence. Write the word on the lines.

you and me
you and me
you and me

I will play with ___you___ . (you) me

You can go with ___me___ . you (me)

Can you run with ___me___ ? (you) me

Page 244

Vocabulary

Directions: Read the words. Trace and write them on the lines. Then, circle the word that completes each sentence. Write it on the line.

over | over over

under | under under

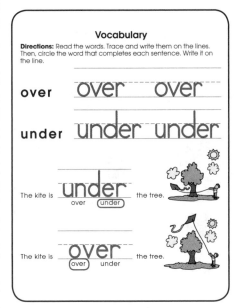

The kite is **under** the tree.
over (under)

The kite is **over** the tree.
(over) under

Page 245

Vocabulary

Directions: Read the words. Trace and write them on the lines. Then, circle the word that completes each sentence. Write it on the line.

above | above above

below | below below

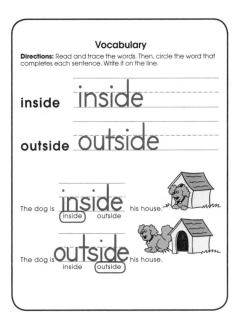

The fish is **below** the water.
above (below)

The fish is **above** the water.
(above) below

Page 246

Vocabulary

Directions: Read and trace the words. Then, circle the word that completes each sentence. Write it on the line.

inside | inside

outside | outside

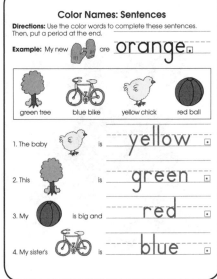

The dog is **inside** his house.
(inside) outside

The dog is **outside** his house.
inside (outside)

Page 247

Vocabulary

Directions: Read the words. Trace and write them on the lines. Then, circle the word that completes each sentence. Write it on the line.

up | up up

down | down down

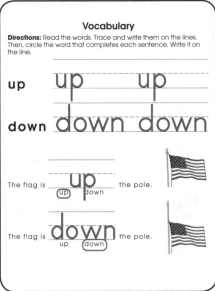

The flag is **up** the pole.
(up) down

The flag is **down** the pole.
up (down)

Page 248

Color Names

Directions: Trace the letters to write the name of each color. Then, write the name again by yourself.

Example:

orange | orange
blue | blue
green | green
yellow | yellow
red | red
brown | brown

Page 250

Color Names: Sentences

Directions: Use the color words to complete these sentences. Then, put a period at the end.

Example: My new [mittens] are **orange.**

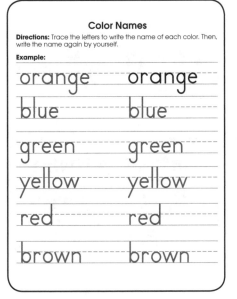

green tree | blue bike | yellow chick | red ball

1. The baby [chick] is **yellow.**

2. This [tree] is **green.**

3. My [ball] is big and **red.**

4. My sister's [bike] is **blue.**

Page 251

Color Names: Sentences

Directions: Some of these sentences tell a whole idea. Others have something missing. If something is missing, draw a line to the word that completes the sentence. Put a period at the end of each sentence.

He is holding up his

book .

1. Kenji has a new puppy.

hand .

2. I can read a

3. We like to play games.

tree .

4. Abby wants to eat some

5. I will color the

cake .

6. This is my birthday.

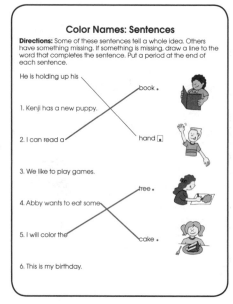

Page 252

Color Names: Capital Letters

A sentence begins with a capital letter.

Directions: The words by each picture are mixed up. Write them to make a sentence that tells about the picture. Begin each sentence with a capital letter, and end it with a period.

Example: coat she has a red

She has a red coat.

1. box sees he a blue

He sees a blue box.

2. her is yellow flower

Her flower is yellow.

3. red draws he a door

He draws a red door.

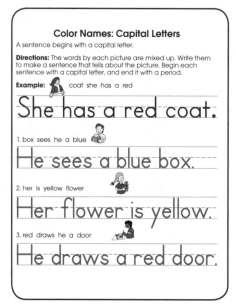

Page 253

Color Names: Crossword Puzzle

Directions: Complete each color name. Some words go down, and some go across. Try to spell each word by yourself.

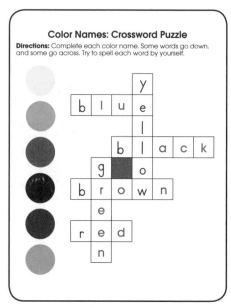

Page 254

Color the Eggs

Directions: Read the words. Color the pictures with the correct colors.

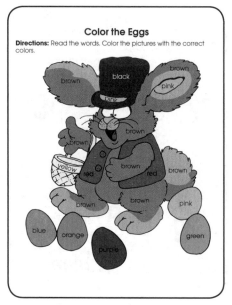

Page 255

Finish the Pictures

Directions: Read the words. Finish the pictures.

a red ball

a black hat

a yellow sun

a pink kite

an orange balloon

a blue umbrella

Page 256

Animal Names

Directions: Fill in the missing letters for each word.

Example:

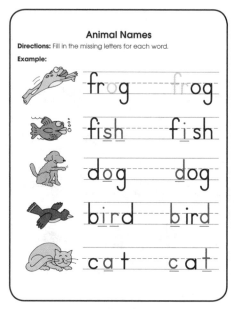

frog   frog

fish   fish

dog   dog

bird   bird

cat   cat

Page 257

Animal Names

Directions: The letters in the name of each animal are mixed up. Write each word correctly.

Example:

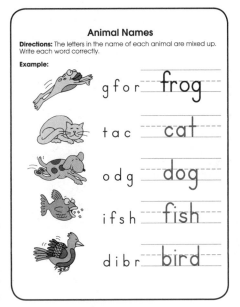

g f o r   frog

t a c   cat

o d g   dog

i f s h   fish

d i b r   bird

Page 258

Animal Names: Beginning Sounds

Directions: Say the name of each animal. Write the beginning sound under its name. Find two pictures in each row that begin with the same sound as the animal. Write the same first letter under them.

Example:

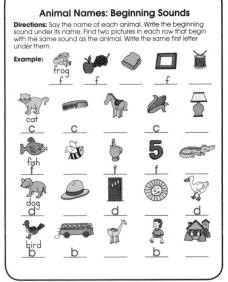

frog
f   f   f

cat
c   c   c

fish
f   f   f

dog
d   d   d

bird
b   b   b

Page 259

Animal Names: Sentences

A **sentence** tells about something.

Directions: These sentences tell about animals. Write the word that completes each sentence.

Example:

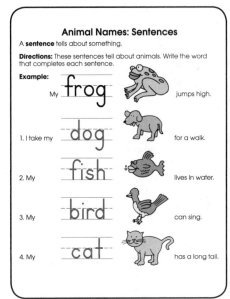

My   frog   jumps high.

1. I take my   dog   for a walk.

2. My   fish   lives in water.

3. My   bird   can sing.

4. My   cat   has a long tail.

Page 260

Animal Names: Sentences

Directions: Finish writing the name of each animal on the line. Draw a line from the first part of the sentence to the part that completes it. Put a period at the end of each sentence.

Example:

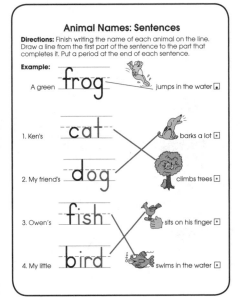

A green   frog   jumps in the water .

1. Ken's   cat   barks a lot .

2. My friend's   dog   climbs trees .

3. Owen's   fish   sits on his finger .

4. My little   bird   swims in the water .

Page 261

Review

Directions: Use the words in the pictures to write a sentence about each animal. Put a period at the end of each sentence.

Example: The   eats bugs.

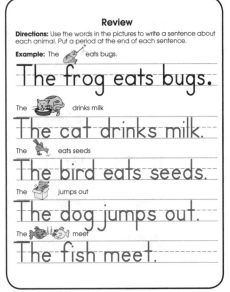

The frog eats bugs.

The   drinks milk

The cat drinks milk.

The   eats seeds

The bird eats seeds.

The   jumps out

The dog jumps out.

The   meet

The fish meet.

Page 262

Things That Go

Directions: Trace the letters to write the name of each thing. Write each name again by yourself. Then, color the pictures.

Example:

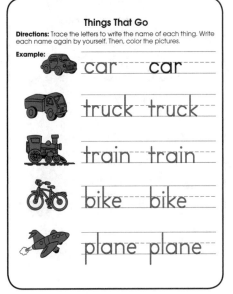

car   car

truck   truck

train   train

bike   bike

plane   plane

Page 263

Things That Go

Directions: Fill in the missing letters for each word.

Example:

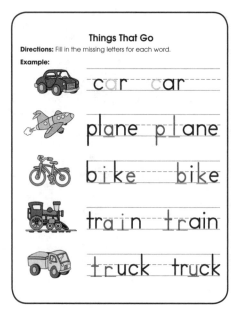

Things That Go

Directions: The letters in the name of each thing are mixed up. Unscramble the letters, and write each word correctly below.

Example:

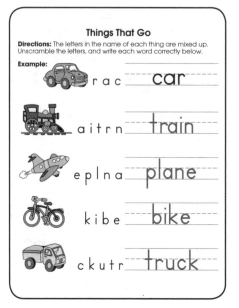

Things That Go: Beginning Sounds

Directions: Say the name of each thing. Write the beginning sound under its name. Find two pictures in each row that begin with the same sound as the first picture. Write the same first letter under them.

Example:

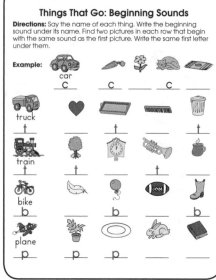

Page 264

Page 265

Page 266

Things That Go: Sentences

Directions: These sentences tell about things that go. Write the word that completes each sentence.

Example:

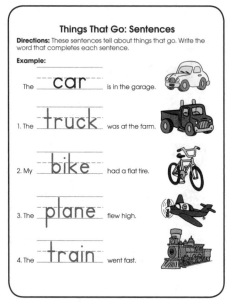

Things That Go: Sentences

Directions: Finish writing the names of the things that go. Draw a line from the first part of the sentence to the part that completes it. Put a period at the end of each sentence.

Example:

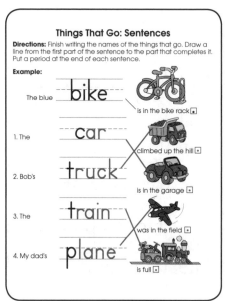

Things That Go: Sentences

Directions: Draw a line from the first part of each sentence to the part that completes it. Put a period at the end of each sentence.

Example:

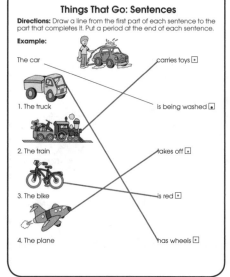

Page 267

Page 268

Page 269

Review

Directions: Use the words in the pictures to write a sentence about each thing that goes. Put a period at the end of each sentence.

Example:

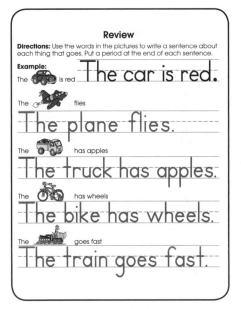

The ___ is red   **The car is red.**

The ___ flies

The plane flies.

The ___ has apples

The truck has apples.

The ___ has wheels

The bike has wheels.

The ___ goes fast

The train goes fast.

Page 270

Clothing Words

Directions: Trace the letters to write the name of each clothing word. Then, write each name again by yourself.

Example:

shirt   shirt

pants   pants

jacket   jacket

socks   socks

shoes   shoes

dress   dress

hat   hat

Page 271

Clothing Words: Beginning Sounds

Directions: Circle the words that begin with the same sound as the first word in each row.

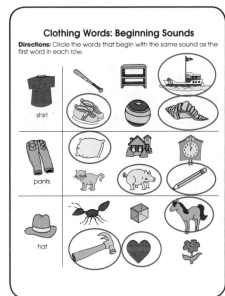

Page 272

Clothing Words: Sentences

Directions: Some of these sentences tell a whole idea. Others have something missing. If something is missing, draw a line to the word that completes the sentence. Put a period at the end of each sentence.

Example:

She is wearing a polka-dot

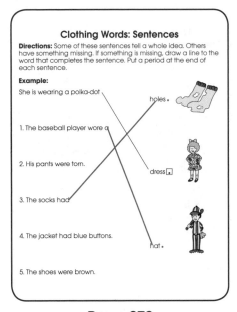

1. The baseball player wore a

2. His pants were torn.

3. The socks had

4. The jacket had blue buttons.

5. The shoes were brown.

holes .

dress .

hat .

Page 273

Clothing Words: Sentences

Directions: The words by each picture are mixed up. Write them to make a sentence that tells about the picture. Begin each sentence with a capital letter, and end it with a period.

Example: is shirt a drying

A shirt is drying.

1. ties his shoes he

He ties his shoes.

2. red wear I a jacket

I wear a red jacket.

3. blue are pants his

His pants are blue.

Page 274

Clothing Words: Sentences

Directions: Use the clothing words to complete these sentences. Then, put a period at the end.

Example:

Mike is wearing a **hat** .

1. Put on your socks before your ___   **shoes** .

2. When it's cold, wear a ___   **jacket** .

3. The little girl liked to wear a pink ___   **dress** .

4. He wore jeans with the ___   **shirt** .

5. The man wore a suit coat and ___   **pants** .

6. The clown wore long, striped ___   **socks** .

Page 275

Comprehensive Curriculum - **Grade 1**

Review

Directions: Write three sentences that tell about this picture. Begin each sentence with a capital letter, and end it with a period.

Answers may include:

1. They are shopping.

2. A woman is working.

3. She sells shirts.

Page 276

Food Names

Directions: Trace the letters to write each food word. Write each name again by yourself. Then, color the pictures.

Example:

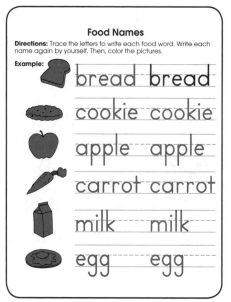

bread bread

cookie cookie

apple apple

carrot carrot

milk milk

egg egg

Page 277

Food Names: Beginning Sounds

Directions: Write the food names that answer the questions.

| egg | milk | ice cream | apple | cookie | cake |

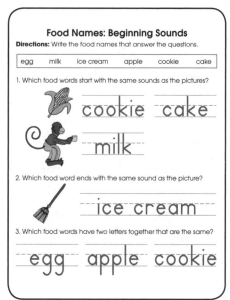

1. Which food words start with the same sounds as the pictures?

cookie cake

milk

2. Which food word ends with the same sound as the picture?

ice cream

3. Which food words have two letters together that are the same?

egg apple cookie

Page 278

Food Names: Asking Sentences

An **asking sentence** asks a question. Asking sentences end with a question mark.

Directions: Write each sentence on the line. Begin each sentence with a capital letter. Put a period at the end of the telling sentences and a question mark at the end of the asking sentences.

Example: do you like carrots

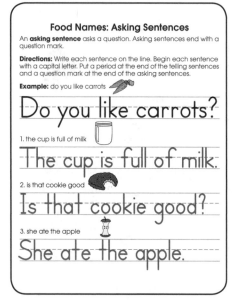

Do you like carrots?

1. the cup is full of milk

The cup is full of milk.

2. is that cookie good

Is that cookie good?

3. she ate the apple

She ate the apple.

Page 279

Food Names: Asking Sentences

Directions: Change each telling sentence into an asking sentence by moving the words. Put a question mark at the end of each question.

Example: The girl is eating.

Is the girl eating?

1. He is sharing.

Is he sharing?

2. He is drinking.

Is he drinking?

3. She is baking.

Is she baking?

Page 280

Food Names: Asking Sentences

Directions: Use the food names to answer each question.

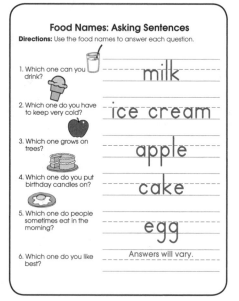

1. Which one can you drink?

milk

2. Which one do you have to keep very cold?

ice cream

3. Which one grows on trees?

apple

4. Which one do you put birthday candles on?

cake

5. Which one do people sometimes eat in the morning?

egg

6. Which one do you like best?

Answers will vary.

Page 281

Food Names: Sentences

Directions: In each sentence, write a word in the first blank to tell who is doing something. Write one of the food names in the second blank. Then, draw a picture to go with each sentence.

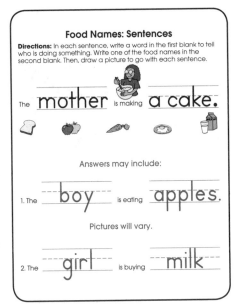

The mother is making a cake.

Answers may include:

1. The boy is eating apples.

Pictures will vary.

2. The girl is buying milk

Page 282

Food Names: Completing a Story

Directions: Write the food names in the story.

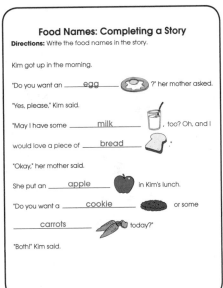

Kim got up in the morning.

"Do you want an ___egg___ ?" her mother asked.

"Yes, please," Kim said.

"May I have some ___milk___ , too? Oh, and I

would love a piece of ___bread___ ."

"Okay," her mother said.

She put an ___apple___ in Kim's lunch.

"Do you want a ___cookie___ or some

___carrots___ today?"

"Both!" Kim said.

Page 283

Review

Directions: Write two telling sentences and one asking sentence about this picture. Use the food, color, and animal words you know.

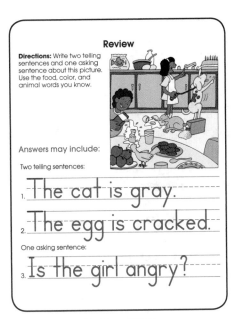

Answers may include:

Two telling sentences:

1. The cat is gray.

2. The egg is cracked.

One asking sentence:

3. Is the girl angry?

Page 284

Number Words

Directions: Trace the letters to write the name of each number. Write the numbers again by yourself. Then, color the number pictures.

Example: Colors will vary.

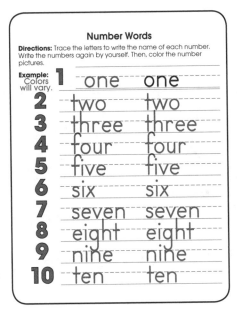

1 one one
2 two two
3 three three
4 four four
5 five five
6 six six
7 seven seven
8 eight eight
9 nine nine
10 ten ten

Page 285

Number Words: Asking Sentences

Directions: Write each sentence on the line. Begin each sentence with a capital letter. Put a period at the end of the telling sentences and a question mark at the end of the asking sentences.

Example: may I eat two crackers

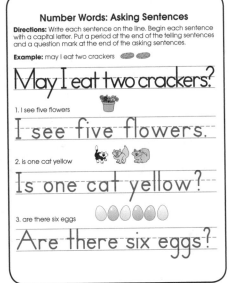

May I eat two crackers?

1. I see five flowers

I see five flowers.

2. is one cat yellow

Is one cat yellow?

3. are there six eggs

Are there six eggs?

Page 286

Number Words: Asking Sentences

Directions: Use a number word to answer each question.

| one | five | seven | three | eight |

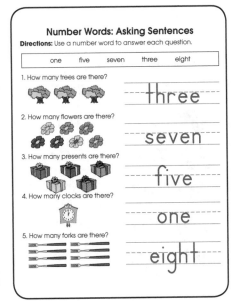

1. How many trees are there? three

2. How many flowers are there? seven

3. How many presents are there? five

4. How many clocks are there? one

5. How many forks are there? eight

Page 287

Number Words: Asking Sentences

Directions: Use the number words to answer each question.

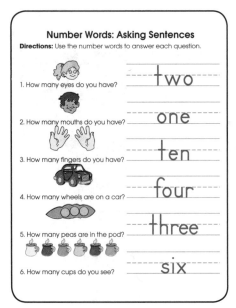

1. How many eyes do you have? — two
2. How many mouths do you have? — one
3. How many fingers do you have? — ten
4. How many wheels are on a car? — four
5. How many peas are in the pod? — three
6. How many cups do you see? — six

Page 288

Number Words: Asking Sentences

Directions: Change each telling sentence into an asking sentence by rearranging the words and adding new ones. Put a question mark at the end of each question.

Example: He ate one egg.

Is he eating one egg?

1. She has two dogs.

Does she have two dogs?

2. Three balls can bounce.

Can three balls bounce?

3. One balloon is red.

Is one balloon red?

Page 289

Review

Directions: Write two telling sentences and one asking sentence about this picture. Use the number words you know.

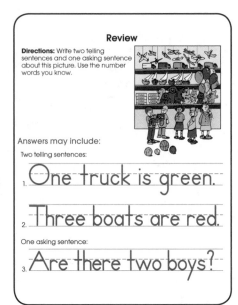

Answers may include:

Two telling sentences:

1. One truck is green.
2. Three boats are red.

One asking sentence:

3. Are there two boys?

Page 290

Action Words

Action words tell things we can do.

Directions: Trace the letters to write each action word. Then, write the action word again by yourself.

Example:

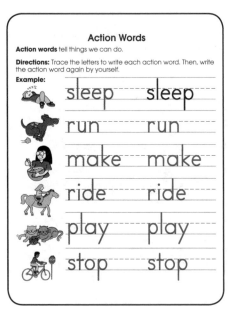

sleep — sleep
run — run
make — make
ride — ride
play — play
stop — stop

Page 291

Action Words

Directions: Circle the word that is spelled correctly. Then, write the correct spelling in the blank.

Example:

seep
(sleep)
slep — sleep

paly
pay
(play) — play

seee
cee
(see) — see

rum
(run)
runn — run

(jump)
jumb
junp — jump

mack
maek
(make) — make

Page 292

Action Words

Directions: Read each sentence, and write the correct words in the blanks.

Example:

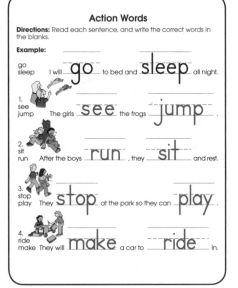

go
sleep — I will go to bed and sleep all night.

1.
see
jump — The girls see the frogs jump.

2.
sit
run — After the boys run, they sit and rest.

3.
stop
play — They stop at the park so they can play.

4.
ride
make — They will make a car to ride in.

Page 293

Action Words: Beginning and Ending Sounds

Directions: Write the action words that answer the questions.

sit	run	make	see	jump	stop	play	ride

1. Which words begin with the same sound as ☀ ?

sit   see   stop

2. Which words begin with the same sound as 🐰 ?

run   ride

3. Which words begin with the same sound as each of these words?

play   jump   make

4. Which words end with the same sound as these?

jump   make   sit

Page 294

Action Words: More Than One

To show more than one of something, add **s** to the end of the word.

Example: one cat   two cats

Directions: In each sentence, add **s** to show more than one. Then, write the action word that completes each sentence.

sit	jump	stop	ride

Example:

The frog   s   sleep   in the sun.

1. The boy   s   sit   on the fence.

2. The car   s   stop   at the sign.

3. The girl   s   jump   in the water.

4. The dog   s   ride   in the wagon.

Page 295

Action Words: Asking Sentences

Directions: Write an asking sentence about each picture. Begin each sentence with **can**. Add an action word. Begin each asking sentence with a capital letter, and end it with a question mark.

Example:

I with you can

Can I sit with you?

she can

Can she cook?

with you can I

Can I play with you?

can she fast

Can she run fast?

Page 296

Review

Directions: Write three telling sentences and one asking sentence about this picture. Put an action word in each sentence.

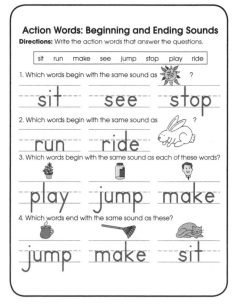

Answers may include:

Three telling sentences:

1. The children play.

2. She flies a kite.

3. The dogs run.

One asking sentence:

4. Is the sun shining?

Page 297

Sense Words

Directions: Circle the word that is spelled correctly. Then, write the correct spelling in the blank.

Example:

tast
(taste)
tste

taste

(touch)
tuch
touh

touch

smel
smll
(smell)

smell

her
(hear)
har

hear

(see)
se
sea

see

Page 298

Sense Words: Sentences

Directions: Read each sentence, and write the correct words in the blanks.

Example:

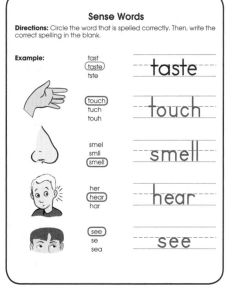

taste
mouth   I can taste things with my mouth.

touch
hands   1. I can touch things with my hands.

nose
smell   2. I can smell things with my nose.

hear
ears   3. I can hear with my ears.

see
eyes   4. I can see things with my eyes.

Page 299

Sense Words: Beginning Sounds

Directions: Use the sense words in the box to answer each question.

smell	see	taste	hear	touch

1. Which word begins with the same sound as [chimney] ?

smell

2. Which word begins with the same sound as [sun] ?

see

3. Which words begin with the same sound as [turtle] ?

taste   touch

4. Which word begins with the same sound as [hat] ?

hear

Page 300

Sense Words: More Than One

Directions: In each sentence, add **s** to show more than one. Then, write the sense word that completes each sentence.

Example: The dog s taste the food.

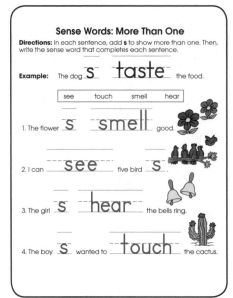

see	touch	smell	hear

1. The flower s smell good.

2. I can see five bird s.

3. The girl s hear the bells ring.

4. The boy s wanted to touch the cactus.

Page 301

Sense Words: Asking Sentences

Directions: Write an asking sentence about each picture. Begin each sentence with **can**. Add a sense word. Begin each asking sentence with a capital letter, and end it with a question mark.

Example: can rose I a

Can I smell a rose?

1. can I the dog

Can I touch the dog?

2. can I pie the

Can I taste the pie?

3. can he car the

Can he see the car?

4. he can bell the

Can he hear the bell?

Page 302

Review

Directions: Write three telling sentences and one asking sentence about this picture. Use a sense word in each sentence.

Three telling sentences: Answers may include:

1. We see the beach.

2. We hear the waves.

3. We touch the sand.

One asking sentence:

4. Do you see a bird?

Page 303

Weather Words: Beginning Sounds

Directions: Say the sound of the letter at the beginning of each row. Find the pictures in each row that begin with the same letter. Write the letter under the pictures.

Example:

s		S	S	
w		w		w
c	c	c		
p	p			p
s	s			S
r	r			

Page 304

Weather Words: Sentences

Directions: Write the weather word that completes each sentence. Put a period at the end of the telling sentences and a question mark at the end of the asking sentences.

Example:
Do flowers grow in the sun ?

rain	water	wet	hot

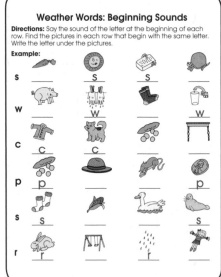

1. The sun makes me hot .

2. When it rains, the grass gets wet .

3. Do you think it will rain on our picnic ?

4. Should you drink the water from the rain ?

Page 305

Weather Words: Sentences

Directions: Read the sentence parts below. Draw a line from the first part of the sentence to the second part that completes it.

Example: When I'm cold, ——— I put on my coat.
I take off my shoes.

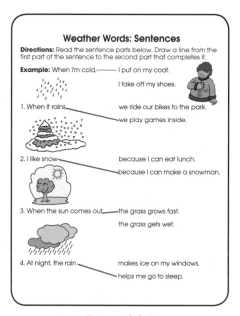

1. When it rains, — we ride our bikes to the park.
— we play games inside.

2. I like snow — because I can eat lunch.
— because I can make a snowman.

3. When the sun comes out — the grass grows fast.
— the grass gets wet.

4. At night, the rain — makes ice on my windows.
— helps me go to sleep.

Page 306

Weather Words: Completing a Story

Directions: Write the missing words to complete the story. The first letter of each word is written for you.

"Please may I go outside?" I asked.

"It's too __cold__," my father told

me. "Maybe later the sun will come

out." Later, the sun did come out. Then, it began to __rain__

again. "May I go out now?" I asked again. Dad looked out the

window. "You will get __wet__," he said. "But I want to

see if the __rain__ helped our flowers grow," I said. "You

mean you want to play in the __water__," Dad said with

a smile. How did Dad know that?

Page 307

Weather Words: Sentences

Directions: Read the two sentences on each line, and draw a line between them. Then, write each sentence again on the lines below. Begin each sentence with a capital letter, and end each one with a period or a question mark.

Example: will it rain | the sky is dark

Will it rain?
The sky is dark.

1. she fell in the pond | she got wet

She fell in the pond.
She got wet.

2. do you like my hat | it is red

Do you like my hat?
It is red.

Page 308

Review

Directions: Write a telling sentence about each of these pictures. Then, write an asking sentence about one of the pictures. Use the weather words and other words you know.

Telling sentences: Answers may include:

1. They are cold.
2. Rain can be fun.

Asking sentence:

3. Is it still snowing?

Page 309

My World

Directions: Fill in the missing letters for each word.

tree   tree
grass   grass
flower   flower
pond   pond
sand   sand
sky   sky

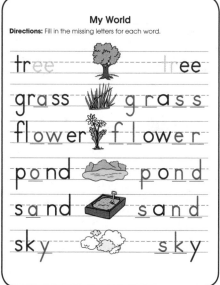

Page 310

My World

Directions: The letters in the words below are mixed up. Unscramble the letters, and write each word correctly.

etre — tree
srags — grass
loefwr — flower
dnop — pond
dnsa — sand
yks — sky

Page 311

ANSWER KEY

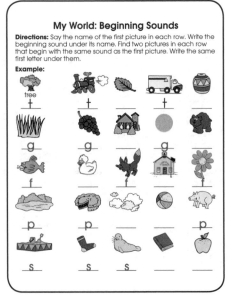

My World: Beginning Sounds
Directions: Say the name of the first picture in each row. Write the beginning sound under its name. Find two pictures in each row that begin with the same sound as the first picture. Write the same first letter under them.

Page 312

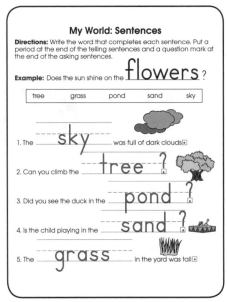

My World: Sentences
Directions: Write the word that completes each sentence. Put a period at the end of the telling sentences and a question mark at the end of the asking sentences.

Example: Does the sun shine on the flowers?

tree grass pond sand sky

1. The sky was full of dark clouds.
2. Can you climb the tree?
3. Did you see the duck in the pond?
4. Is the child playing in the sand?
5. The grass in the yard was tall.

Page 313

My World: Sentences
Directions: Read the two sentences on each line, and draw a line between them. Then, write each sentence again on the lines below. Begin each sentence with a capital letter, and end each one with a period or a question mark.

Example: the tree has leaves|can we rake some

The tree has leaves.
Can we rake some?

1. the lake is fun|we swim in it
The lake is fun.
We swim in it.

2. the sky is so blue|isn't it pretty
The sky is so blue.
Isn't it pretty?

Page 314

Review
Directions: Write three telling sentences about the picture. Then, write an asking sentence about the picture. Use the words that tell about your world and other words you know.

Answers may include:
Telling sentences:
1. The grass is green.
2. There are two trees.
3. The pool is pink.
Asking sentence:
4. Is the sky clear?

Page 315

The Parts of My Body: Sentences
Directions: Write the word that completes each sentence. Put a period at the end of the telling sentences and a question mark at the end of the asking sentences.

Example: I wear my hat on my head.

arms legs feet hands

1. How strong are your arms?
2. You wear shoes on your feet.
3. If you're happy and you know it, clap your hands.
4. My pants covered my legs.

Page 316

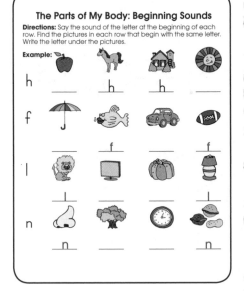

The Parts of My Body: Beginning Sounds
Directions: Say the sound of the letter at the beginning of each row. Find the pictures in each row that begin with the same letter. Write the letter under the pictures.

h / h / h
f / f / f
l / l
n / n / n

Page 317

The Parts of My Body: Sentences

Directions: Read the sentence parts below. Draw a line from the first part of the sentence to the second part that completes it.

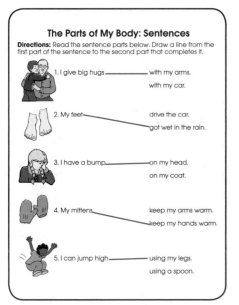

1. I give big hugs — with my arms.
   with my car.

2. My feet — drive the car.
   got wet in the rain.

3. I have a bump — on my head.
   on my coat.

4. My mittens — keep my arms warm.
   keep my hands warm.

5. I can jump high — using my legs.
   using a spoon.

Page 318

The Parts of My Body: Sentences

Directions: Read the two sentences on each line, and draw a line between them. Then, write each sentence again on the lines below. Begin each sentence with a capital letter, and end each one with a period or a question mark.

Example: wash your hands|they are dirty

Wash your hands.

They are dirty.

1. you have big arms|are you very strong

You have big arms.

Are you very strong?

2. I have two feet|I can run fast

I have two feet.

Page 319

Review

Directions: Write a telling sentence about each of these pictures. Then, write an asking sentence about one of the pictures. Use the words that name the parts of your body and other words you know.

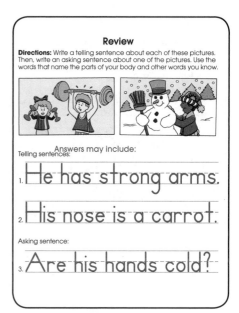

Answers may include:

Telling sentences:

1. He has strong arms.

2. His nose is a carrot.

Asking sentence:

3. Are his hands cold?

Page 320

Opposite Words

Some words are opposites. **Opposites** are things that are different in every way. **Dark** and **light** are opposites.

Directions: Trace the letters to write each word. Then, write the word again by yourself.

Example:

new   new
old   old
big   big
little little
lost   lost
found found

Page 321

Opposite Words

Directions: Circle one word in each sentence that is not spelled correctly. Then, write the word correctly.

| dark | found | old | first | lost |

Example:
The house is (little).   little

1. Are those your (olde) shoes?   old

2. I (fond) your book.   found

3. She is (frist) in line.   first

4. She (loss) her lunch.   lost

5. I am afraid of the (drak).   dark

Page 322

Opposite Words: Beginning and Ending Sounds

Directions: Write the opposite words that answer the questions.

| dark | found | old | light | new | first | lost | last |

1. Which words begin with the same sound as 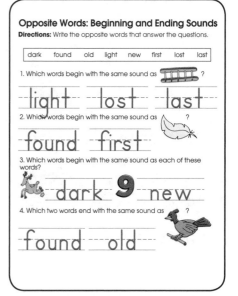 ?

light   lost   last

2. Which words begin with the same sound as ?

found   first

3. Which words begin with the same sound as each of these words?

dark   9   new

4. Which two words end with the same sound as ?

found   old

Page 323

Comprehensive Curriculum - **Grade 1**

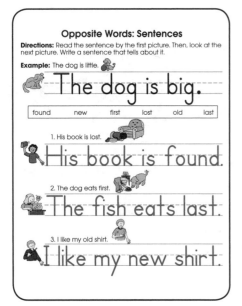

Opposite Words: Sentences

Directions: Read the sentence by the first picture. Then, look at the next picture. Write a sentence that tells about it.

Example: The dog is little.

The dog is big.

found	new	first	lost	old	last

1. His book is lost.

His book is found.

2. The dog eats first.

The fish eats last.

3. I like my old shirt.

I like my new shirt.

Page 324

Opposite Words: Sentences

Directions: Read the sentence about the first picture. Write another sentence about the second picture. Use the opposite words.

Example: This apple is little.

This apple is big.

dark	old	first	new	light	last

1. This coat is light.

This coat is dark.

2. This woman is first.

This woman is last.

3. This car is old.

This car is new.

Page 325

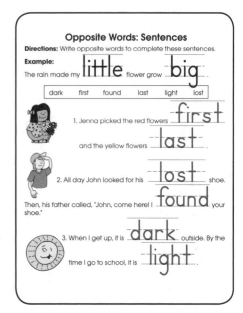

Opposite Words: Sentences

Directions: Write opposite words to complete these sentences.

Example:

The rain made my **little** flower grow **big**.

dark	first	found	last	light	lost

1. Jenna picked the red flowers **first**

and the yellow flowers **last**.

2. All day John looked for his **lost** shoe.

Then, his father called, "John, come here! I **found** your shoe."

3. When I get up, it is **dark** outside. By the time I go to school, it is **light**.

Page 326

Review

Directions: Look at the pictures in each row. Write one sentence about the last picture in each row. Begin each sentence with a capital letter, and end it with a period.

Answers may include.

The sandwich is gone.

The barn is red.

Page 327

More Action Words

Directions: Fill in the missing letters for each word.

Example:

paint   paint

catch   catch

color   color

eat   eat

grow   grow

fly   fly

Page 328

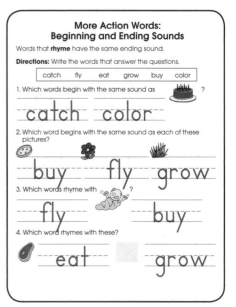

More Action Words: Beginning and Ending Sounds

Words that **rhyme** have the same ending sound.

Directions: Write the words that answer the questions.

catch	fly	eat	grow	buy	color

1. Which words begin with the same sound as ?

catch   color

2. Which word begins with the same sound as each of these pictures?

buy   fly   grow

3. Which words rhyme with ?

fly   buy

4. Which word rhymes with these?

eat   grow

Page 329

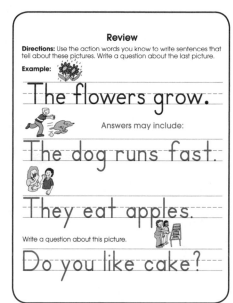

More Action Words: Sentences

Directions: Write a sentence that tells about the picture. Use the words next to the picture. Remember to begin each sentence with a capital letter, and end it with a period.

Example: likes boy to paint the

The boy likes to paint.

1. boy see grow the

See the boy grow.

2. bird the can fly

The bird can fly.

3. she will color

She will color.

Page 330

More Action Words: Sentences

Directions: Put the two sentences together to make one new sentence.

Example: The ball is red. The ball is blue.

The ball is red and blue.

1. I eat apples. I eat cookies.

I eat apples and cookies.

2. We buy milk. We buy eggs.

We buy milk and eggs.

Page 331

Review

Directions: Use the action words you know to write sentences that tell about these pictures. Write a question about the last picture.

Example:

The flowers grow.

Answers may include:

The dog runs fast.

They eat apples.

Write a question about this picture.

Do you like cake?

Page 332

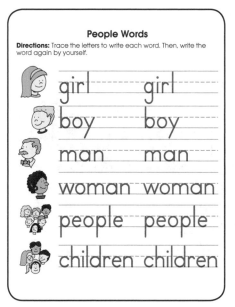

People Words

Directions: Trace the letters to write each word. Then, write the word again by yourself.

girl girl

boy boy

man man

woman woman

people people

children children

Page 333

People Words

Directions: Write a people word in each sentence to tell who is doing something.

1. The **boy** was last in line at the toy store.

2. The **people** took a walk in the woods.

3. The **girl** had to help her father.

4. The **woman** had a surprise for the children.

5. Some **children** like to eat outside.

6. Something came out of the box when the **man** opened it.

Page 334

People Words

Sometimes, we use other words in place of people names. For **boy** or **man**, we can use the word **he**. For **girl** or **woman**, we can use the word **she**. For two or more people, we can use the word **they**.

Directions: Write the words **he**, **she**, or **they** in these sentences.

Example: The boy likes soccer. **He** likes soccer.

1. The girl is running fast. **She** is running fast.

2. The man reads the paper. **He** reads the paper.

3. The woman has a cold. **She** has a cold.

4. Two children came to school. **They** came to school.

Page 335

Comprehensive Curriculum - **Grade 1**

People Words: Sentences

Directions: Write the people word that completes each sentence.

| people | man | girl | children | boy | woman |

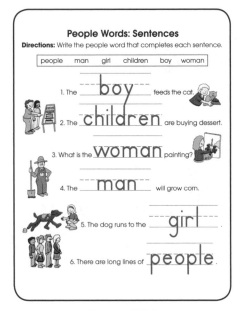

1. The **boy** feeds the cat.

2. The **children** are buying dessert.

3. What is the **woman** painting?

4. The **man** will grow corn.

5. The dog runs to the **girl**

6. There are long lines of **people**

Page 336

Number Recognition

Directions: Write the numbers 1-10. Color the bear.

1 2 3 4 5 6 7 8 9 10

Colors will vary.

Page 338

Number Recognition 1, 2, 3, 4, 5

Directions: Use the color codes to color the parrot.

Color:
1s red
2s blue
3s yellow
4s green
5s orange

Page 339

Number Recognition 6, 7, 8, 9, 10

Directions: Use the code to color the carousel horse.

Color:
6s purple
7s yellow
8s black
9s pink
10s brown

Page 340

Number Recognition

Directions: Count the number of objects in each group. Draw a line to the correct number.

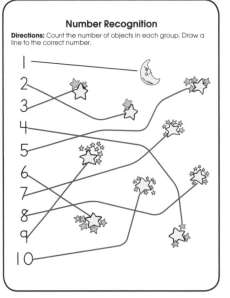

Page 341

Counting

Directions: How many are there of each picture? Write the answers in the boxes. The first one is done for you.

Page 342

Counting

Directions: How many are there of each picture? Write the answers in the boxes. The first one is done for you.

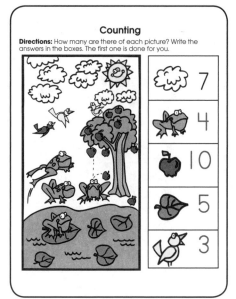

Page 343

Review

Directions: Count the flowers, and write the answers.

Directions: Fill in the missing numbers. Connect the dots to finish the picture.

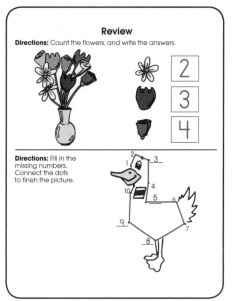

Page 344

Number Word Find

Directions: Find the number words for 0 through 12 hidden in the box.

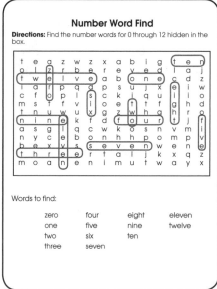

Words to find:

zero	four	eight	eleven
one	five	nine	twelve
two	six	ten	
three	seven		

Page 347

Number Words

Directions: Number the buildings from one to six.

Directions: Draw a line from the word to the number.

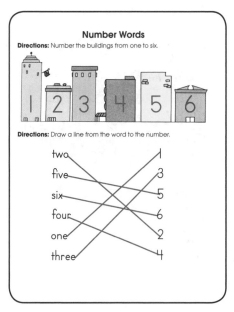

Page 348

Number Words

Directions: Number the buildings from five to ten.

Directions: Draw a line from the word to the number.

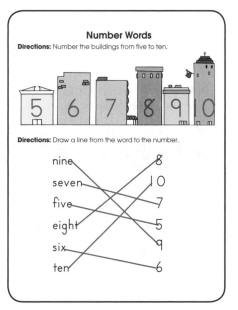

Page 349

Number Recognition Review

Directions: Match the correct number of objects with the number. Then, match the number with the word.

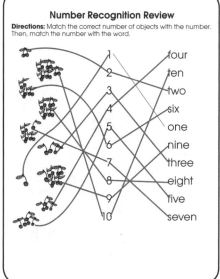

Page 350

Comprehensive Curriculum - **Grade 1**

Sequencing Numbers

Sequencing is putting numbers in the correct order.

1, 2, 3, 4, 5, 6, 7, 8, 9, 10

Directions: Write the missing numbers.

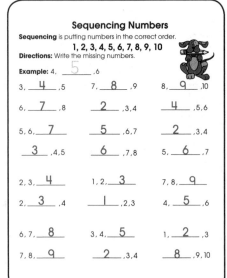

Example: 4, _5_, 6

3, _4_, 5   7, _8_, 9   8, _9_, 10

6, _7_, 8   _2_, 3, 4   _4_, 5, 6

5, 6, _7_   _5_, 6, 7   _2_, 3, 4

_3_, 4, 5   _6_, 7, 8   5, _6_, 7

2, 3, _4_   1, 2, _3_   7, 8, _9_

2, _3_, 4   _1_, 2, 3   4, _5_, 6

6, 7, _8_   3, 4, _5_   1, _2_, 3

7, 8, _9_   _2_, 3, 4   _8_, 9, 10

Page 353

Number Crossword Puzzle

Directions: Write the correct number word in the boxes provided.

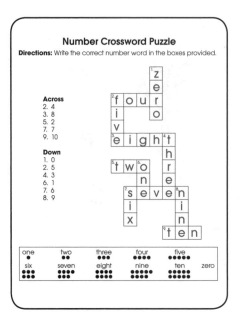

Across
2. 4
3. 8
5. 2
7. 7
9. 10

Down
1. 0
2. 5
4. 3
6. 1
7. 6
8. 9

Page 354

Review

Directions: Count the objects and write the number.

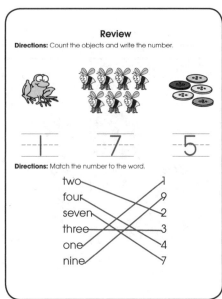

1   7   5

Directions: Match the number to the word.

two — 1
four — 9
seven — 2
three — 3
one — 4
nine — 7

Page 355

Ordinal Numbers

Ordinal numbers are used to indicate order in a series, such as **first**, **second**, or **third**.

Directions: Draw a line to the picture that corresponds to the ordinal number in the left column.

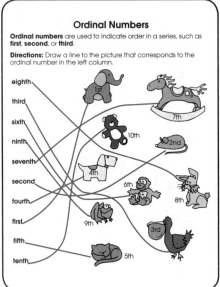

eighth
third
sixth
ninth
seventh
second
fourth
first
fifth
tenth

Page 356

Ordinal Numbers

Directions: Draw an **X** on the first vegetable, draw a circle around the second vegetable, and draw a square around the third vegetable.

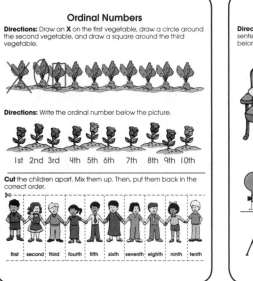

Directions: Write the ordinal number below the picture.

1st 2nd 3rd 4th 5th 6th 7th 8th 9th 10th

Cut the children apart. Mix them up. Then, put them back in the correct order.

first second third fourth fifth sixth seventh eighth ninth tenth

Page 357

Sequencing: At the Movies

Directions: The children are watching a movie. Read the sentences. Cut out the pictures below. Glue them where they belong in the picture.

1. The first child is eating popcorn.
2. The third child is eating candy.
3. The fourth child has a cup of fruit punch.
4. The second child is eating a big pretzel.

Page 359

Sequencing: Standing in Line

Directions: These children are waiting to see a movie. Look at them and follow the instructions.

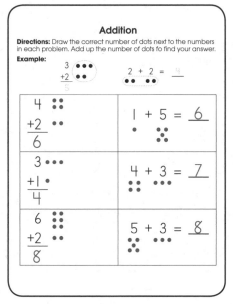

1. Color the person who is first in line yellow.
2. Color the person who is last in line orange.
3. Color the person who is second in line pink.
4. Circle the person who is at the end of the line.

Page 361

Addition 1, 2

Addition means "putting together" or adding two or more numbers to find the sum. "+" is a plus sign. It means to add the 2 numbers. "=" is an equal sign. It tells how much they are together.

Directions: Count the objects and write the number.

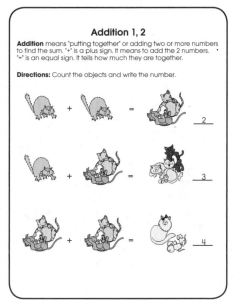

Page 362

Addition

Directions: Count the shapes, and write the numbers below to tell how many in all.

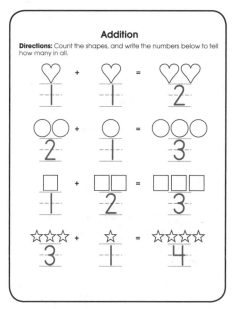

$$1 + 1 = 2$$
$$2 + 1 = 3$$
$$1 + 2 = 3$$
$$3 + 1 = 4$$

Page 363

Addition

Directions: Draw the correct number of dots next to the numbers in each problem. Add up the number of dots to find your answer.

Example:

$$\begin{array}{r} 3 \\ +2 \\ \hline 5 \end{array}$$

$$2 + 2 = 4$$

$$\begin{array}{r} 4 \\ +2 \\ \hline 6 \end{array}$$

$$1 + 5 = 6$$

$$\begin{array}{r} 3 \\ +1 \\ \hline 4 \end{array}$$

$$4 + 3 = 7$$

$$\begin{array}{r} 6 \\ +2 \\ \hline 8 \end{array}$$

$$5 + 3 = 8$$

Page 364

Addition 3, 4, 5, 6

Directions: Practice writing the numbers, and then add. Draw dots to help, if needed.

3 3 3 3
4 4 4 4
5 5 5 5
6 6 6 6

$$\begin{array}{r} 2 \\ +4 \\ \hline 6 \end{array}$$

$$\begin{array}{r} 1 \\ +4 \\ \hline 5 \end{array}$$

$$\begin{array}{r} 3 \\ +2 \\ \hline 5 \end{array}$$

$$\begin{array}{r} 1 \\ +2 \\ \hline 3 \end{array}$$

Page 365

Addition 4, 5, 6, 7

Directions: Practice writing the numbers, and then add. Draw dots to help, if needed.

4 4 4 4
5 5 5 5
6 6 6 6
7 7 7 7

$$\begin{array}{r} 2 \\ +5 \\ \hline 7 \end{array}$$

$$\begin{array}{r} 3 \\ +1 \\ \hline 4 \end{array}$$

$$\begin{array}{r} 4 \\ +1 \\ \hline 5 \end{array}$$

$$\begin{array}{r} 2 \\ +4 \\ \hline 6 \end{array}$$

Page 366

Addition 6, 7, 8

Directions: Practice writing the numbers, and then add. Draw dots to help, if needed.

6   6 6 6

7   7 7 7   3   5

8   8 8 8   +4   +1

           7   6

           2   4

          +6   +4

           8   8

Page 367

Addition 7, 8, 9

Directions: Practice writing the numbers, and then add. Draw dots to help, if needed.

7   7 7 7

8   8 8 8   8   3

9   9 9 9   +1   +5

           9   8

           2   6

          +7   +1

           9   7

Page 368

Addition Table

Directions: Add across and down with a friend. Fill in the spaces.

+	0	1	2	3	4	5
0	0	1	2	3	4	5
1	1	2	3	4	5	6
2	2	3	4	5	6	7
3	3	4	5	6	7	8
4	4	5	6	7	8	9
5	5	6	7	8	9	10

Do you notice any number patterns in the addition table?

Page 369

Subtraction 1, 2, 3

Subtraction means "taking away" or subtracting one number from another. "–" is a minus sign. It means to subtract the second number from the first.
Directions: Practice writing the numbers, and then subtract. Draw dots and cross them out, if needed.

1   1 1 1

2   2 2 2   3   4

3   3 3 3   –1   –3

           2   1

           2   3

          –1   –2

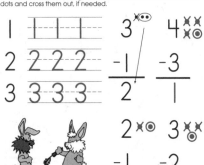

Page 370

Subtraction 3, 4, 5, 6

Directions: Practice writing the numbers, and then subtract. Draw dots and cross them out, if needed.

3   3 3 3   5   6

4   4 4 4   –2   –1

5   5 5 5   3   5

6   6 6 6   6   5

          –3   –1

           3   4

Page 371

Subtraction

Directions: Draw the correct number of dots next to the numbers in each problem. Cross out the ones subtracted to find your answer.
Example:

5
–2
3

2 – 1 = 1

4 – 2 = __2__

8
–6
2

6
–1
5

3 – 1 = __2__

9 – 6 = __3__

4
–3
1

Page 372

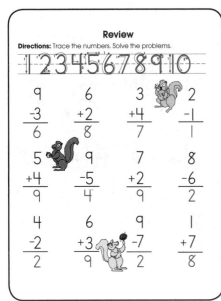

Review

Directions: Trace the numbers. Solve the problems.

1 2 3 4 5 6 7 8 9 10

```
  9      6      3        2
 -3     +2     +4       -1
 ___    ___    ___      ___
  6      8      7        1

  5      9      7        8
 +4     -5     +2       -6
 ___    ___    ___      ___
  9      4      9        2

  4      6      9        1
 -2     +3     -7       +7
 ___    ___    ___      ___
  2      9      2        8
```

Page 373

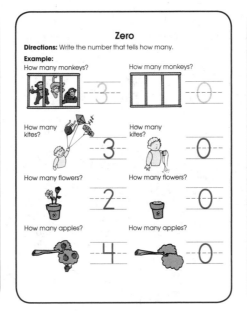

Zero

Directions: Write the number that tells how many.

Example:

How many monkeys?   3   How many monkeys?   0

How many kites?   3   How many kites?   0

How many flowers?   2   How many flowers?   0

How many apples?   4   How many apples?   0

Page 374

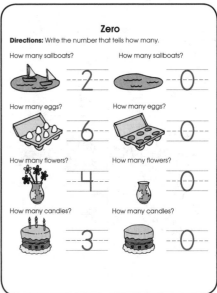

Zero

Directions: Write the number that tells how many.

How many sailboats?   2   How many sailboats?   0

How many eggs?   6   How many eggs?   0

How many flowers?   4   How many flowers?   0

How many candles?   3   How many candles?   0

Page 375

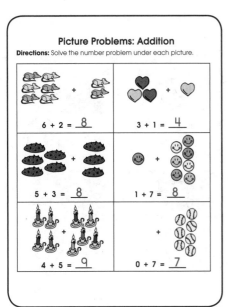

Picture Problems: Addition

Directions: Solve the number problem under each picture.

6 + 2 = 8   3 + 1 = 4

5 + 3 = 8   1 + 7 = 8

4 + 5 = 9   0 + 7 = 7

Page 376

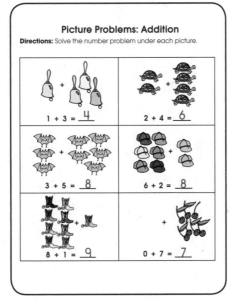

Picture Problems: Addition

Directions: Solve the number problem under each picture.

1 + 3 = 4   2 + 4 = 6

3 + 5 = 8   6 + 2 = 8

8 + 1 = 9   0 + 7 = 7

Page 377

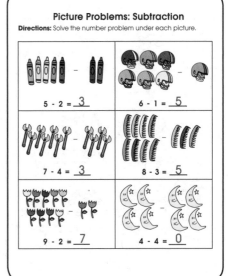

Picture Problems: Subtraction

Directions: Solve the number problem under each picture.

5 - 2 = 3   6 - 1 = 5

7 - 4 = 3   8 - 3 = 5

9 - 2 = 7   4 - 4 = 0

Page 378

ANSWER KEY

Picture Problems: Subtraction

Directions: Solve the number problem under each picture.

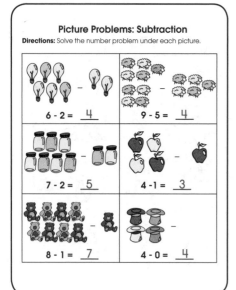

6 - 2 = 4

9 - 5 = 4

7 - 2 = 5

4 - 1 = 3

8 - 1 = 7

4 - 0 = 4

Page 379

Picture Problems: Addition and Subtraction

Directions: Solve the number problem under each picture.

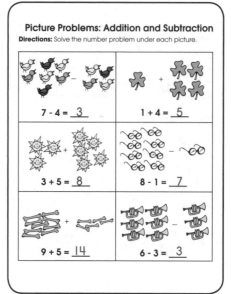

7 - 4 = 3

1 + 4 = 5

3 + 5 = 8

8 - 1 = 7

9 + 5 = 14

6 - 3 = 3

Page 380

Picture Problems: Addition and Subtraction

Directions: Solve the number problem under each picture. Write + or – to show if you should add or subtract.

How many s in all?
4 + 5 = 9

How many s in all?
7 + 5 = 12

How many s are left?
12 – 3 = 9

How many s are left?
15 – 8 = 7

How many s in all?
5 + 8 = 13

How many s are left?
11 – 4 = 7

Page 381

Picture Problems: Addition and Subtraction

Directions: Solve the number problem under each picture. Write + or – to show if you should add or subtract.

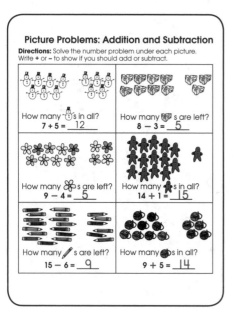

How many s in all?
7 + 5 = 12

How many s are left?
8 – 3 = 5

How many s are left?
9 – 4 = 5

How many s in all?
14 + 1 = 15

How many s are left?
15 – 6 = 9

How many s in all?
9 + 5 = 14

Page 382

Review: Addition and Subtraction

Directions: Solve the number problem under each picture. Write + or – to show if you should add or subtract.

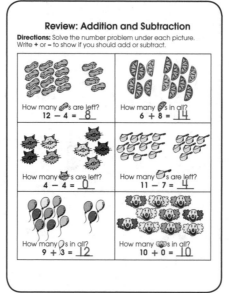

How many s are left?
12 – 4 = 8

How many s in all?
6 + 8 = 14

How many s are left?
4 – 4 = 0

How many s are left?
11 – 7 = 4

How many s in all?
9 + 3 = 12

How many s in all?
10 + 0 = 10

Page 383

Addition 1-5

Directions: Count the tools in each tool box. Write your answers in the blanks. Circle the problem that matches your answer.

4

6

2
+2

2
+1

5
+0

4
+2

8

5

6
+2

4
+3

3
+1

2
+3

Page 384

Addition 1-5

Directions: Look at the red numbers, and draw that many more flowers in the pot. Count them to get your total.

Example: 3 + 2 = 5

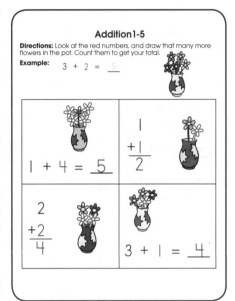

1 + 4 = 5

1
+1
2

2
+2
4

3 + 1 = 4

Page 385

Addition 1-5

Directions: Add the numbers. Put your answers in the nests.

Example: 2 + 3 = 5

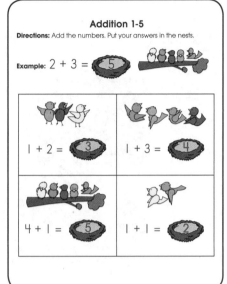

1 + 2 = 3

1 + 3 = 4

4 + 1 = 5

1 + 1 = 2

Page 386

Addition 6-10

Directions: Add the numbers. Put your answers in the doghouses.

Example: 4 + 2 = 6

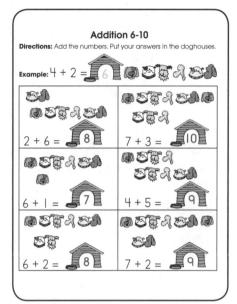

2 + 6 = 8

7 + 3 = 10

6 + 1 = 7

4 + 5 = 9

6 + 2 = 8

7 + 2 = 9

Page 387

Subtraction 1-5

Directions: Subtract the red numbers by crossing out that many flowers in the pot. Count the ones not crossed out to get the answer.

Example: 2 - 1 = 1

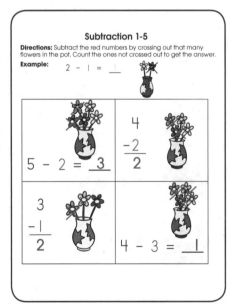

5 - 2 = 3

4
-2
2

3
-1
2

4 - 3 = 1

Page 388

Subtraction 1-5

Directions: Count the fruit in each bowl. Write your answers on the blanks. Circle the problem that matches your answer.

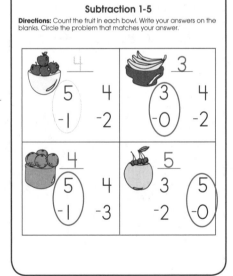

4

5
-1

4
-2

3

3
-0

4
-2

4

5
-1

4
-3

5

5
3
-2

5
-0

Page 389

Subtraction 6-10

Directions: Count the flowers. Write your answer on the blank. Circle the problem that matches your answer.

9

10
-1

9
-1

6

7
-2

9
-3

8

9
-6

8
-0

7

10
-2

8
-1

Page 390

Page 391

Addition and Subtraction

Directions: Solve the problems. Remember, addition means "putting together" or adding two or more numbers to find the sum. Subtraction means "taking away" or subtracting one number from another.

$1 + 3 = \underline{4}$ $4 - 3 = \underline{1}$ $4 + 5 = \underline{9}$

$6 + 1 = \underline{7}$ $7 - 2 = \underline{5}$ $8 - 4 = \underline{4}$

$9 - 1 = \underline{8}$ $10 - 3 = \underline{7}$

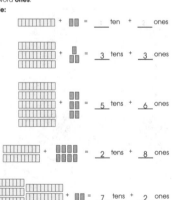

$5 - 2 = \underline{3}$ $6 + 3 = \underline{9}$

$8 + 2 = \underline{10}$ $5 + 5 = \underline{10}$

Page 392

Addition and Subtraction

Remember, addition means "putting together" or adding two or more numbers to find the sum. Subtraction means "taking away" or subtracting one number from another.

Directions: Solve the problems. From your answers, use the code to color the quilt.

Color:
6 = blue
7 = yellow
8 = green
9 = red
10 = orange

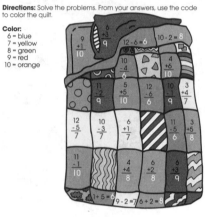

Page 393

Place Value: Tens and Ones

The **place value** of a digit, or numeral is shown by where it is in the number. For example, in the number **23**, **2** has the place value of **tens**, and **3** is **ones**.

Directions: Count the groups of ten crayons, and write the number by the word **tens**. Count the other crayons, and write the number by the word **ones**.

Example:

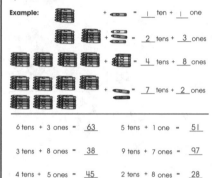

= $\underline{1}$ ten + $\underline{1}$ one

= $\underline{2}$ tens + $\underline{3}$ ones

= $\underline{4}$ tens + $\underline{8}$ ones

= $\underline{7}$ tens + $\underline{2}$ ones

6 tens + 3 ones = $\underline{63}$ 5 tens + 1 one = $\underline{51}$

3 tens + 8 ones = $\underline{38}$ 9 tens + 7 ones = $\underline{97}$

4 tens + 5 ones = $\underline{45}$ 2 tens + 8 ones = $\underline{28}$

Page 394

Place Value: Tens and Ones

Directions: Count the groups of ten blocks, and write the number by the word **tens**. Count the other blocks, and write the number by the word **ones**.

Example:

= $\underline{}$ ten + $\underline{}$ ones

= $\underline{3}$ tens + $\underline{3}$ ones

= $\underline{5}$ tens + $\underline{6}$ ones

= $\underline{2}$ tens + $\underline{8}$ ones

= $\underline{7}$ tens + $\underline{2}$ ones

Page 395

Place Value: Tens and Ones

Directions: Write the answers in the correct spaces.

	tens	ones		
3 tens, 2 ones	3	2	=	32
3 tens, 7 ones	3	7	=	37
9 tens, 1 one	9	1	=	91
5 tens, 6 ones	5	6	=	56
6 tens, 5 ones	6	5	=	65
6 tens, 8 ones	6	8	=	68
2 tens, 8 ones	2	8	=	28
4 tens, 9 ones	4	9	=	49
1 ten, 4 ones	1	4	=	14
8 tens, 2 ones	8	2	=	82
4 tens, 2 ones	4	2	=	42

28 = $\underline{2}$ tens, $\underline{8}$ ones
64 = $\underline{6}$ tens, $\underline{4}$ ones
56 = $\underline{5}$ tens, $\underline{6}$ ones
72 = $\underline{7}$ tens, $\underline{2}$ ones
38 = $\underline{3}$ tens, $\underline{8}$ ones
17 = $\underline{1}$ ten, $\underline{7}$ ones
63 = $\underline{6}$ tens, $\underline{3}$ ones
12 = $\underline{1}$ ten, $\underline{2}$ ones

Page 396

Review: Place Value

The place value of each digit or numeral is shown by where it is in the number. For example, in the number **123**, **1** has the place value of **hundreds**, **2** is **tens**, and **3** is **ones**.

Directions: Count the groups of crayons and add.

Example:

           Hundreds Tens Ones

= $\underline{1}$ $\underline{1}$ $\underline{3}$

1 Hundred + 1 Ten + 3 Ones

= $\underline{1}$ $\underline{2}$ $\underline{4}$

= $\underline{1}$ $\underline{3}$ $\underline{6}$

Counting by Fives
Directions: Count by fives to draw the path to the playground.

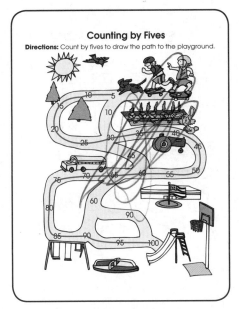

Page 397

Counting by Fives
Directions: Use tally marks to count by fives. Write the number next to the tallies.
Example: A tally mark stands for one (1). Five tally marks look like this: 卌.

卌	5	卌 卌 卌 卌 卌 卌 卌	35
卌 卌	10	卌 卌 卌 卌 卌 卌 卌 卌	40
卌 卌 卌	15	卌 卌 卌 卌 卌 卌 卌 卌 卌	45
卌 卌 卌 卌	20	卌 卌 卌 卌 卌 卌 卌 卌 卌 卌	50
卌 卌 卌 卌 卌	25		
卌 卌 卌 卌 卌 卌	30		

Page 398

Counting by Tens
Directions: Count in order by tens to draw the path the boy takes to the store.

Page 399

Counting by Tens
Directions: Use the groups of tens to count to 100.

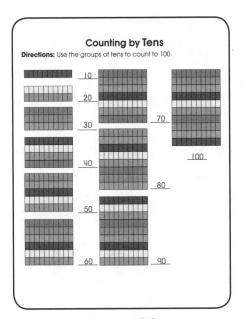

10
20
30
40
50
60
70
80
90
100

Page 400

Addition: 10-15
Directions: Count groups of ten crayons. Add the remaining ones to make the correct number.

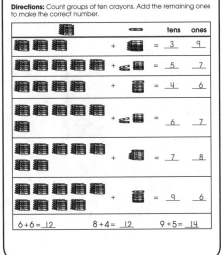

	tens	ones
+ =	3	9
+ =	5	7
+ =	4	6
+ =	6	7
+ =	7	8
+ =	9	6

6+6 = 12   8+4 = 12   9+5 = 14

Page 401

Subtraction: 10-15
Directions: Count the crayons in each group. Put an **X** through the number of crayons being subtracted. How many are left?

		-		=	
		-	5	=	10
		-	4	=	7
		-	7	=	6
		-	6	=	8
		-	5	=	7
		-	8	=	6

13 - 8 = 5   11 - 5 = 6   12 - 9 = 3
14 - 7 = 7   10 - 7 = 3   13 - 3 = 10
15 - 9 = 6   11 - 8 = 3   12 - 10 = 2

Page 402

Comprehensive Curriculum - **Grade 1**

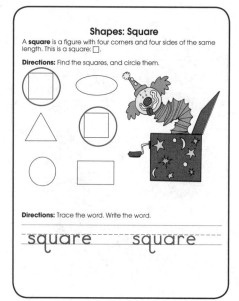

Shapes: Square

A **square** is a figure with four corners and four sides of the same length. This is a square: □.

Directions: Find the squares, and circle them.

Directions: Trace the word. Write the word.

square square

Page 403

Shapes: Circle

A **circle** is a figure that is round. This is a circle: ○.

Directions: Find the circles, and put a square around them.

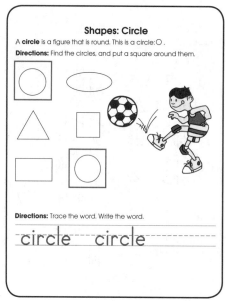

Directions: Trace the word. Write the word.

circle circle

Page 404

Shapes: Square and Circle

Directions: Practice drawing squares. Trace the samples, and make four of your own.

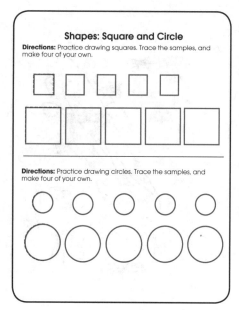

Directions: Practice drawing circles. Trace the samples, and make four of your own.

Page 405

Shapes: Triangle

A **triangle** is a figure with three corners and three sides. This is a triangle: △.

Directions: Find the triangles, and put a circle around them.

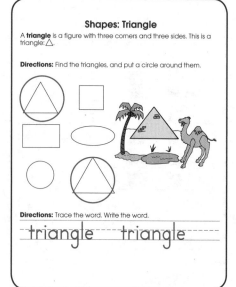

Directions: Trace the word. Write the word.

triangle triangle

Page 406

Shapes: Rectangle

A **rectangle** is a figure with four corners and four sides. Sides opposite each other are the same length. This is a rectangle: ▭.

Directions: Find the rectangles, and put a circle around them.

Directions: Trace the word. Write the word.

rectangle rectangle

Page 407

Shapes: Triangle and Rectangle

Directions: Practice drawing triangles. Trace the samples, and make four of your own.

Directions: Practice drawing rectangles. Trace the samples, and make four of your own.

Page 408

Patterns: Rectangles

Directions: In each picture, there is more than one rectangle. Trace each rectangle with a different color crayon. Under each picture, write how many rectangles you found.

__3__ rectangles

__3__ rectangles

Page 409

Patterns: Triangles

Directions: In each picture, there is more than one triangle. Trace each triangle with a different color crayon. Under each picture, write how many triangles you found.

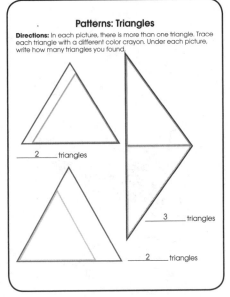

__2__ triangles

__3__ triangles

__2__ triangles

Page 410

Shapes: Oval and Rhombus

An **oval** is an egg-shaped figure. A rhombus is a figure with four sides of the same length. Its corners form points at the top, side, and bottom. This is an oval: ◯. This is a rhombus: ◇.

Directions: Color the ovals red. Color the rhombuses blue.

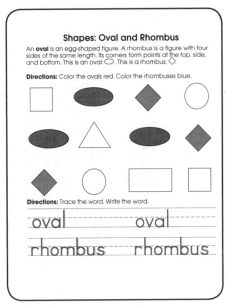

Directions: Trace the word. Write the word.

oval   oval

rhombus   rhombus

Page 411

Shapes: Oval and Rhombus

Directions: Practice drawing ovals. Trace the samples, and make four of your own.

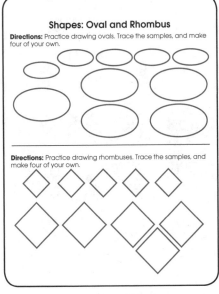

Directions: Practice drawing rhombuses. Trace the samples, and make four of your own.

Page 412

Following Directions: Shapes and Colors

Directions: Color the squares ☐ purple.

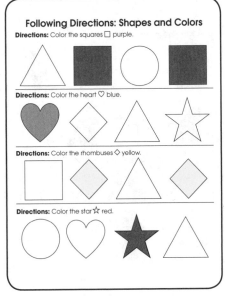

Directions: Color the heart ♡ blue.

Directions: Color the rhombuses ◇ yellow.

Directions: Color the star ☆ red.

Page 413

Shape Review

Directions: Color the shapes in the picture as shown.

black

red

orange

yellow

blue

green

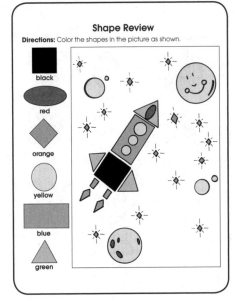

Page 414

Comprehensive Curriculum - **Grade 1**

Shape Review

Directions: Trace the circles
Trace the squares
Trace the rectangles
Trace the triangles
Trace the ovals
Trace the rhombuses

red
blue
yellow
green
purple
orange

Page 415

Classifying: Stars

Help Connor find the stars.

Directions: Color all the stars blue.

How many stars did you and Connor find? ___10

Page 416

Classifying: Shapes

Mary and Rudy are taking a trip into space. Help them find the stars, moons, circles, and rhombuses.

Directions: Color the shapes.
Use yellow for ☆s.   Use blue for ☾s.
Use red for ○s.   Use purple for ◇s.

How many stars? ___5   How many moons? ___5
How many circles? ___4   How many rhombuses? ___4

Page 417

Classifying: Shapes

Directions: Look at the shapes. Answer the questions.

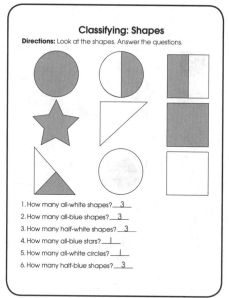

1. How many all-white shapes? ___3
2. How many all-blue shapes? ___3
3. How many half-white shapes? ___3
4. How many all-blue stars? ___1
5. How many all-white circles? ___1
6. How many half-blue shapes? ___3

Page 418

Same and Different: Shapes

Directions: Color the shape that looks the same as the first shape in each row.

Page 419

Same and Different: Shapes

Directions: Draw an **X** on the shapes in each row that do not match the first shape.

Page 420

Copying: Shapes and Colors

Directions: Color your circle to look the same.

Directions: Color your square to look the same.

Directions: Trace the triangle. Color it to look the same.

Directions: Trace the star. Color it to look the same.

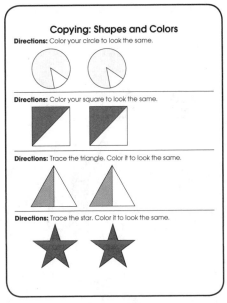

Page 421

Copying: Shapes and Colors

Directions: Color the second shape the same as the first one. Then, draw and color the shape two more times.

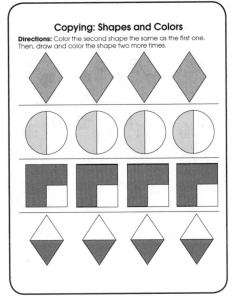

Page 422

Patterns: Shapes

Directions: Draw a line from the box on the left to the box on the right with the same shape and color pattern.

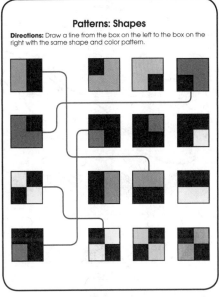

Page 423

Patterns: Shapes

Directions: Draw a line from the box on the left to the box on the right with the same shape and color pattern.

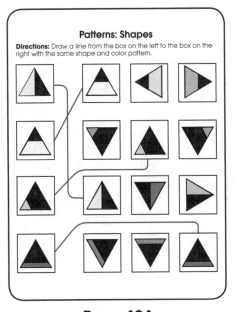

Page 424

Patterns: Find and Copy

Directions: Circle the shape in the middle box that matches the one on the left. Draw another shape with the same pattern in the box on the right.

Page 425

Patterns

Directions: Draw what comes next in each pattern.
Example:

Page 426

Comprehensive Curriculum - Grade 1

Patterns

Directions: Fill in the missing shape in each row. Then, color it.

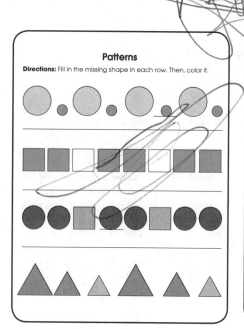

Page 427

Patterns

Directions: Color to complete the patterns.

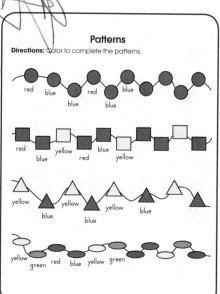

red blue red blue
blue blue

red blue
blue yellow red yellow

yellow yellow yellow yellow
blue blue

yellow green red blue yellow green

Page 428

Fractions: Whole and Half

A **fraction** is a number that names part of a whole, such as $\frac{1}{2}$ or $\frac{3}{4}$.

Directions: Color half of each object.

Example:

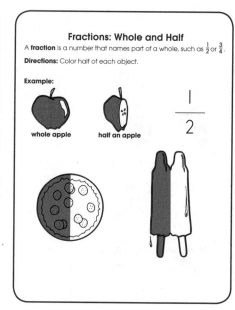

whole apple   half an apple

$\frac{1}{2}$

Page 429

Fractions: Halves $\frac{1}{2}$

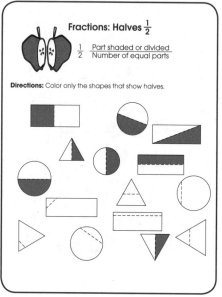

$\frac{1}{2}$ $\frac{\text{Part shaded or divided}}{\text{Number of equal parts}}$

Directions: Color only the shapes that show halves.

Page 430

Fractions: Thirds $\frac{1}{3}$

Directions: Circle the objects that have 3 equal parts.

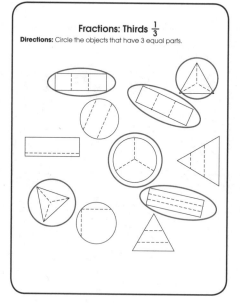

Page 431

Fractions: Fourths $\frac{1}{4}$

Directions: Circle the objects that have 4 equal parts.

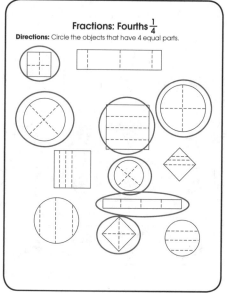

Page 432

Fractions: Thirds and Fourths

Directions: Each object has 3 equal parts. Color one section.

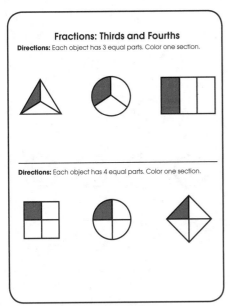

Directions: Each object has 4 equal parts. Color one section.

Page 433

Review: Fractions

Directions: Count the equal parts, then write the fraction.

Example:

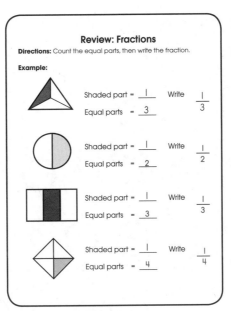

Shaded part = $\underline{1}$ Write $\dfrac{1}{3}$
Equal parts = $\underline{3}$

Shaded part = $\underline{1}$ Write $\dfrac{1}{2}$
Equal parts = $\underline{2}$

Shaded part = $\underline{1}$ Write $\dfrac{1}{3}$
Equal parts = $\underline{3}$

Shaded part = $\underline{1}$ Write $\dfrac{1}{4}$
Equal parts = $\underline{4}$

Page 434

Review

Directions: Write the missing numbers by counting by tens and fives.

$\underline{10}$, 20, $\underline{30}$, $\underline{40}$, $\underline{50}$, $\underline{60}$, 70, $\underline{80}$, $\underline{90}$, 100

5, $\underline{10}$, 15, $\underline{20}$, $\underline{25}$, 30, $\underline{35}$, $\underline{40}$, $\underline{45}$, $\underline{50}$

Directions: Color the object with thirds red. Color the object with halves blue. Color the object with fourths green.

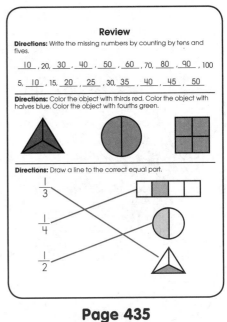

Directions: Draw a line to the correct equal part.

$\dfrac{1}{3}$ $\dfrac{1}{4}$ $\dfrac{1}{2}$

Page 435

Tracking: Straight Lines

Directions: Draw a straight line from A to B. Use a different color crayon for each line.

B   B
   A triangle   A square

B   A
A rectangle   odd shape B

What shapes do you see hidden in these shapes? _triangles_

Page 436

Tracking: Different Paths

Directions: Trace three paths from A to B.

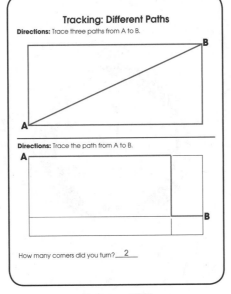
B

A

Directions: Trace the path from A to B.

A

B

How many corners did you turn? _2_

Page 437

Tracking: Different Paths

Help Megan find Mark.

Directions: Trace a path from Megan to Mark.
Paths may vary.

How many different paths can she follow to reach him? _5_

Page 438

Tracking: Different Paths

Directions: Use different colors to trace three paths the bear could take to get the honey.

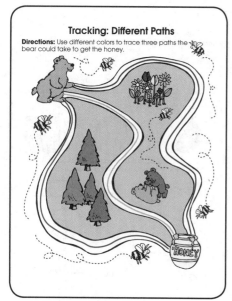

Page 439

Time: Hour

The short hand of the clock tells the hour. The long hand tells how many minutes after the hour. When the minute hand is on the **12**, it is the beginning of the hour.

Directions: Look at each clock. Write the time.

Example:

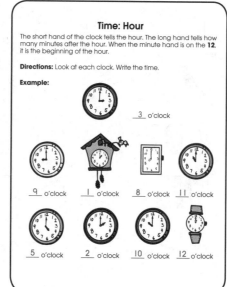

3 o'clock

9 o'clock   1 o'clock   8 o'clock   11 o'clock

5 o'clock   2 o'clock   10 o'clock   12 o'clock

Page 440

Time: Hour, Half-Hour

The short hand of the clock tells the hour. The long hand tells how many minutes after the hour. When the minute hand is on the **6**, it is on the half-hour. A half-hour is thirty minutes. It is written **:30**, such as **5:30**.

Directions: Look at each clock. Write the time.

Example:

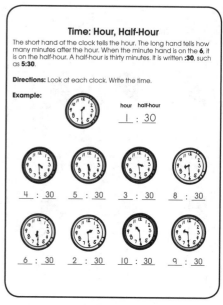

hour   half-hour
1 : 30

4 : 30   5 : 30   3 : 30   8 : 30

6 : 30   2 : 30   10 : 30   9 : 30

Page 441

Time: Hour, Half-Hour

Directions: Draw the hands on each clock to show the correct time.

2:30   9:00

7:00   4:30

3:00   1:30

Page 442

Time: Counting by Fives

Directions: Fill in the numbers on the clock face. Count by fives around the clock.

60

55   5
50   10
45   15
40   20
35   25

30

There are 60 minutes in one hour.

Page 443

Time: Review

Directions: Look at the time on the digital clocks and draw the hands on the clocks.

10:00   5:00

Directions: Look at each clock. Write the time.

3 o'clock   2 o'clock

Directions: Look at each clock. Write the time.

1 : 30   10 :30   4 :30

Page 444

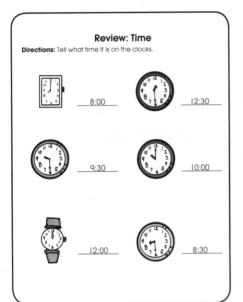

Review: Time

Directions: Tell what time it is on the clocks.

8:00   12:30

9:30   10:00

12:00   8:30

Page 445

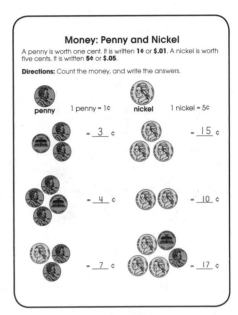

Review: Time

Directions: Match the time on the clock with the digital time.

10:00

5:00

3:00

9:00

2:00

Page 446

Money: Penny and Nickel

A penny is worth one cent. It is written **1¢** or **$.01**. A nickel is worth five cents. It is written **5¢** or **$.05**.

Directions: Count the money, and write the answers.

penny   1 penny = 1¢   nickel   1 nickel = 5¢

= _3_ ¢   = _15_ ¢

= _4_ ¢   = _10_ ¢

= _7_ ¢   = _17_ ¢

Page 447

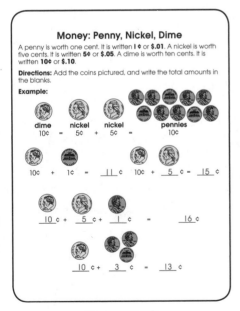

Money: Penny, Nickel, Dime

A penny is worth one cent. It is written **1¢** or **$.01**. A nickel is worth five cents. It is written **5¢** or **$.05**. A dime is worth ten cents. It is written **10¢** or **$.10**.

Directions: Add the coins pictured, and write the total amounts in the blanks.

Example:

dime = 10¢ + nickel = 5¢ + nickel = 5¢ = pennies = 10¢

10¢ + 1¢ = _11_ ¢   10¢ + _5_ ¢ = _15_ ¢

_10_ ¢ + _5_ ¢ + _1_ ¢ = _16_ ¢

_10_ ¢ + _3_ ¢ = _13_ ¢

Page 448

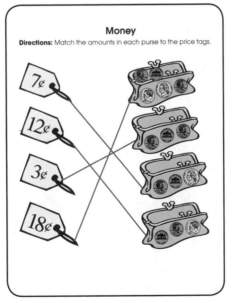

Money

Directions: Match the amounts in each purse to the price tags.

7¢

12¢

3¢

18¢

Page 449

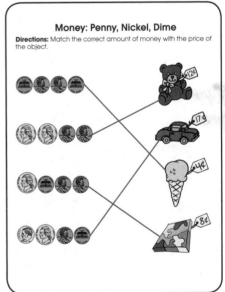

Money: Penny, Nickel, Dime

Directions: Match the correct amount of money with the price of the object.

Page 450

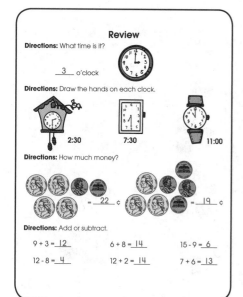

Review

Directions: What time is it?

___3___ o'clock

Directions: Draw the hands on each clock.

2:30   7:30   11:00

Directions: How much money?

= __22__ ¢   = __19__ ¢

Directions: Add or subtract.

9 + 3 = _12_   6 + 8 = _14_   15 - 9 = _6_

12 - 8 = _4_   12 + 2 = _14_   7 + 6 = _13_

Page 451

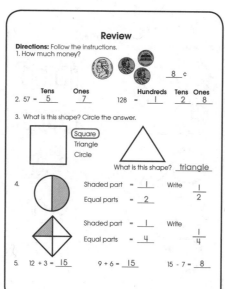

Review

Directions: Follow the instructions.
1. How much money?

__8__ ¢

Tens	Ones		Hundreds	Tens	Ones
2. 57 = __5__ __7__   128 = __1__ __2__ __8__

3. What is this shape? Circle the answer.

(Square)
Triangle
Circle

What is this shape? __triangle__

4.

Shaded part = __1__   Write $\frac{1}{2}$

Equal parts = __2__

Shaded part = __1__   Write $\frac{1}{4}$

Equal parts = __4__

5.   12 + 3 = _15_   9 + 6 = _15_   15 - 7 = _8_

Page 452

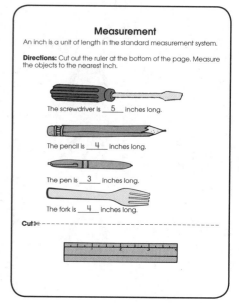

Measurement

An inch is a unit of length in the standard measurement system.

Directions: Cut out the ruler at the bottom of the page. Measure the objects to the nearest inch.

The screwdriver is __5__ inches long.

The pencil is __4__ inches long.

The pen is __3__ inches long.

The fork is __4__ inches long.

Cut ✂ -

Page 453

Addition

Make your own "plus" sign. Glue two toothpicks or popsicle sticks together. Then, your child can create groups of objects on either side of the "plus" sign to add.

$$4 + 1 = 5$$

Use dry beans or other small objects to practice counting. Have your child divide ten beans into two separate groups and combine them by adding. Have your child write the number problem on paper and read it to you.

$$3 + 4 = 7$$

Look through magazines with your child. Encourage him to create addition problems from the pictures. For example: "One Mommy plus two children equals three people!"

Alphabetical (ABC) Order

Write three or four words (names of family members, color words, objects found in the kitchen) on a sheet of paper. Space them so they can be cut out and rearranged in random order. Have your child move them around so that they are in the correct order. At first, you will need to be careful not to include two words that begin with the same letter. As your child masters ABC order, however, you can show her how to use the second letter of a word when doing alphabetical order. Words such as *brown* and *blue* both begin with the letter *b*, so your child would need to look at the *r* and the *l* to help her determine which word would come first.

Give your child a copy of your weekly grocery list, and let her rewrite it for you in alphabetical order.

Show your child a dictionary. Lead her to discover that the words are listed in alphabetical order. Purchase an inexpensive picture dictionary for your child to use in her writing, and encourage her to look up words she wants to spell correctly.

Classifying

Classifying involves putting objects, words, or ideas that are alike into categories. Objects can be classified in more than one way. For example, hats could be sorted by size, color, or season worn. If your child creates a category you had not considered, praise him for thinking creatively.

Your child could sort the clothing in his closet. He could sort it according to the season in which each item is worn, by color, type of clothing, or even likes and dislikes. You could also have your child help you sort laundry.

At the grocery store, talk about the layout of the store and how items are arranged. For example, fruits are together, vegetables are together, cooking supplies are together, soups are together, etc. Talk about why items would be arranged in groups like that. What would happen if they were not arranged in groups? Have your child help you find what you need by having him decide what section of the store it would be in. After finding the item, talk about alternate places the item could be found.

When planning a family vacation, print out travel brochures on possible destinations and sites to see. Have your child classify the brochures according to location, activity, or places you may or may not want to visit. Use these groupings to plan your trip.

Recycling is a good way to practice classifying. Label recycling containers clearly (paper, plastic, glass, metal). Your child's job can be to sort the recyclables and put them in the correct containers.

Let your child help you organize the kitchen cupboards, a closet, or a dresser drawer. Food could be organized into food groups. Clothes and shoes could be sorted by season or color.

Help your child take a poll while riding in the car. Decide on a topic (color of cars, types of vehicles seen, color of houses, etc.). Have your child draw columns on a sheet of paper and label the columns. Each time you or your child spots an object that belongs in a category, have him make a tally mark in that column.

Encourage your child to help you as you prepare meals in the kitchen. Talk about the places where kitchen utensils are kept—silverware, glasses, plates, etc. As you dry the dishes or empty the dishwasher, your child can sort the forks, spoons, and knives or the plates and glasses. Helping to sort and fold the laundry is another practical way to reinforce this skill.

Arrange an assortment of "like" objects, such as buttons, safety pins, paper clips (all used to fasten things) or chalk, pens, markers (things used to write with), and have your child find something that also belongs in that grouping. You could also arrange an assortment of "like" materials with one object that doesn't belong and have your child remove the wrong one.

Colors

Fill six clear plastic glasses half full with water. Have your child experiment with mixing drops of food coloring into each cup. Talk about the colors created and how they were created. Help your child record her findings. For example, red + yellow = orange.

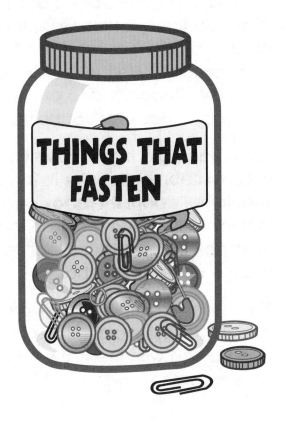

Compound Words

Look for compound words in newspapers and magazines, or write compound words on cards, and cut them apart for your child. Challenge your child to match the word parts, glue them together, and illustrate them.

Comprehension

Your child can make a poster for a book or movie. Have her include the important events, the most exciting parts, her favorite part, and reasons why someone else should view or read it.

Comprehension involves understanding what is seen, heard, or read. To help your child with this skill, talk about a book, picture, movie, or television program. Ask your child if she likes it and the reasons why or why not. By listening to what she says, you can tell whether the material was understood. If your child does not fully understand part of it, discuss that section further. Reread the book or watch the program again, if possible.

Discuss the job of a news reporter with your child. After your child understands what reporters do, create your own newscast. You can be the reporter, and your child can pretend to be a character from a book or movie. Make up the questions together, based on a book she has read or a movie she has watched. Use the questions for an interview. Record video of your interview, and play it back for your child to watch.

After reading a book, have your child create a book cover for it. The picture should tell about the book and include a brief summary on the back. If the book belongs to your child, she could use the cover on the book.

Find a comic strip without words, or use a comic strip from the newspaper and cut off the words. Have your child look at the pictures and create words to go along with them. If your child has difficulty writing, you may want to write what she says.

Consonants/Vowels

Have your child write the names of family members and graph the number of consonants and vowels in each person's name. Then, ask questions to help your child interpret the graph. For example: "Whose name has the most vowels? The most consonants? Whose name has the most letters?"

Play "Letter Bingo" or "Word Bingo" with your child. Cut pictures from magazines, and glue them on a Bingo board. Start by calling out beginning consonant sounds. For example, "Cover words that start with the letter *t*." You can make the game more difficult by asking your child to identify words by both their beginning and ending sound, as in "Cover the word that begins with a *t* and ends with a *d*."

Have your child brainstorm a list of words that have the short *a* sound (or whatever vowel you're working on) in the beginning or middle. Looking at pictures in books or magazines may help spark ideas.

Counting

Have your child write her name. Have her count the number of letters in her name and the number of times each letter appears. Have your child do the same with your name and other family members' names.

Buy or make a calendar for your child to keep in her room. Have your child number the calendar. Put stickers on or draw pictures to mark special days. Have your child cross out each day.

Play the card game "War" with your child. Each player needs an equal number of cards. Explain the value of face cards to your child. Each player places a card facedown and turns it over at the same time. The player with the higher number gets to keep both cards.

Comprehensive Curriculum - **Grade 1**

Following Directions

Give your child a set of three directions to follow. For example, you could say, "Go to the refrigerator and get a carrot stick. Put it on a small plate. Take it to your father in the garage." You may be able to increase the steps in the sequence, but do not make the skill so difficult that your child gets frustrated. Then, reverse your roles! Have your child give you a set of directions to follow. This change is not only fun for him, it is also good practice in giving clear directions.

When playing a new game, read the directions with your child. Then, have him explain how to play the game. When a friend visits, let your child explain the rules of the game.

Write a note for your child, giving step-by-step directions on how to do something. If he cannot read yet, use pictures to show what needs to be done. Encourage your child to follow the directions to complete the task.

Fractions

Let your child help you cut pie or pizza into equal slices.

Peel an orange. Separate the sections, and talk about "fractions" as parts of a whole.

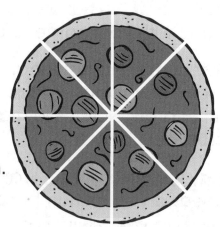

Pick clovers. Talk about equal parts as you pull off the leaves.

Fold a sheet of paper into four equal sections. Have your child shade three sections blue and one brown. Explain that $\frac{3}{4}$ of Earth is covered by water, and $\frac{1}{4}$ is land.

Letter Sounds

Write each consonant letter on a large index card. Choose four to eight of the cards, and lay them out on a table. Say a word that begins with one of the letters, and have your child identify the beginning sound. (At first, avoid naming words that begin with blends and digraphs, such as *frog* or *shop*.) Repeat with other consonant letters.

To help your child develop her skill in recognizing beginning and ending sounds, play a game of "I Spy" together. Say, for example,"I see something in this room that starts with the sound of *t*," or "I spy something that ends with the same sound as *top*." Your child should respond with an appropriate object. You can make the game more challenging by using consonant blends, as in "Can you spy something that begins with the same beginning blend as *glove*?"

Make up letter riddles. Example: "I'm thinking of an animal that hops and whose name begins with *r*." Have your child guess the answer.

Letter Sounds and ABC Order

Create an ABC scavenger hunt for your child. Provide your child with a list of words and pictures representing each of the 26 letters of the alphabet. For example:

a   apple
b   ball
c   cat
d   doll

Let her collect the items for the scavenger hunt from around your home or neighborhood and label them.

Letter Recognition and Formation

Use glue to write the capital and lowercase letters of the alphabet. After the glue dries, encourage your child to trace the letters with her fingers. Then, encourage her to identify the letters with her eyes closed!

Using white liquid glue, have your child write words in large letters on drawing paper. Then, have your child place thick yarn in the glue to form each letter of the word. When the words dry, your child can trace them with her fingers while spelling the words.

On a trip to the beach, encourage your child to write the entire alphabet in the sand before the waves wash the letters away!

TEACHING SUGGESTIONS

Making Inferences

Talk about daily events with your child. Ask your child questions about what he thinks might happen next or how a person might have felt about an event. Ask your child how he arrived at that answer.

Use questions to encourage your child to think about why people do things. For example, "Why do you think that man is scraping the paint off the house?" Why do you think we are buying chicken at the store today?" Based upon what your child sees, he can come up with information without being told.

Measurement

Purchase a plastic or wooden ruler for your child. Let her measure various objects around the house. Record her findings, and talk about length.

Money

Practice counting by fives with nickels and by tens with dimes.

Let your child label canned goods in your home with prices. He will gain valuable practice counting and exchanging money by playing store.

Give your child small amounts of money to purchase items when you go shopping. Encourage your child to count his change after each transaction.

Encourage your child to create other combinations of money for the same amount. For example, ten cents can be made with one dime, two nickels, ten pennies, or one nickel and five pennies.

Number Recognition

Have your child read the numbers on the license plates of other vehicles as you drive around town. This will not only reinforce number recognition but letter recognition as well!

Safety Tip: Make sure your child knows her address. Have your child write her address (with your assistance) and keep it with her:

> My Child
> 12345 Oak Street
> Any City, Any State 12345

Help your child memorize her phone number, as well. Have her practice writing it and dialing it on the phone.

Number Words

Play hopscotch with your child. Instead of using numbers, write a number word in each hopscotch square.

Patterns

Patterns can be made from beads, blocks, paper clips, pencils, and any other small objects, either alone or combined (blue block, red block, blue block, red block, . . . pencil, paper clip, paper clip, pencil . . .). Begin a pattern with objects, and have your child continue the pattern.

Place Value (Tens and Ones)

Rubber band or glue ten toothpicks together to represent "tens," and let your child practice counting by tens.

Let your child practice trading with pennies, dimes, and a dollar to reinforce the concept of ones, tens, and hundreds. Roll a die, and let your child take as many pennies from the "pot" as the die indicates. When he has ten pennies, he can trade them in for a dime. Continue playing and trading pennies for dimes. When your child gets ten dimes, he can trade them in for a dollar!

Predicting

When reading a story to your child, pause often and ask,"What do you think will happen next?" This can also be done when watching movies or shows.

You can also help your child practice predicting by giving clues about where you are going. For example, you might say that you are going to visit someone who lives in a white house. If your child needs more information, give additional clues.

Rhyming Words

Read familiar nursery rhymes to your child, and leave out the last word or line. For example:

> Jack and Jill
> Went up the ____ .

Same and Different, Similarities, Opposites

Play a game with your child by giving her a clue, such as, "Can you bring me something that looks like a book?" or "Can you find a shirt that is the opposite of white?"

In the car, you can play "I Spy." Take turns with your child finding things that are opposite or similar, and then give your child a clue, such as, "I spy a sign that is the opposite of go." Have your child guess the object.

Give your child two similar objects, such as a baseball and a balloon. Ask her to tell you ways the two are alike and ways they are different. Do the same with objects that are not very much alike, such as a ball and a toy truck. Again, ask your child to tell you how they are alike and different.

Sequencing

A daily activity, like setting the table, can help your child practice sequencing. Develop an order in which objects should be put on the table. You can also have your child put away toys according to size, such as from smallest to largest. Words could be put into alphabetical order.

After reading a story, ask your child to retell the story in his own words. Listen to see if he orders the events correctly. If not, relate an event in the story, and ask your child to tell you what happened next.

Talk to your child about order and sequencing in everyday life. Make lists together.

> Example: 1. Go to the bank.
> 2. Go to the grocery store.

Shapes

Encourage your child to look at the different shapes of traffic signs and road signs. What shapes does your child see?

Shapes are part of our everyday lives. What shapes does your child see in his home, yard, etc.? List the shapes and objects. Add more as you find them.

Purchase or make a geoboard. To make a geoboard, pound sixteen 2-inch nails an equal distance apart into a 1-inch thick piece of wood. Pull rubber bands over the nails to create various geometric shapes. Talk with your child about the shapes he has created.

When going for a walk, have your child look around for shapes in the environment. For example, the front of a house might be a square, etc. Suggest a shape for your child to find.

Cut a long piece of yarn or string for your child. He can use it to make shapes. Draw a shape on a sheet of paper, and have your child put the yarn on top of it to trace it. Then, have him make the shape without tracing it first. Do this with other shapes.

Spelling

Purchase magnetic alphabet letters, and let your child practice spelling words and reading them to you. You can spell a word for your child, leaving out the vowel, as in "c _ t." Have your child add a vowel to complete the word.

Have your child write words on an index card with a black marker. Using a different colored crayon or marker to write the word again, have her "shadow" the first spelling. Let your child repeat this using several colors to create a rainbow effect.

Have your child spell words with alphabet soup letters, alphabet cereal letters, or alphabet pasta letters.

Let your child spell words with bread dough letters. To make bread dough, help your child mix together the ingredients listed below.

$3\frac{3}{4}$ cups whole wheat flour
2 cups buttermilk
$\frac{1}{4}$ cup wheat germ
2 teaspoons baking soda
1 cup molasses
1 cup raisins

On wax paper, have your child roll out each piece of dough like a snake. Then, help her form each piece into a letter of the alphabet. Place the letters on a greased cookie sheet, and bake at 350 degrees for 20 minutes or until golden brown.

Story Order

Encourage your child to tell you about his day. Write each event of your child's day on a separate strip of paper as he relates them to you. Then, cut the strips apart, and challenge him to rearrange the events in the correct order.

Tracking

To practice tracking, your child can make a road out of blocks, cardboard, or paper. Then, she can "drive" a toy car on the road.

If your child has a bike or tricycle, you can set up a course for her to follow. This could also be done on in-line skates or a skateboard. She can practice tracking by following a jogging path. Mazes also provide practice in tracking. Provide a city map, or draw one of your own. Point out where you are and where you are going. Let your child help find the shortest route to follow.

Writing

Fold a sheet of construction paper into a large cube-shaped block. Before folding, write a word on each side of the cube. Have your child throw the block, read the word that is faceup, and write a sentence using the word.

INDEX

INDEX